MONETARY REMEDIES FOR BREACH OF HUMAN RIGHTS

This book constructs a framework which allows a greater understanding of domestic causes of action for breaches of human rights sounding in a monetary remedy. The first part describes the cause of action in three jurisdictions: the United States of America, India and New Zealand.

The second part discusses two insights resulting from a comparative analysis of these three jurisdictions. The first is a list of four common questions that, when answered, structure the cause of action. These questions address what the cause of action protects, who the cause of action protects, against whom the cause of action is directed, and what the court orders. The second is a list of four overarching influences that affected the answers given to those questions in the three jurisdictions, so completing the structure of the causes of action. These influences are the cause of action's source, age, wider context and internal context. Putting these two chapters together provides a generalized outline of the causes of action.

In the third part of the book the analysis is turned around. The generalized framework is assessed as a way in which to categorise the development and shape of the cause of action in England under the Human Rights Act 1998.

The book concludes that a generic structure of the cause of action is common to the three jurisdictions studied and that the differences between the jurisdictions can be explained by influences that affect the causes of action in different ways. Further, this generalized framework is of relevance beyond the three jurisdictions from which it was drawn; it can be used as a guide by other jurisdictions in which such a cause of action either exists or will develop in the future.

Volume 9 in the series Human Rights Law in Perspective

Human Rights Law in Perspective

General Editor: Colin Harvey

The language of human rights figures prominently in legal and political debates at the national, regional and international levels. In the UK the Human Rights Act 1998 has generated considerable interest in the law of human rights. It will continue to provoke much debate in the legal community and the search for original insights and new materials will intensify.

The aim of this series is to provide a forum for scholarly reflection on all aspects of the law of human rights. The series will encourage work which engages with the theoretical, comparative and international dimensions of human rights law. The primary aim is to publish over time books which offer an insight into human rights law in its contextual setting. The objective is to promote an understanding of the nature and impact of human rights law. The series is inclusive, in the sense that all perspectives in legal scholarship are welcome. It will incorporate the work of new and established scholars.

Human Rights Law in Perspective is not confined to consideration of the UK. It will strive to reflect comparative, regional and international perspectives. Work which focuses on human rights law in other states will therefore be included in this series. The intention is to offer an inclusive intellectual home for significant scholarly contributions to human rights law.

Volume 1. Importing the Law in Post-Communist Transitions *Catherine Dupré*

Volume 2. The Development of the Positive Obligations Under the European Convention on Human Rights by the European Court of Human Rights *Alastair Mowbray*

Volume 3. Human Rights Brought Home: Socio-Legal Studies of Human Rights in the National Context *edited by Simon Halliday and Patrick Schmidt*

Volume 4. Corporations and Transnational Human Rights Litigation *Sarah Joseph*

Volume 5. Human Rights in the Community: Rights as Agents for Change *edited by Colin Harvey*

Volume 6. Human Rights, Culture and the Rule of Law *Jessica Almqvist*

Volume 7. Property and the Human Rights Act 1998 *Tom Allen*

Volume 8. Gender, Culture and Human Rights *Siobhán Mullally*

Volume 9. Monetary Remedies for Breach of Human Rights: A Comparative Study *Lisa Tortell*

Monetary Remedies for Breach of Human Rights

A Comparative Study

Lisa Tortell

• HART •
PUBLISHING

OXFORD AND PORTLAND, OREGON
2006

Published in North America (US and Canada) by
Hart Publishing
c/o International Specialized Book Services
920 NE 58th Avenue, Suite 300
Portland, OR 97213-3786
USA
Tel: +1 503 287 3093 or toll-free: (1) 800 944 6190
Fax: +1 503 280 8832
E-mail: orders@isbs.com
Website: www.isbs.com

Hart Publishing, 16C Worcester Place, Oxford, OX1 2JW
Telephone: +44 (0)1865 517530 Fax: +44 (0) 1865 510710
E-mail: mail@hartpub.co.uk
Website: http//:www.hartpub.co.uk

British Library Cataloguing in Publication Data

Data Available

ISBN-13: 978-1-84113-511-3 (hardback)
ISBN-10: 1-84113-511-9 (hardback)

Typeset by Forewords, Oxford
Printed and bound in Great Britain by
TJ International Ltd, Padstow, Cornwall

Series Editor's Preface

This book is a timely and welcome examination of the use of monetary remedies in the context of constitutional rights. The comparative work undertaken is of particular value in, for example, placing debates in Britain on the Human Rights Act 1998 in perspective. The premise is that monetary remedies are a reality in the human rights world and represent an international practice worthy of detailed analysis. The focus on judicial decision-making links directly to recent reflections on the extent and nature of transnational legal conversations in human rights law. This work is another fine addition to *Human Rights Law in Perspective* and will contribute significantly to current discussions

Colin Harvey
Belfast
October 2006

Acknowledgements

This book is based upon a thesis submitted for a DPhil at the University of Oxford. My thanks go to all those who helped and supported me during my time at Oxford. I am particularly grateful to Paul Craig, who was a generous, encouraging and challenging supervisor. Thank you also to all those at Wadham College, and especially Jeffrey Hackney and Laura Hoyano. My thanks also to DINÂMIA–Centro de Estudos sobre a Mudança Sócio-económica at the Instituto Superior de Ciências do Trabalho e da Empresa in Lisbon for practical support, Maria Eduarda Gonçalves for her warm encouragement, and the Portuguese Fundação para a Ciência e a Tecnologia for its financial support during the final stages of this process.

Sanjay Bavikatte, David Boldt, Ramapriya Gopalakrishnan, Sara Hossein, Marie Levontine, Sharon Percival, and Arun Thiruvengadam helped me with the practical difficulties of researching the law of jurisdictions other than the one in which I studied. Brigit Laidler provided invaluable comments. I am grateful to the Law Librarians at the Bodleian for their help throughout and to my doctoral examiners, Roderick Bagshaw and Duncan Fairgrieve, for their useful comments. It has been a true pleasure to deal with Richard Hart and I am delighted to be associated with Hart Publishing.

My biggest debt goes to my family: my parents, my sister, my husband and my daughters, the wonderful constants in my life. In particular, I would not have started the process without my parents' support and encouragement, and without Guilherme's wisdom and incisive thought I would not have finished it.

Contents

Table of Cases

1. India

2. New Zealand

3. United States of America

4. United Kingdom

5. European Union

6. Other jurisdictions

1

Introduction

And if the concept of a constitutional right is to have any meaning, it must surely sound in the protection which the law affords to it.[1]

THIS BOOK IS a comparative analysis of the monetary remedy for breach of constitutional rights in the United States of America, India and New Zealand, and a consideration of its relevance to England. It is concerned with the interplay in law of human rights and money: the remedying of human rights breaches by a judicial award of money. It addresses the shape of the domestic monetary remedy for breach of constitutional-type human rights as an international phenomenon. The intention is to construct a framework which allows a greater understanding of the domestic cause of action.

The idea of a monetary remedy is a relatively new feature of constitutional rights law and money may not always be the best remedy for human rights breaches. For this reason, declarations and similar remedies are often seen as more appropriate in the human rights context. Nevertheless, money is a usual way to ascribe value to things in general, and the use of monetary remedies is increasingly commonplace in relation to human rights breaches domestically and internationally. As Shelton has commented, in the human rights context, the monetary remedy is often symbolic of vindication of the rights and a governmental admission of wrongdoing: '[m]oney is the tangible confirmation of responsibility'.[2]

The fundamental nature of human rights guarantees, combined perhaps with their governmental aspect, mean that breaches of such rights are taken seriously and remedies are an extremely important part of rights jurisprudence. The sentiments of the Indian Chief Justice in *Fertilizer Corporation* are echoed in other jurisdictions: 'It is meaningless to confer fundamental rights without providing an effective remedy for their enforcement, if and when they are violated. A right without a remedy is a legal conundrum of a most grotesque kind.'[3]

Having said that, there are many thorny questions concerning constitu-

1 *R v Lord Chancellor, ex p Witham* [1997] 2 All ER 779, 783.
2 D Shelton, *Remedies in International Human Rights Law* (Oxford, OUP, 1999) 51.
3 *Fertiliser Corporation Kamgar Union v Union of India* (1981) 1 SCC 568, 574.

tional rights, extending to their definition and how breaches are best remedied. The rights relevant to this book exist or are codified in domestic constitutional-type legal documents. Neither the scope of the rights themselves, nor the desirability or effectiveness of a monetary remedy is addressed; this book considers the nature of the remedy, by identifying the features that are common across jurisdictions and the features that are unique to each jurisdiction. The focus is on the lessons that one jurisdiction may learn from another in relation to the cause of action.

A comparative analysis of the monetary remedy is timely in recognition of 'a growing sense that legal developments are less and less the product of wholly domestic processes, but often owe their form, if not their existence, to the laws and practices of other places.'[4]

Such interaction between legal systems has been described by Slaughter as 'transjudicial communication: communication among courts—whether national or supranational—across borders'.[5] Clearly, there is also a great deal of interaction and transnational communication in legal scholarship.[6]

While there is more to constitutional rights law than case law—and more to rights than the law—this book is concerned with the reasoning and decisions of judges, and not the nature of the statutory or constitutional guarantees. Judicial decisions have an indirect effect beyond the parties and specialist readers: 'judicial doctrine sensitizes people to their rights and forms an important bargaining tool in legal, social and political negotiations in day-to-day matters'.[7] From a practical level, comparing judicial pronouncements is more useful than a comparison of statutory instruments when considering the shape of a new cause of action and remedy internationally. The analysis in this book is limited to a reading of the judgments, and only rarely considers the enforcement of judgments or assesses their success. While this might not tell us the whole story of constitutional rights in the United States, India, New Zealand and England, it will tell an important part of the story.

There are some preliminary matters of terminology that ought to be addressed. The phrase 'constitutional rights' is used to encompass those human rights which are protected through a domestic instrument of constitutional value. The sort of rights that are covered are those that exist

[4] B Opeskin, 'Constitutional Modelling: The Domestic Effect of International Law in Commonwealth Countries—Part I' [2000] *PL* 607.

[5] A Slaughter, 'A Typology of Transjudicial Communication' (1994) 29 *U Richmond L Rev* 99, 101.

[6] Eg Opeskin (n 4 above); C McCrudden, 'A Common Law of Human Rights? Transnational Judicial Conversations on Constitutional Rights' (2000) 20 *OJLS* 499; Slaughter (n 5 above); S Abrahamson and M Fischer, 'All the World's a Courtroom: Judging in the New Millennium' (1997) 26 *Hofstra L Rev* 273; C Osakwe, 'Introduction: The Problems of the Comparability of Notions in Constitutional Law' (1985) 59 *Tulane L Rev* 875.

[7] J Cooper and R Dhavan, 'Introduction' in J Cooper and R Dhavan, (eds), *Public Interest Law* (London, Blackwell, 1986) 3, 13.

in domestic constitutions or statutes and 'seek to protect and advance rights of the type typically found in international and regional rights conventions'.[8] The intention is to bypass the questions of terminology which surround 'human rights' or 'fundamental rights', or even 'constitutional'. Rather, these rights are taken for granted, and the way in which they are enforced through the monetary remedy is examined.

Second, reference is generally made to the 'monetary remedy' and not to 'damages', 'compensation', or 'reparations'. By doing so, the intention is to avoid the assumptions inherent in each of these terms. This aspect is addressed further in chapter 6.

Third, it should be acknowledged that it is not necessarily obvious that this is a cause of action and not simply a remedy. It is, nevertheless, most appropriate to consider the matter as a cause of action, sounding in this particular remedy as no remedy can be awarded without consideration of the legal aspects that make up a cause of action. In this case, many of those aspects are specific to the particular remedy sought and so deserve consideration as a unique cause of action.[9]

Finally, there is a tension between the internationalization of constitutional rights law, and the importance of socio-legal context.[10] In fact, this comparison highlights the important lesson that the cause of action and remedy must be particular to jurisdiction, as there are a multitude of influences on all aspects of the cause of action that result in a unique remedy in each jurisdiction, but that at the same time the commonality of much of the constitutional rights monetary remedy cannot be ignored. While it does not address the discussion in comparative law about the globalization of law, the book aims to provide a culturally neutral set of questions setting out the structure of the cause of action, and to properly weight the jurisdiction-specific overarching influences.

The book is divided into three parts. The first part describes the cause of action in three jurisdictions: the United States of America, India and New Zealand. These three jurisdictions all enjoy a legal system based in the British common law and share some aspects of a common legal tradition, language and system of governance. The intention, then, is to adopt something resembling the scientific approach of constructing controls for experiments. To ensure a meaningful comparison it is important to keep the differences to a minimum when choosing case studies. Thus, it is assumed that these jurisdictions are similar enough to make a comparison useful and fruitful, while encompassing enough differences and potential influences, that the results reached will have relevance for other jurisdictions. In this way, it may be that the comparison of these

[8] McCrudden (n 6 above) 499–500.

[9] I am grateful to David Boldt for a useful discussion on this point in relation to the New Zealand cause of action.

[10] McCrudden (n 6 above) summarises this debate.

three jurisdictions provides some insight into the fledgling United Kingdom monetary remedy under Section 8 of the Human Rights Act 1998, as well as having some application to jurisdictions beyond England. Each of these first chapters has been organized in the way which is most appropriate to that jurisdiction to provide an overview for the analysis that follows. Most of the analysis is limited to discussion of authorities from the highest courts.

The second part of the book discusses the following two aspects of a comparative analysis of the United States, India and New Zealand. At first blush, it seems that the causes of action differ greatly between the jurisdictions. A deeper look, however, shows that the differences between jurisdictions are superficial and, at their base, the causes of action are surprisingly similar. The same questions are asked in each jurisdiction, and the same issues raised. It seems clear that there is a finite number of legal responses to constitutional rights breaches and a great deal of commonality in domestic human rights law. This insight is the basis for chapter 5, which sets out a list of four common questions: what the cause of action protects, who the cause of action protects, against whom the cause of action is directed, and what the court orders. These questions, when answered, structure the cause of action.

Despite very similar questions being asked and issues being raised in the way discussed in chapter 5, the initial observation that each jurisdiction has a relatively unique cause of action remains true. A second insight is, therefore, that those questions are answered, and the issues resolved, in different ways dependent upon certain influences of an overarching nature. This insight is explored in chapter 6, which lists the overarching influences that largely determined the answers given to those questions in the three jurisdictions. The four influences that affected the answers, so completing the structure of the causes of action are its source, its age, its wider context, and its internal context.

In this way, a layering effect becomes visible: the domestic causes of action, when considered as an international phenomenon, are both very similar to one another and very different. This contradictory statement is the observation that best fits the results of this comparative study. The conglomerate of the ideas set out in these two chapters, therefore, provides an outline of the causes of action, and the interplay of the questions and the influences amounts to a template with wider use.

In the final part of the book, the analysis is turned around to consider how the generalized framework, developed to explain the causes of action in the three jurisdictions explored, may work in application to another jurisdiction. That is, it is used to categorise and explain the early development of the new monetary remedy under Section 8 of the United Kingdom Human Rights Act 1998 and, perhaps, to suggest ways in which it may continue to develop. This is not an exercise in crystal ball gazing, but rather aims to provide a way of looking at the cause of action and, specifically, to suggest outstanding questions as it develops. To do this, the content of the overarching influences for England is compiled and 'applied' to the structure, indicating the likely outline of the Section 8 cause of action.

The issues raised by this book are timely in England. Even prior to the enactment of the Human Rights Act and the plethora of writing on the subject, judicial comment had been made as to the importance of remedies for breach of constitutional rights.[11] The cause of action for breach of the Human Rights Act sounding in a monetary remedy will be an important part of human rights litigation in England, and is likely to evolve incrementally through judicial decision-making. This book aims to provide a framework for the discussion of the legal protection of the rights in the Human Rights Act.

The book concludes that a generic structure of the cause of action is common to the three jurisdictions studied and that the differences between the jurisdictions can be explained by four influences, that are also common to some extent, but that affect the causes of action in different ways. This analysis will have value for such domestic causes of action internationally as was shown by its application to England. In other words, the generalized framework both explains and orders existing causes of action, and serves as a template suggesting the future of evolving causes of action.

11 Eg *Witham* (n 1 above) 783.

PART I

JURISDICTIONS

2

United States of America: Section 1983 and Bivens

A. INTRODUCTION

CONSTITUTIONAL RIGHTS JURISPRUDENCE in the United States is highly developed and complex. The questions considered are usually those of a clearly first world nature, involving abstract interpretations of the rights and freedoms guaranteed. These features are perhaps attributable to the age of the Constitution and constitutional jurisprudence; the Supreme Court and legislature have had 200 years to sculpt the reality that now exists.

The United States Constitution consists of a preamble, six articles and 27 amendments, all of equal standing. The articles of the Constitution establish a democratic, republican and federal system of government. The amendments create a bill of rights. The guarantees include the right to freedom of religion[1]; the right to bear arms[2]; the freedom from search and seizure[3]; various criminal and civil justice rights[4]; a prohibition against slavery[5]; the right to equal protection of the law and to due process of the law in relation to life, liberty and property[6]; and the right to vote.[7]

The Constitution is, of course, federal and certain federal statutes provide the means by which the Constitution is actionable. Remedies available include injunctive relief, evidence-related relief, judicial review of legislation, and the prerogative remedies, in addition to the monetary remedy.

The federal statute of primary importance in this area is 42 USC Section 1983, the first of the two principal causes of action through which individuals can seek a monetary remedy for breach of constitutional rights.

1 Amendment I.
2 Amendment II.
3 Amendment IV.
4 Amendments V, VI, VII and VIII.
5 Amendment XIII.
6 Amendment XIV.
7 Amendments XV, XIX and XXVI.

This section provides a cause of action in the federal courts against state officials and state governments. The other principal cause of action sounding in a monetary remedy for breach of constitutional rights was implied by the Supreme Court in the decision of *Bivens*.[8] This common law cause of action provides a remedy for breach by federal actors.

In this way, the monetary remedy for breach of constitutional rights in the United States is divided into two separate causes of action, dependant upon whether it is alleged that the rights were breached at the federal or at the state level. Both these causes of action are based on federally-protected rights, and are brought in federal courts, despite the fact that one cause of action is solely reserved for litigating acts of individual states.

While the state constitutions and statutes which must conform with federal civil rights provisions are of no little importance, the analysis that follows will address only federal rights and federal jurisprudence of the Supreme Court. The following description will provide an overall impression of the monetary remedy for breach of rights in the United States.[9] It has been suggested that constitutional interpretation in the United States is best described as a pyramid, with the Supreme Court at the apex.[10] It is for this reason that this analysis will be limited to a discussion of Supreme Court jurisprudence and will not address the many decisions of the lower courts.[11]

It is worth noting the existence of two federal statutes which are outside the scope of this book. The first is the Federal Aliens Tort Act.[12] This statute grants jurisdiction to United States federal courts to hear suits by aliens for torts that violate international law or treaties. In practice, although its use has increased dramatically in the past 20 years, awards are rarely enforced and disagreement exists about its scope.[13] The second statute is the Federal Tort Claims Act, which provides the main mechanism by which tort liability is imposed upon the United States, so over-riding the

[8] *Bivens v Six Unknown Named Agents of Federal Bureau of Narcotics* 403 US 388, 91 S Ct 1999 (1971).

[9] D Schuman, 'The Right to a Remedy' (1992) 65 *Temple L Rev* 1197: 'State constitutional law, even as it moves from the margins toward the mainstream of American legal culture, remains for the most part a collection of variations on federal constitutional themes'.

[10] R Spurrier, *To Preserve These Rights: Remedies for the Victims of Constitutional Deprivations* (New York, National University Publications, 1977) 11–12.

[11] It would be close to impossible to assess all the United States case law on this subject due to the 'sheer volume of reports': G Hammona, 'Rethinking Remedies: The Changing Concept of the Relationship Between Legal and Equitable Remedies' in J Berryman, (ed), *Remedies: Issues and Perspectives* (Ontario, Carswell, 1991) 87, 89.

[12] 28 USC §1350.

[13] In *Tel Oren v Libyan Arab Republic* 726 F2d 774 (US Ct of Apps, District of Columbia, 1984) 775 the provision was described as 'aged but little-noticed' and as conferring 'jurisdiction over a minute class of cases.' See generally B Stephens and M Ratner, *International Human Rights Litigation in United States Courts* (New York, Transnational Publishers, 1996).

general sovereign immunity accorded to the state.[14] The Act authorizes tort actions against the United States based on the conduct of its agencies and agents as if the government were a private party.[15] A later amendment stated that the government would be solely liable for nonconstitutional torts committed by any employee acting within the scope of their office or employment.[16] While it is by no means easy to determine whether a particular action is a constitutional or nonconstitutional tort,[17] Congress 'explicitly declined to transfer liability for constitutional torts committed by federal employees in the scope of their duties' to the FTCA and so to the United States government.[18]

B. ACTIONS AGAINST STATE GOVERNMENTS

1. Historical Background

The federal statute 42 USC Section 1983 'is the basis for most suits in federal courts against local governments and state and local government officers to redress violations of federal law'.[19] Section 1983 creates a cause of action by which individuals may claim monetary redress for breach of federal rights by the state. Its importance has 'fluctuated', from being seldom used in the first 50 years following its enactment, to becoming 'one of the most litigated federal provisions'.[20] It has been stated that '[n]o statute is more important in contemporary American law':

> Every person who, under color of any statute, ordinance, regulation, custom, or usage of any State or Territory or the District of Columbia, subjects, or causes to be subjected, any citizen of the United States or other person within the jurisdiction thereof to the deprivation of any rights, privileges, or immunities secured by the Constitution and laws, shall be liable to the party injured in an action at law, suit in equity, or other proper proceeding for redress.[21]

14 Codified as 28 USC §1346 and §§2671–80. See K Davis and R Pierce, *Administrative Law Treatise*, Vol III, 3rd edn, (Boston, MA, Little Brown, 1994) 229. There is a plethora of other statutes which impose liability in specific circumstances.

15 Davis and Pierce (n 14 above) 202.

16 Federal Employees Liability Reform and Tort Compensation Act.

17 Eg *DeShaney v Winnebago County Department of Social Services* 489 US 189, 109 S Ct 998 (1989) in which the Supreme Court held that the particular facts (child abuse by a foster parent) was not a breach of due process; it was, therefore, a non constitutional breach and so subject only to the FTCA.

18 Davis and Pierce (n 14 above) 233.

19 E Chemerinsky, *Federal Jurisdiction*, 2nd edn, (Boston, MA, Little Brown, 1994) 422.

20 L Levy, *et al*, *Encyclopedia of the American Constitution*, Vol IV (New York, MacMillan, 1986) 1640.

21 M Schwartz and J Kirklin, *Section 1983 Litigation: Claims, Defences and Fees* (New York, Wiley Law Publications, 1986) 3.

The section was enacted in 1871, in response to the strength of the Ku Klux Klan in the southern states of the United States. State governments in the South were perceived as being unable or unwilling to prevent rights abuses, and state courts as being ineffective in enforcing or punishing these breaches. In such circumstances, the section was enacted to enable individuals to bring a claim in the federal courts against the state government for its failure to enforce constitutional guarantees.

Despite these expansive intentions, the statute remained largely unused for the first 50 years. The causes for this varied, but it seems that the socio-political climate of the time was reflected both in the fact that few cases were brought, and in the decisions of the courts. It has been suggested that not only were southern federal judges no more likely to enforce constitutional guarantees than their state counterparts, but that the Supreme Court was loathe to interfere in even these state matters.[22]

Further, decisions in other areas of constitutional interpretation may have indirectly limited the interpretation of this section. Most obviously, the rights and freedoms in the Constitution were interpreted much more narrowly at the time, so that many of the cases which now are brought under Section 1983 could not have been brought at its commencement. The expansion of the section has occurred, to some extent, because of an expansion in the rights that individuals have against the federal and state administrations.[23]

Other aspects of constitutional interpretation more directly stunted the potential of Section 1983. For example, in relation to the Fourteenth Amendment, the phrase 'rights, privileges and immunities secured by the Constitution' had been interpreted as including only a small subclass of rights, rather than all constitutional rights, an interpretation which was carried over into some Section 1983 cases.[24] The Supreme Court had suggested that the Court's jurisdiction as set out in Section 1343(3) should be limited to cases involving personal rights, and not extend to property rights: again this limitation narrowed the initial use of Section 1983.[25] Finally, the phrase 'under color of any law' was assumed to have a narrow meaning, limited to authorised actions and not extending to unauthorised actions of state officials, potentially reducing the number of cases which were brought.

Thus, between 1871, when it was enacted, and the 1920s, Section 1983 was used very rarely.[26] From the 1920s until the 1960s, the section was used rather more often, in particular in a series of voting registration

22 Chemerinsky (n 19 above) 427.

23 Eg equal protection and due process clauses, fourth amendment, and the strict interpretation of the state action doctrine: Levy (n 20 above) 1640.

24 Levy (n 20 above) 1640 referring to the *Slaughterhouse Cases* 16 Wallace 36 (1873).

25 Levy (n 20 above) 1640.

26 In fact only 21 cases were so decided: Comment, 'The Civil Rights Act: Emergence of an Adequate Federal Civil Remedy?' (1951) 26 *Ind LJ* 361, 363.

cases.[27] The total overall figures remained low, however, with only 287 such cases brought by 1961.[28]

The scope of the section began to increase, and likewise its usage, in the 1960s.[29] This was in the context of an increasing societal awareness of both civil rights issues and the possibility of the legal system being used to provide a remedy. As a result, there has been a general increase in the number of cases brought at federal level, of which the Section 1983 cases are merely one part, albeit 'the centrepiece'.[30] In the mid-1960s, Section 1983 began to be used for public interest litigation, so that the section became one way in which the legal system was used to benefit classes of people.[31] In turn, this led to an increase in the number of Section 1983 actions filed by individuals.[32]

2. *Monroe v Pape*: A Seminal Decision

Such social and legal change was notably reflected in the Supreme Court's decision in *Monroe v Pape*,[33] which was a watershed, after which the section was much-used: '[t]he dramatic increase in Section 1983 actions has generated a comprehensive and intricate body of law'.[34] The case raised a number of issues, around which much of the following jurisprudence has centred.

First, the decision changed the definition of 'under color of any law', the most significant finding for the cause of action. In holding that Section 1983 was actionable against unauthorised actions of officials employed by the state governments, in addition to the previously held authorised actions, the scope of the section was dramatically increased.[35] In relation to the instant case, it meant that an illegal search and seizure could found a cause of action under the section.

The issue of what amounts to 'under color of law' has continued to receive judicial attention following *Monroe v Pape*. Clearly, the official conduct of state and local officials amounts to actions made under color of law,[36] so long as the actions were made under official authority and not in a personal capacity. The exception to prove the rule was outlined by the Supreme Court in *Polk County v Dodson* in which it was held that a

27 Chemerinsky (n 19 above) 428.
28 *Ibid.*
29 Schwartz and Kirklin (n 21 above) 4: 270 cases were filed in 1961 and over 30,000 in 1981.
30 Chemerinsky (n 19 above) 429.
31 Schwartz and Kirklin (n 21 above) 5.
32 *Ibid.*
33 *Monroe v Pape* 365 US 167, 81 S Ct 473 (1961).
34 Schwartz and Kirklin (n 21 above) 5.
35 *Monroe* (n 33 above) 476.
36 Schwartz and Kirklin (n 21 above) 94.

public defender's representation of a criminal defendant was not an action under color of law as it was an essentially private act, apart from the way in which the lawyer was paid.[37]

The Courts have determined that 'under color of law' is equivalent to the phrase 'state action', which has been much litigated in relation to the question of private entities and individuals whose involvement with state and local government has made them subject to the Fourteenth Amendment.[38] Simply put, the doctrine requires an aspect of state involvement for liability to attach to the state.

The cases consider 'state action' to be proved if it is fair to attribute the impugned conduct to the state. This breaks into two components: 'the deprivation must be caused by the exercise of some right or privilege created by the State or by a rule of conduct imposed by the State or by a person for whom the State is responsible'[39]; and the defendant must 'fairly be said to be a state actor'.[40] Thus, an individual may be a state actor for one purpose but not another and neither state regulation, assistance nor authorisation is sufficient, unless the state can be said to have encouraged the action. The importance of a function is not determinative to the decision, as the function must be an 'historically and exclusively governmental function'.[41] Nowadays, determinations will involve 'a totality of circumstances approach'.[42]

Second, the majority decision in *Monroe v Pape* set out three principal objectives of Section 1983: to override certain kinds of state laws; to provide a remedy where state law was inadequate; and to provide a federal remedy where the state remedy, although adequate in theory, was not available in practice.[43]

This analysis allowed the court to find that there was no requirement for claimants to exhaust available state remedies before using the Section 1983 cause of action: '[t]he federal remedy is supplementary to the state remedy, and the latter need not be first sought and refused before the federal one is invoked.'[44]

This matter has been important in contemporary cases and was finally determined in *Patsy v Board of Regents of the State of Florida*,[45] when the Court deferred to congressional history and intent, which it considered showed clearly that individuals would not be compelled to exhaust state

37 *Polk County v Dodson* 454 US 312, 102 S Ct 445 (1981).
38 *Lugar v Edmondson Oil Co* 457 US 922, 102 S Ct 2744 (1982).
39 *Ibid*, p 2753.
40 *Ibid*, p 2754.
41 Schwartz and Kirklin (n 21 above) 103.
42 S Kean, 'Municipal Liability for Off-duty Police Misconduct Under §1983: The "Under Color of Law" Requirement' (1999) 79 *Boston U L Rev* 195, 211.
43 *Monroe* (n 33 above) 477.
44 *Ibid*, p 482.
45 *Patsy v Board of Regents of the State of Florida* 457 US 496, 102 S Ct 2557 (1982).

administrative remedies as a prerequisite to Section 1983 cases. The related doctrines of *res judicata* and collateral estoppel generally apply in Section 1983 cases.[46]

The aims set out in *Monroe v Pape* illustrate another theme in constitutional interpretation in general, and tension within the section: the balance between federal and state responsibility. There is a 'special delicacy', it has been said, between federal power and the state's administration of its own law.[47] While in the earlier years of the section's existence the balance was tipped in favour of state autonomy, by the 1960s the federal government's responsibility for constitutional guarantees was enhanced and overcame such concerns. While individual rights accordingly became paramount, this tension has continued to be relevant in the Section 1983 jurisprudence.[48]

Finally, *Monroe v Pape* raised the question of which 'persons' are covered by the section. In the Court's opinion, 'Congress did not undertake to bring municipal corporations within the ambit'.[49] Clearly the section requires a state component to the action.[50] This much obviously accords with the purposes of enacting the section to provide a remedy against the misuse of state power. Courts have attempted to provide some boundaries to the word 'persons' in Section 1983, in a series of cases in which historical and policy elements were closely scrutinised to determine what common law immunities would have existed at the time the section was enacted. This issue has generated the majority of jurisprudence under Section 1983: 'Immunity doctrine has expanded to the point that Section 1983 and *Bivens* actions are barely able to serve their purposes. The true litigation explosion in Section 1983 is in immunity claims, not filings.'[51]

3. Range of Bodies that can be Sued: Extension by *Monell*

In a case concerning discrimination against pregnant state employees, *Monell v Department of Social Services of the City of New York*, the Supreme Court expressly overruled *Monroe v Pape* to the extent that it had held that municipalities were immune from suit under Section 1983.[52] Rather, the Court considered that local governing bodies—local govern-

[46] Schwartz and Kirklin (n 21 above) 193 et seq.

[47] *Stefanelli v Minard* 342 US 117, 72 S Ct 118 (1951) 120.

[48] See later discussion of *Will v Michigan Department of State Police* (see text accompanying n 69 above).

[49] *Monroe* (n 33 above) 484.

[50] C Antieau and W Rich, *Modern Constitutional Law*, Vol III, 2nd edn, (St Paul, MN, West Group, 1997) 672.

[51] A Burris, 'Qualifying Immunity in §1983 and *Bivens* Actions' (1992) 71 *Texas L Rev* 123, 186.

[52] *Monell v Department of Social Services of the City of New York* 436 US 658, 98 S Ct 2018 (1978). Municipalities include 'all government bodies below the state level': Kean (n 42 above) 196 (n 2).

ments and municipalities—would be liable under Section 1983 'when execution of a government's policy or custom, whether made by its lawmakers or by those whose edicts or acts may fairly be said to represent official policy, inflicts the injury'.[53]

In other words, municipalities may be sued pursuant to Section 1983 on the basis of their policies, laws or customs. There is, however, difficulty in defining exactly which actions fall within these concepts although it is clear that such actions must truly be governmental in kind. Courts must determine which officials can be said to have the authority that their acts or edicts amount to official policy, whether a practice is sufficiently persistent to amount to a policy, and which policies are 'moving forces' behind a violation of federal rights.[54]

The doctrine of *respondeat superior* was held not to apply, so that the mere employment of a tortfeasor would not be enough to make a municipality liable. The rule extends to all Section 1983 cases.[55] Despite that limitation, *Monell* was a watershed second only to *Monroe v Pape*, opening up the section to numerous new suits. In deciding that no absolute immunity applied, the decision left open the question of whether other qualified immunities could apply to municipalities and their officials.

4. Range of Bodies that can be Sued: Immunities

This area has received much jurisprudential attention, not least because judges have considered it to be interchangeable between Section 1983 and the *Bivens* action.[56] It should be noted that much of the immunity question is related to tort law as Section 1983 is silent as to such aspects.[57] Section 1983 immunities will be available where such immunities existed at common law at the time that the section was enacted, and if no policy reasons exist to suggest they should not apply now.[58]

Owen v City of Independence Missouri reaffirmed *Monell's* finding that municipalities could be sued under the section.[59] The Court noted that

[53] *Monell* (n 52 above) 2037–38.

[54] *City of Oklamahoma v Tuttle* 471 US 808, 105 S Ct 2427 (1985) and *Pembaur v City of Cincinnati* 475 US 469, 106 S Ct 1292 (1986) make it clear that proof must be provided that a policy exists as the basis of an impugned action.

[55] According to *Rizzo v Goode* 423 US 362, 96 S Ct 598 (1976), absent a pattern of unconstitutional behaviour, hierarchically superior officers cannot be liable for the behaviour of certain police officers; rather, these police officers should have been named and sued themselves (note that this is a case seeking injunctive, not monetary, relief under §1983).

[56] *Butz v Economou* 438 US 478, 98 S Ct 2894 (1978) 2909; *Harlow v Fitzgerald* 457 US 800, 102 S Ct 2727 (1982) 2733.

[57] M Wells, 'Constitutional Remedies, Section 1983 and the Common Law' [1998] *Mississippi LJ* 157. *City of Newport v Facts Concerts* 453 US 247, 101 S Ct 2748 (1981) positions constitutional tort law within the historical context of common law tort.

[58] Eg *Wyatt v Cole* 504 US 158, 112 S Ct 1827 (1992) 1831.

[59] *Owen v City of Independence Missouri* 445 US 622, 100 S Ct 1398 (1980).

immunities had been held to exist to prevent or limit the personal liability of various government officials. For example, there is an absolute immunity for judges[60] and for prosecutors in initiating and presenting the state's case.[61] Qualified good faith immunities have been held to exist for prison officers,[62] state hospital superintendents,[63] local school board members,[64] police officers,[65] and state governors and other executive officers performing discretionary acts in the course of official conduct.[66] In fact, almost all officials will enjoy some immunity: 'Although the Supreme Court has acknowledged that not all government officials can be immune from Section 1983 actions, it has proceeded apace to grant either absolute or qualified immunity to every government official.'[67]

Further, there are suggestions that a qualified immunity does not differ greatly in effect from an absolute immunity. The recent case law has been said to result in the situation that qualified immunity immunizes all 'but the plainly incompetent or those who knowingly violate the law'.[68]

Will v Michigan Department of State Police extended the immunities available for defendants, to create an absolute immunity for state governments and state officials acting within their official capacity.[69] It held that states and state officials acting in their official capacity are not 'persons' subject to liability pursuant to Section 1983 despite municipalities being held so liable.

The Court considered the Eleventh Amendment, which provides an absolute immunity for states and their agencies from federal liability in damages,[70] and extended it to Section 1983 cases against states brought in state courts. The Court in *Will* was concerned with protecting sovereign immunity and ensuring that Section 1983 did not alter the federal-state balance. It held that states were not liable for damages in Section 1983 cases brought in state courts, as well as those brought in federal courts. As it was held that 'a suit against a state official in his or her official capacity

60 *Pierson v Ray* 386 US 547, 87 S Ct 1213 (1967) 1217–18.

61 *Imbler v Pachtman* 424 US 409, 96 S Ct 984 (1976) 993.

62 *Procunier v Navarette* 434 US 555, 98 S Ct 855 (1978) 859.

63 *O'Connor v Donaldson* 422 US 563, 95 S Ct 2486 (1975) 2494–95.

64 *Wood v Strickland* 420 US 308, 95 S Ct 992 (1975) 997–1001.

65 *Pierson v Ray* (n 60 above) 1218–19.

66 *Scheuer v Rhodes* 416 US 232, 94 S Ct 1683 (1974) 1692.

67 Burris (n 51 above) 140–41; J Jeffries, 'In Praise of the Eleventh Amendment and §1983' (1998) 84 *Virg L Rev* 47, 54.

68 *Malley v Briggs* 475 US 335, 106 S Ct 1092 (1986) 1096.

69 *Will v Michigan Department of State Police* 491 US 58, 109 S Ct 2304 (1989). See P Prygoski, '*Will v Michigan Department of State Police*: The Eleventh Amendment in State Courts' (1990) 43 *Oklahoma L Rev* 429; W Burnham and M Fayz, 'The State as a "Non-person" Under §1983: Some Comments on *Will* and Suggestions for the Future' (1991) 70 *Oregon L Rev* 1.

70 In *Edelman v Jordan* 419 US 651, 94 S Ct 1347 (1974) the Supreme Court had already held that states were immune from damages under §1983 actions brought in a federal court, in accordance with the Eleventh Amendment.

is not a suit against the official but rather is a suit against the official's office',[71] state officials were likewise not considered 'persons' subject to liability pursuant to Section 1983.

Thus, following this judgment, Section 1983 suits may only be brought against either municipalities whose official policy caused the breach,[72] against state officials in their personal capacity,[73] or against 'co-conspiritors', private individuals acting in cohorts with state officials who had acted under colour of law.[74]

The 'arm of state doctrine' was set out in the *Mt Healthy* decision as a way in which to determine which state entities would be entitled to rely upon the immunities.[75] There, the Court distinguished between, on the one hand, state entities and, on the other hand, municipal corporations or other political subdivisions, such as counties and municipalities. The Court held that 'a local school board ... is more like a county or city than it is like an arm of the State'.[76] It could not, therefore, assert any Eleventh Amendment immunity from suit in the federal courts and was not immune from Section 1983 suit.

5. Range of Bodies that can be Sued: Persons

The question of suing individual officials is of great importance as it is almost the only way in which liability can be held to attach to actions of states or state officials, or to the actions of municipalities which are not based upon official policy or custom.[77] As discussed above, the Courts have determined that a qualified, good faith immunity is available for all government officials sued in their official capacity under Section 1983. *Scheuer v Rhodes* held that a qualified immunity would be available to varying degrees 'dependant upon the scope of discretion and responsibilities of the office and all the circumstances as they reasonably appeared at the time of the action on which liability is sought to be based'.[78]

The test for good faith was restated in *Harlow* as a substantially objective test: 'government officials performing discretionary functions generally are shielded from liability for civil damages insofar as their

71 *Will* (n 69 above) 2312.

72 The limitation in *Monell* (n 52 above).

73 All other state officials, not to mention states, are excluded by *Will* (n 69 above).

74 In *Dennis v Sparks* 449 US 24, 101 S Ct 183 (1980) 186, the Supreme Court noted that private individuals may be liable under §1983 if they are 'wilful participant[s] in joint action with the State or its agents' regardless of the fact that the state actors will be immune from liability itself or themselves.

75 *Mt Healthy City School District Board of Education v Doyle* 429 US 274, 97 S Ct 568 (1977) 572–73.

76 *Ibid*, p 573.

77 Antieau (n 50 above) 667.

78 *Scheuer* (n 66 above).

conduct does not violate clearly established statutory or constitutional rights of which a reasonable person would have known.'[79]

This definition of qualified immunity both allowed officials to avoid the burdens of trial and created a shield for officials whether or not they acted wrongly, rather than a mere defence.[80] In *Butz*, a qualified immunity was again seen as the best balance between protection of the administration from unnecessary suits and the importance of rights suits. Federal executive officers were entitled to a qualified immunity except in exceptional situations where an absolute immunity 'is essential for the conduct of the public business'.[81] Thus, not only is qualified immunity widely available but, once it applies, most defendants enjoy what amounts to an absolute immunity due to the element of intention that has been imported into the test.

Significantly, private actors sued under Section 1983 do not have the qualified immunity protection of government officials exercising discretionary functions. The Court has determined 'that the rationales mandating qualified immunity for public officers are not applicable to private parties' in the case of private persons who conspire with state officials.[82] In *Wyatt* the Supreme Court held that private actors will not automatically be immune from Section 1983 simply because the liability attaches:

> Qualified immunity strikes a balance between compensating those who have been injured by official conduct and protecting government's ability to perform its traditional functions ... . In short, the qualified immunity recognised in *Harlow* acts to safeguard government, and thereby to protect the public at large, not to benefit its agents.[83]

Richardson concerned the question of whether prison officers employed in a private prison, under private management, and sued pursuant to Section 1983, were able to claim the protection of qualified immunity that applied to governmental officials.[84] As usual, the Court considered the historical and policy elements, concluding that such private actors were not eligible to enjoy the immunity. It should be noted that the Court did not express a view on whether the private prison officers were actually covered by Section 1983: it was for the District Court to determine whether the defendants acted under color of law.[85]

79 *Harlow* (n 56 above).

80 *Johnson v Fankell* 520 US 911, 117 S Ct 1800 (1997) 1803; *Richardson v McKnight* 521 US 399, 117 S Ct 2100 (1997) 2103.

81 *Butz* (n 56 above) 2911.

82 *Wyatt* (n 58 above) 1833.

83 *Ibid.*

84 *Richardson* (n 80 above).

85 *Ibid*, p 2108.

Further, the Court left open the question of whether an immunity would apply to private individuals associated only briefly with a government entity acting as an adjunct to government in an essential government activity, or acting under close official supervision. Finally, like the court in *Wyatt*, *Richardson* did not express a view as to whether a weaker good faith defence, rather than the more powerful qualified immunity, was open to such defendants.

The jurisprudence makes another important distinction which serves to limit the liability even of state officials. *Kentucky v Graham* set out the distinction between personal capacity suits and official capacity suits: 'Personal-capacity suits seek to impose personal liability upon a government official for actions he takes under color of state law ... . Official-capacity suits, in contrast, "generally represent only another way of pleading an action against an entity of which an officer is an agent".'[86]

Thus, if officials are sued in their official capacity, the Eleventh Amendment prevents the claim, but if officials are sued in their personal capacity, no immunities apply.[87] As an official capacity suit is in reality against the state entity, it is the state entity which will pay any award of damages. In contrast, awards against officials sued in their personal capacity will be executed against them in their personal capacity.[88] For example, in *Brandon* the action was held to be properly against the public servant in his official capacity, and not against the particular individual. This meant that liability fell to the entity, rather than the individual.[89]

Determining whether a claim is a personal or official capacity suit seems to be a matter solely of pleading and not of substance. As a result, 'a damages action brought against a state officer in his or her official capacity is a serious pleading error'.[90] It seems fair to conclude that this is a distinction of form only, as an officer can only be sued if there is a state element to his or her action[91] and so a 'personal' capacity suit will still involve an official element.

In summary, the question of who will be liable for Section 1983 breaches is equivalent to the question of immunities. Municipalities enjoy no general immunity; the Eleventh Amendment creates an absolute immunity for states, and correspondingly, for state officials in their official capacity sued in federal courts (which has been extended to those sued in state courts); qualified good faith immunity applies to all other executive and administrative officials sued in their official capacity, except for judges, prosecutors and legislators who have an absolute immunity; no

86 *Kentucky* 473 US 159, 105 S Ct 3099 (1985) 3105 quoting *Monell* (n 52 above).
87 Chemerinsky (n 19 above) 463.
88 *Kentucky* (n 86 above). See Jeffries (n 67 above) 50, who argues that 'functionally' any suit against a state officer is a suit against the state, primarily due to indemnification.
89 *Brandon v Holt* 469 US 464, 105 S Ct 873 (1985).
90 Jeffries (n 67 above) 62.
91 *Ibid*, p 63.

immunity exists for individuals sued in their personal capacity, although a weaker good faith defence may exist.

6. Nature of Protected Rights

The early question of which rights are covered by Section 1983 has resurfaced. In *Lynch v Household Finance Corporation*, the Supreme Court held that Section 1983 covers both personal and property rights, so overruling earlier decisions that only personal rights could found a constitutional action.[92] While most federal constitutional rights are actionable under Section 1983,[93] it will only cover violations of state law and violations of tort duties of care if they also amount to constitutional violations.[94]

Despite this, in 1980, in *Maine v Thiboutot*,[95] the Supreme Court held that Section 1983 was actionable for the breach by state officials of not only constitutional rights, but also federal statutory law, including those sourced in statutes which relate to other than civil rights. This was based on the wording of Section 1983 which relates to 'rights, privileges, or immunities secured by the Constitution *and laws*'.[96] The scope of this decision was subsequently reduced by suggestions of two exceptions: for a federal statute to be actionable, it must confer substantive rights and its statutory remedies must not be exclusive of any others.[97]

Paul v Davis distinguished between common law tort and constitutional tort.[98] In that case, it was held that defamation by a state official did not in itself ground a constitutional tort under Section 1983; the claimant would have needed to show that the impugned actions also breached a constitutional guarantee. Without evidence of the breach of a constitutional right, the Court considered that such action breached interests only, which were protected by resort to tort and not to constitutional law.[99]

92 *Lynch* 405 US 538, 92 S Ct 1113 (1972).

93 Schwartz and Kirklin (n 21 above) 36–37.

94 *Baker v McCollan* 443 US 137, 99 S Ct 2689 (1979) makes this explicit: The first inquiry must be whether the plaintiff has been deprived of any right secured by the Constitution and laws of the United States. In this case, what amounted to a tort did not also amount to a constitutional breach.

95 *Maine v Thiboutot* 448 US 1, 100 S Ct 2502 (1980): Re social security benefits payable by a state department.

96 Emphasis added.

97 *Pennhurst State School and Hospital v Halderman* 451 US 1, 101 S Ct 1531 (1981); and *Middlesex County Sewerage Authority v National Sea Clammers Association* 453 US 1, 101 S Ct 2615 (1981).

98 *Paul* 424 US 693, 96 S Ct 1155. It has been suggested that the true reason for this case was one of pragmatism; had the certainty of a damages award not featured, then the Court would have decided otherwise: Jeffries (n 67 above) 78–79.

99 *Paul* (n 98 above) 1165–66.

7. Standard of Liability

The question of which standard of liability applies is a vexed one.[100] While the Supreme Court has stated that Section 1983 'has never been found ... to contain a state-of-mind requirement',[101] it has been convincingly argued that, in essence, a fault requirement does exist.[102] Brown suggests that requirements for both 'institutional fault' and 'official fault' exist in Section 1983 cases.[103]

Notably, the previous discussion of qualified immunity illustrates that an element of knowledge or intention is required so that fault has been incorporated into the cause of action under Section 1983. For example, for a municipality to be sued, a deliberate act of policy or custom must be instanced: according to Brown, this is institutional fault.[104] In relation to officials sued on the basis of actions made under colour of law, it is necessary to show that officers reasonably knew that they were violating a clearly established constitutional right: this is official fault.[105]

Further, in any Section 1983 case, 'the plaintiff must establish the state of mind required to prove the underlying violation' as Section 1983 itself does not create a right.[106] This means that sometimes negligence will not be sufficient because the particular right breached may itself require intention.[107] In particular, it has been held that negligence is not sufficient in due process cases as unintended loss or injury does not 'deprive' a person of life, liberty or property.[108] Mere negligence is not, therefore, sufficient for a Section 1983 claim to succeed. The suggestion that it is necessary to prove a 'constitutional injury' which at least 'shocks the conscience', as set out in due process cases, also imports an intention element into Section 1983 cases.[109]

In relation to proximity, the Supreme Court has held that the defendant's conduct must have had a sufficiently close relationship with the alleged violation, as otherwise it would not be possible to conclude that a

100 Antieau (n 50 above) 675–77.

101 *Parratt v Taylor* 451 US 527, 101 S Ct 1908 (1981) 1912; over-ruled in relation to the sufficiency of negligence by *Daniels v Williams* 474 US 327, 106 S Ct 662 (1986).

102 M Brown, 'The Failure of Fault Under §1983: Municipal Liability for State Law Enforcement' (1999) 84 *Cornell L Rev* 1503.

103 *Ibid*, pp 1503–4.

104 *Monell* (n 52 above); *Board of County Commissioners of Bryan County v Brown* 520 US 397, 117 S Ct 1382 (1997) 1388–89.

105 *Harlow* (n 56 above).

106 *Bryan County* (n 104 above) 1389.

107 *Estelle v Gamble* 429 US 97, 97 S Ct 285 (1976) re Eighth Amendment and medical mistreatment of a prisoner.

108 *Daniels v Williams* 474 US 327, 106 S Ct 662 (1986) (re substantive due process); and *Davidson v Cannon* 474 US 344, 106 S Ct 668 (1986) (re procedural due process).

109 *County of Sacramento v Lewis* 523 US 833, 118 S Ct 1708 (1998) 1718: 'Conduct intended to injure in some way unjustifiable by any government interest is the sort of official action most likely to rise to the conscience-shocking level'. See Kean (n 42 above) 227.

defendant had 'subjected' a plaintiff 'to the deprivation of rights', in the words of Section 1983.[110] In *Martinez*, the parole officer's decision to release a prisoner was held to be too distant from that prisoner's murder of a young woman five months later to allow a Section 1983 action to stand.[111] The Court considered that it was necessary for the breach to have been caused by a state actor; that a state defendant will only be responsible under Section 1983 for the actions of a third party 'when the third person's conduct was a reasonably foreseeable consequence of the defendant's conduct'; and, finally, that the defendant must have engaged in constitutionally impermissible behaviour.[112]

8. Identity of the Plaintiff

It is necessary to determine who falls within the category of 'a citizen or other person' and so is entitled to bring a Section 1983 action. First, it should be noted that not only citizens, but also permanent residents and even illegal immigrants in the United States are entitled to bring such actions. Claims by a deceased's estate in relation to actions that took place when the deceased was alive are allowed, but not cases in relation to actions that occurred after death or before birth. A relative may claim for the wrongful death of a person not on the basis of the deceased's rights, but on the basis of their own rights.[113]

The phrase has been held to extend beyond real people, to both business and non-profit voluntary membership organisations.[114] Organisations may bring claims to redress their own injuries,[115] and probably also to assert the civil rights of their members.[116] The Supreme Court set out the requirements for organisational standing in *Hunt v Washington State Apple Advertising Commission*.[117] First, members must have the standing to sue on their own behalf; second, the interests sought to be protected must be germane to the organisation's purposes; and third, neither the claim asserted nor the relief sought should require the participation of

110 *Martinez v California* 444 US 277, 100 S Ct 553 (1980). Wells (n 57 above) does not believe that this case answers the question sufficiently.

111 *Martinez* (n 110 above) 559.

112 Schwartz and Kirklin (n 21 above) 71.

113 *Ibid*, pp 21–24.

114 Eg *Allee v Medrano* 416 US 802, 94 S Ct 2191 (1974) 2202, (n 13 above) in which a union was able to raise the same claims as would any of its members.

115 *Village of Arlington Heights v Metropolitan Housing Development Corporation* 429 US 252, 97 S Ct 555 (1977); *Warth v Seldin* 422 US 490, 95 S Ct 2197 (1975) 2211.

116 *Warth* (n 115 above) 2211.

117 *Hunt v Washington State Apple Advertising Commission* 432 US 333, 97 S Ct 2434 (1977).

individual members in the law suit.[118] Overall, however, the section is intended for private actions against public institutions.

The essence of the standing question has been described as determining 'whether the litigant is entitled to have the court decide the merits of the dispute or of particular issues'.[119] The question focuses on the person bringing the claim and not on either the issues or the defendant.[120] It will be determined by considering constitutional and prudential elements. Under the constitutional ground, only actual cases or controversies will be litigated.[121] This amounts to requirements for injury, causation and redressability.[122] The prudential ground predominantly relates to whether the plaintiffs are the proper people to bring the action.[123] Put simply, a claimant must be alleging some injury[124]; the general rules of standing require an element of causation so that there must be a connection between the injury and the conduct.[125] An individual should have suffered an injury, and should be asserting his or her own rights or interests.[126]

While a general rule exists against third party standing,[127] this is relaxed in certain circumstances. These include special relationships such as sellers and prospective purchasers, doctors and patients, and schools and parents and children.[128] It also includes situations in which there are practical reasons preventing third parties from bringing the action themselves.[129] In general, third party standing requires an actionable causal relationship to be established.[130] In the case of a class action, the named plaintiffs must meet the standing requirements and so be able to

118 *Ibid*, p 2441. The third requirement has been interpreted as allowing unions to seek damages awards on behalf of members when Congress authorized such actions: *United Food and Commercial Workers Union Local 751 v Brown Group* 517 US 544, 116 S Ct 1529 (1996) 1537.

119 *Warth* (n 115 above) 2205. For a general discussion of standing see Chemerinsky (n 19 above) 53–113.

120 *Simon v Eastern Kentucky Welfare Rights Organization* 426 US 26, 96 S Ct 1917 (1976) 1924 quoting from *Flast v Cohen* 392 US 83, 88 S Ct 1942 (1968).

121 To fulfil the requirement of Art III, the plaintiff must allege an 'injury in fact' or, in other words, 'a sufficiently concrete interest in the outcome of their suit': *Singleton v Wulff* 428 US 106, 96 S Ct 2868 (1976) 2873. See also *Simon* (n 120 above) 1924.

122 *Northeastern Florida Chapter of the Associated General Contractors of America v City of Jacksonville* 508 US 656, 113 S Ct 2297 (1993) 2301–2.

123 *Singleton* (n 121 above) 2873: Are the plaintiffs the 'proper proponents of the particular legal rights on which they base their suit'.

124 *Arlington Heights* (n 115 above) 561; *Simon* (n 120 above) 1924–25. A pure injury to the right, rather than actual injury, may be sufficient for this threshold issue.

125 *Allen v Wright* 468 US 737, 104 S Ct 3315 (1984) 3324.

126 *Warth* (n 115 above) 2205.

127 *Singleton* (n 121 above) 2874: This general rule exists for two reasons. First, the holders of these rights may not wish, or need, them to be adjudicated and rights should not be adjudicated unnecessarily. Second, rights-holders are usually the best proponents of their own rights.

128 Schwartz and Kirklin (n 21 above) 31.

129 *Singleton* (n 121 above) 2875.

130 See *Warth* (n 115 above); and *Arlington Heights* (n 115 above).

prove injury to themselves.[131] Such plaintiffs can seek remedies on behalf of all other people similarly affected only if the requirements of the class action rule are met.[132] Standing will not be denied simply because many people suffer the same injury.[133]

Public interest litigation[134] as a movement was important in the United States in the 1960s and 1970s. Its transformative potential was lauded and its use 'seemed to be on the rise and gathering momentum'.[135] The impact on who could bring the cause of action was potentially large. However, by 1982, 'counter-tendencies' to public interest litigation in the United States were identified, in particular in relation to issues of standing, class actions and relief.[136] By 1987, an assessment suggested that 'the counter-reaction to PIL has, if anything, become stronger'.[137]

These standing issues are closely related to the requirements of ripeness, mootness and justiciability. These elements relate to the question of subject matter and, in particular, the constitutional element of the standing requirement. Ripeness concerns ensuring the suit is not premature, and mootness concerns the requirement for the litigation to be live. Standing, on the other hand, concerns asking whether this particular person is the appropriate person to bring the case.[138]

9. The Remedy

The section is not specific as to remedy, but clearly mandates both legal and equitable relief; relief with a monetary aspect encompasses compensatory and punitive damages and attorney fees.

The first point to note is that remedies will not be awarded automatically upon claimants showing that their rights were breached under colour of law. Rather, the claimant must show an entitlement to the particular relief sought, as well as defeat any jurisdictional defences such as the Eleventh Amendment and the standing requirement.[139]

Damages for breach of Section 1983, according to *Bivens*, are the 'ordinary remedy' for invasions of personal liberty[140] and, according to

131 *Simon* (n 120 above) 1924; *Warth* (n 115 above) 502.

132 Rule 23 of the Federal Rules of Civil Procedure.

133 *United States and Interstate Commerce Commission v Students Challenging Regulatory Agency Procedures* 412 US 669, 93 S Ct 2405 (1973) 2415–17.

134 Or 'public law litigation' as it was termed in 1976: A Chayes, 'The Role of Judges in Public Law Litigation' (1976) 89 *Harv L Rev* 1281.

135 A Chayes, 'The Supreme Court 1981 Term Forward: Public Law Litigation and the Burger Court' (1982) 96 *Harv L Rev* 4, 5.

136 *Ibid*; C Cunningham, 'Public Interest Litigation in the Indian Supreme Court: A Study in the Light of American Experience' (1987) 29 *JILI* 494.

137 Cunningham (n 136 above) 495.

138 K Ripple, *Constitutional Litigation* (Virginia, MD, Michie, 1984) 88.

139 Schwartz and Kirklin (n 21 above) 287–88.

140 *Bivens* (n 8 above) 2004.

Owen, are 'vital' for vindicating constitutional guarantees.[141] Primarily, damages awarded pursuant to Section 1983 should be intended to compensate and, usually as a secondary aim, to prevent other such breaches.[142] *Carey v Piphus* made it clear that the awarding of constitutional damages should be based on the principles developed in tort law at least as a 'starting point'.[143] While in some cases, where the constitutional rights parallel tort law interests, tort law rules can be directly applied, in other cases common law rules of damages will have to be 'adapted' to constitutional rights.[144] In fact, the Court suggested that: 'the rules governing compensation for injuries caused by the deprivation of constitutional rights should be tailored to the interests protected by the particular right in question—just as the common-law rules of damages themselves were defined by the interests protected in the various branches of tort law.'[145]

In *Carey*, the Supreme Court held that it was necessary for the victim of a deprivation of due process to prove actual injury—which would include distress or suffering—for compensatory damages to be awarded. Otherwise, only nominal damages would be available; here the award was 'not to exceed one dollar'.[146] This is equivalent to the requirement for a constitutional injury which at least 'shocks the conscience', as discussed above in relation to intention.[147]

Had injury been proven, then the second sort of damages would have been awarded: actual damages, which include special damages to compensate for actual loss, and general damages to compensate for emotional pain, suffering or distress. General damages will be calculated according to federal law, with elements from state and common law considered, should it be necessary.[148] As was stated in *Carey v Piphus*, the calculation will attempt to provide compensation only; deterrence will be ensured through the threat inherent in the award of compensatory damages.[149]

The final sort of damages that may be awarded in Section 1983 cases are punitive damages, awarded to punish or deter an official who has engaged in egregious behaviour. Punitive damages will not be available against municipalities. In *Newport v Facts Concerts*,[150] the Court noted that punitive damages are intended to punish the wrongdoer and provide a

141 *Owen* (n 59 above) 1415.
142 *Ibid*, p 1416; *Robertson v Wegmann* 436 US 584, 98 S Ct 1991 (1978) 1995; *Carey v Piphus* 435 US 247, 98 S Ct 1042 (1978) 1047–48.
143 *Carey* (n 142 above) 1049.
144 *Ibid*.
145 *Ibid*, p 1050.
146 *Ibid*, p 1054.
147 Kean (n 42 above) 227.
148 *Robertson* (n 142 above) 1994.
149 *Carey* (n 142 above) 1048.
150 *Facts Concerts* (n 57 above).

deterrence, neither of which were advanced by making municipalities liable in this way. The Court considered that payment of such damages by a municipality only harms the taxpayer. Further, the Court noted that punishment is not a primary purpose under Section 1983, unlike compensation and deterrence. The Court considered that a 'damages remedy recoverable against individuals is more effective as a deterrent than the threat of damages against a government employer'.[151] Thus, the Court concluded that municipalities had an absolute immunity from punitive damages under Section 1983.[152]

Smith v Wade made it clear that punitive damages could be awarded in appropriate Section 1983 cases brought against officials in their personal capacity.[153] The case held that 'appropriate' circumstances would include reckless or callous indifference to the plaintiff's federal rights, as well as intentional breaches.[154] In other words, the standard required is not 'actual intent', but includes recklessness. This will be so even where the underlying standard of liability for compensatory damages is also one of recklessness.[155] The Court pointed out that punitive damages 'are never awarded as of right, no matter how egregious the defendant's conduct'.[156] The jury will be required to find, as a discretionary moral judgment, that the defendant's conduct merited a punitive award in addition to the compensatory award.

These conclusions were reached by a consideration of the common law that existed at the time the section was enacted, and the policy behind Section 1983. Deterrence is the principal aim of punitive damages under Section 1983, and the common law approach accords with ensuring this aim is fulfilled. The jury should, therefore, be instructed to assess punitive damages in Section 1983 cases on these grounds. The Supreme Court held that the jury verdict in *Smith v Wade* of compensation and punitive damages against a prison guard, sued in his individual capacity, should stand.

A number of procedural points are relevant to the nature of the Section 1983 remedy. First, it should be noted that the Seventh Amendment guarantees a right to trial by jury for Section 1983 cases in which damages in excess of $20 are sought.[157] Thus, most Section 1983 cases will involve both judge and jury, and damages awards will reflect this somewhat unpredictable feature. It has been suggested that, in relation to housing

151 *Ibid*, p 2761.
152 *Ibid*, p 2762.
153 *Smith v Wade* 461 US 30, 103 S Ct 1625 (1983).
154 *Ibid*, p 1637.
155 *Ibid*, pp 1638–40.
156 *Ibid*, p 1638.
157 Schwartz and Kirklin (n 21 above) 289 et seq.

discrimination cases, juries tend 'to be more extreme on both the high and low side than judges'.[158]

An important element of monetary relief is the issue of fees.[159] For Section 1983 cases, this is governed by Section 1988. In 1976, the Civil Rights Attorney's Fees Awards Act 'added to the Section 1983 litigation by allowing prevailing plaintiffs to recover the costs of their attorneys' fees'.[160] This statute ensured that Section 1988 fees could be awarded, reducing the money barrier to the litigation of meritorious civil rights claims. Supreme Court jurisprudence has emphasised that fees under Section 1988 are available for any Section 1983 action, including those based on federal statutes.[161]

One important factor is that while the Eleventh Amendment may limit the payment of damages, it will not affect the payment of attorney fees.[162] Further, the payment of fees awards against officials sued in their official capacity will be paid by the state or entity, whether or not it was named as a party.[163] Conversely, for officials sued in their personal capacity, fees cannot be claimed from the governmental entity.[164]

Generally, fees are only awarded to the 'prevailing party' as a matter of policy. To prevail, a party must have won on the merits, or at least in relation to an important claim.[165] Each fees assessment will be made on the facts of the individual case and by determining what is reasonable.[166] Further, to avoid claimants being deterred by the threat of fees in favour of the defendant, fees will only be awarded against a plaintiff if the plaintiff's action was groundless or without foundation: '[t]he fact that a plaintiff may ultimately lose his case is not in itself a sufficient justification for the assessment of fees'.[167]

While fees will not be awarded for unsuccessful claims, there will be no direct link between a fees award and the damages award. In the decision of *City of Riverside v Rivera*, the Supreme Court held that an award of $245,456.25 for attorney's fees was supportable, even though the plaintiffs had recovered only $33,350 in damages.[168] The Court rejected the proposition that a fees award under Section 1988 should necessarily be proportionate to the amount of damages awarded: 'Unlike most private

158 R Schwemm, *Housing Discrimination Law* (Bureau of National Affairs, 1983) 262, cited in Schwartz and Kirklin (n 21 above) 292.

159 Only an overview of the complex body of jurisprudence relating to the litigation of fees in these cases will be discussed here.

160 Chemerinsky (n 19 above) 428.

161 *Thiboutot* (n 95 above) 2507.

162 *Missouri v Jenkins by Agyei* 491 US 274, 109 S Ct 2463 (1989) 2467.

163 *Hutto v Finney* 437 US 678, 98 S Ct 2565 (1978) 2578.

164 *Kentucky* (n 86 above) 3106.

165 *Hensley v Eckerhart* 461 US 424, 103 S Ct 1933 (1983) 1939.

166 *Ibid*, pp 1939–41.

167 *Hughes v Rowe* 449 US 5, 101 S Ct 173 (1980) 178.

168 *Rivera* 477 US 561, 106 S Ct 2686 (1986).

tort litigants, a civil rights plaintiff seeks to vindicate important civil and constitutional rights that cannot be valued solely in monetary terms.'[169] The public has an interest in such cases, and by bringing such a claim, a civil rights litigant also 'secures important social benefits' to the community at large, which will not be reflected in the damages award which is individual.[170] Thus, to link attorney's fees with damages awards in such cases would not make sense.

10. Summary

In summary, Section 1983 has operated as a weathervane for developments in the area of human rights litigation in the United States of America including the tension between the federal system and the state's respective responsibilities. The section itself has been the subject of extensive jurisprudence and, in particular, the theme of immunities has developed a highly sophisticated and complex cause of action.

C. ACTIONS AGAINST FEDERAL OFFICERS

The action for monetary damages for breach of the Constitution by federal officers is an entirely judicial remedy: 'the Constitution does not expressly provide for recovery in money damages for violations of the ... Amendments and Congress has not enacted a statute that does so provide'.[171] The remedy was inferred from the Constitution by the Supreme Court in the 1970s in the *Bivens* case[172] and has evolved since that time through further jurisprudence. The cause of action is based on the premise that the 'Bill of Rights should be self-executing, that rights guarantees have force irrespective of whether Congress provides a vehicle for their enforcement'.[173] Although independent and relating to different potential defendants than the Section 1983 cause of action, the cause of action exists within the context of the Section 1983 constitutional remedial jurisprudence and the two causes of action have become substantially linked.

169 *Ibid*, p 2694.
170 *Ibid.*
171 *Bell v Hood* 327 US 678, 66 S Ct 773 (1946) 775.
172 *Bivens* (n 8 above).
173 S Bandes, 'Reinventing *Bivens*' (1995) 68 *S Cal L Rev* 289, 325, argues that this is one of two far-reaching insights. The other is that 'the Constitution is enforceable regardless of its congruence with state or common law'.

1. History

Before the development of the remedy in the case of *Bivens*, the Supreme Court had considered the possibility of a monetary remedy in 1946. *Bell v Hood* involved allegations of breach of the petitioners' rights by federal officers in relation to which monetary damages were sought.[174] The petitioners based their claim for a monetary remedy on the Constitution, arguing that it was necessary to infer such a remedy when the Fourth and Fifth Amendments were breached.

The Supreme Court allowed an appeal against the federal District Court's decision to dismiss the claim for want of jurisdiction, holding that a federal court must consider a suit drawn to seek relief directly under the Constitution or federal law.[175] The Court based jurisdiction on the availability of a suit to receive monetary relief for breach of the right to vote, of injunctions to protect Constitutional rights and:

> [m]oreover, where federally protected rights have been invaded, it has been the rule from the beginning that courts will be alert to adjust their remedies so as to grant the necessary relief. And it is also well settled that where legal rights have been invaded, and a federal statute provides for a general right to sue for such invasion, federal courts may use any available remedy to make good the wrong done.[176]

2. *Bivens*

In *Bivens v Six Unknown Named Agents of Federal Bureau of Narcotics*, the Supreme Court finally held that the monetary remedy was available in a cause of action based directly upon the Constitution and Amendments.[177] The petitioner alleged breach of the freedom from unreasonable search and seizure by federal agents and sought damages.

The majority decision delivered by Brennan J stressed the difference between the relationship of individuals with one another and the relationship of individuals with federal officials exercising federally sanctioned power.[178] The Court noted that, historically, damages have been regarded as the ordinary remedy for an invasion of personal interests in liberty, while admitting that 'the Fourth Amendment does not in so many words provide for its enforcement by an award of money damages for the consequences of its violation'.[179] The Court considered that there

174 *Bell* (n 171 above).
175 *Ibid*, p 776.
176 *Ibid*, p 777.
177 *Bivens* (n 8 above).
178 *Ibid*, p 2002.
179 *Ibid*, p 2004.

were 'no special factors counselling hesitation' in this case so as to warrant the non-application of the remedy and no alternative remedy developed by Congress was available for this plaintiff.[180] In that context, a cause of action was held to exist under the Fourth Amendment and the particular petitioner was entitled to damages for injuries suffered as a result of the breach.[181]

The concurring judgment of Harlan J is often quoted. He emphasised that federal courts had already inferred such relief in statutory contexts silent as to remedy and that there was no reason for a reduced judicial power in relation to the Constitution.[182] In the circumstances of the case, and after having assessed the policy considerations, the awarding of damages was essential: 'For people in Bivens' shoes, it is damages or nothing'.[183]

The cause of action set out in *Bivens* was developed in subsequent cases. In the early years of the remedy, its development was closely linked with an increasing judicial dissatisfaction with the exclusion of evidence rule.[184] In many of these cases the remedy was cited as a preferable alternative with less costly social implications.[185] In this way, the positive elements of the remedy were closely considered and its scope analysed in cases in which it was not actually used. Nevertheless, three cases, in particular, directly developed the approach that ought to be taken by litigators and the Courts to the *Bivens* cause of action.

3. *Butz, Davis* and *Carlson*: the Approach is Developed

In 1978, the Supreme Court in *Butz v Economou* affirmed the availability of the cause of action sounding in a monetary remedy for the breach of an individual's constitutional rights by federal actors.[186] *Butz* noted the two exceptions to the availability of the remedy set out in *Bivens*: first, when Congress has provided an alternative and equally effective remedy which was clearly intended as a replacement; and second, when special factors counsel hesitation in the absence of affirmative congressional intent. That two-step process has continued to epitomise the *Bivens* action in later

180 *Ibid*, p 2005.
181 *Ibid*.
182 *Ibid*, p 2008.
183 *Ibid*, p 2012.
184 Eg *Coolidge v New Hampshire* 403 US 443, 91 S Ct 2022 (1971) (Burger CJ); *Schneckloth v Bustamonte* 412 US 218, 93 S Ct 2041 (1973); *US v Calandra* 414 US 338, 94 S Ct 613 (1974); *US v Janis* 428 US 433, 96 S Ct 3021 (1976). There was also a link with the question of *habeus corpus*, where the Court had considered the possible social effect of guilty people being released: *Stone v Powell* 428 US 465, 96 S Ct 3037 (1976) and *Brewer v Williams* 430 US 387, 97 S Ct 1232 (1977).
185 See especially *Schneckloth* (n 184 above) and *Janis* (n 184 above).
186 *Butz* (n 56 above). This case is mostly concerned with the question of immunities.

cases. *Davis v Passman* and *Carlson v Green* create a 'trilogy' with *Butz* in the development of the Supreme Court's approach.[187]

In *Davis v Passman*,[188] the *Bivens* cause of action was extended to apply to the Fifth Amendment, which guarantees that no-one will be deprived of life, liberty or property without due process of law. The Court found no difficulty in holding that constitutional rights were different from statutory rights and so, absent evidence of any alternative congressional intent, it was right to assume that the judiciary was empowered to enforce those rights. Thus, anyone whose rights have been breached has, *prima facie*, a cause of action available to them to assert the right.[189]

The Court found that in the circumstances as they existed, the monetary remedy was an appropriate form of relief. First, such relief would be 'judicially manageable'.[190] Although special factors counselling hesitation did exist as the defendant was a Congressman, these were answered by the protections afforded by the Speech or Debate Clause.[191] Finally, the Court noted that there was no explicit legislative declaration that such petitioners should not obtain such relief.[192] The Court did not consider that the floodgates argument had any merit as the Section 1983 cause of action provided exactly the same relief for the same breaches made under colour of state law and the remedy would be available only for violations of constitutional rights, and not for every tort by federal officers.[193]

In *Carlson v Green*,[194] the cause of action and remedy was extended to apply to further constitutional rights. The Supreme Court held that neither special factors counselling hesitation nor any express Congressional intent to the contrary was found to exist.[195] In relation to the last point, the Supreme Court held that the *Bivens* cause of action co-existed with the Federal Tort Claims Act, so that a petitioner would not be required to first exhaust that statute before bringing a *Bivens* claim. In other words, a petitioner can 'pursue both remedies'.[196]

The Supreme Court pointed to four factors which suggested that the *Bivens* remedy was more effective than the statutory cause of action and supported the initial conclusion that Congress did not intend to limit the response in this case to a FTCA action. First, the deterrence purpose of the *Bivens* action; second, the availability of punitive damages; third, the

187 S Speiser, *et al*, *The American Law of Torts*, Vol 5 (Rochester, Lawyers Cooperative, 1998) 121–22.
188 *Davis v Passman* 442 US 228, 99 S Ct 2264 (1979).
189 *Ibid*, p 2275.
190 *Ibid*, p 2277.
191 *Ibid.*
192 *Ibid*, p 2278.
193 *Ibid.*
194 *Carlson v Green* 446 US 14, 100 S Ct 1468 (1980).
195 *Ibid*, p 1472.
196 Davis and Pierce (n 14 above) 255.

option of a jury trial; and fourth, unlike the FTCA, the *Bivens* action does not depend upon the state permitting the cause of action to proceed.[197]

As may be seen equally in the Section 1983 cases, the *Bivens* remedy is to some extent linked with the particular rights and circumstances of individual cases. Thus, it was initially developed in relation to the search and seizure provisions of the Constitution, and it was not immediately obvious that it would be extended further. The first few cases clarified this point, so that it is now clear that the *Bivens* remedy is available for the breach of various other constitutional rights.[198] As an allied point, it seems clear that federal law, and not state law, is the source of a claim for breach of constitutional rights.[199]

McCarthy v Madigan concerned the question of whether a prisoner must exhaust administrative proceedings before bringing a *Bivens* action.[200] The Court held that the petitioner did not need to have exhausted alternative remedies in light of general principles and because it was held that Congress had not meaningfully addressed the appropriateness of requiring exhaustion in this context. The Court felt that the circumstances of the case were such that 'McCarthy's individual interests outweigh countervailing institutional interests favoring exhaustion'.[201]

4. Existence of Alternative Remedies

Alternative remedies were found available, so precluding a *Bivens* action, in two particularly important cases. In the first, *Bush v Lucas*, the Supreme Court held that federal civil servants could not bring damages claims against their employers on the basis of the breach of their First Amendment rights.[202] This decision was based on the existence of an elaborate parallel scheme protecting employers from such actions and providing procedures for such breaches to be remedied, despite the fact that the scheme did not provide total relief for the plaintiff. The Court considered Congress to be in the best position to decide whether a separate damages remedy was necessary in this context.

The Supreme Court somewhat 'conflated' the two exceptions to ask whether Congress had sufficiently created any alternative remedy, or

197 *Carlson* (n 194 above) 1472–74.

198 *Davis* (n 188 above): The Fifth Amendment; *Carlson* (n 194 above): The Eighth Amendment; *Bush v Lucas* 462 US 367, 103 S Ct 2404 (1983): The First Amendment (although not allowed in this case, the Court accepted that such a cause of action existed). *Davis* is generally seen as holding that *Bivens* applies to all constitutional violations: Davis and Pierce (n 14 above) 254.

199 *FDIC v Meyer* 510 US 471, 114 S Ct 996 (1994) 1001.

200 *McCarthy v Madigan* 503 US 140, 112 S Ct 1081 (1992).

201 *Ibid*, pp 1088–89.

202 *Bush* (n 198 above).

whether any other factors counselling hesitation existed.[203] The Supreme Court was wary of 'authorising new kinds of federal litigation'[204] in fact situations which had not previously received the Court's attention.[205] In the view of one commentator, the *Bivens* dissent 'became the majority' in *Bush v Lucas*, so that the notion of deference to the political branches of government was emphasized at the expense of the federal cause of action for damages.[206]

Schweiker v Chilicky, the second important case concerning alternative remedies, involved a social security scheme.[207] The Supreme Court found that adequate remedial mechanisms existed; this was not a context for which the *Bivens* cause of action was created. The Court canvassed the recent judicial decisions that suggested a more wary approach to imposing *Bivens* liability in new contexts and concluded that:

> the concept of 'special factors counselling hesitation in the absence of affirmative action by Congress' has proved to include an appropriate judicial deference to indications that congressional inaction has not been inadvertent. When the design of a Government program suggests that Congress has provided what it considers adequate remedial mechanisms for constitutional violations that may occur in the course of its administration, we have not created additional *Bivens* remedies.[208]

The Court considered that Congress had turned its mind to the instant case, and had determined not to provide such relief, and emphasised that Congress was best placed to decide such matters.[209]

In a third case, the increasingly narrow cause of action suggested by *Bush* and *Schweiker* was further limited by rephrasing the relevant question as whether the individual plaintiff had any effective remedy, rather than whether the existing remedy was equally effective to a constitutional remedy.[210] The Supreme Court in *Malesko* held that Mr Malesko was 'not a plaintiff in search of a remedy as in *Bivens* and *Davis*',[211] although 'the Court recognized that the alternative remedies available would not compensate Malesko fully for the harm that he suffered'.[212] In *Malesko*, unlike *Bush* and *Schweiker*, there was no congressional scheme

203 Bandes (n 173 above) 297.
204 *Bush* (n 198 above) 2411.
205 This wariness is evident in relation to many of the following cases discussed; see especially *FDIC* (n 199 above).
206 Bandes (n 173 above) 297.
207 *Schweiker v Chilicky* 487 US 412, 108 S Ct 2460 (1988).
208 *Ibid*, p 2468.
209 *Ibid*, pp 2468–70.
210 *Correctional Services Corporation v Malesko* 534 US 61, 122 S Ct 515 (2001) 522.
211 *Malesko* (n 210 above) 523.
212 M Mazefsky, '*Correctional Services Corporation v Malesko*: Unmasking the Implied Damage Remedy' (2003) 37 *U Rich L Rev* 639, 656.

to provide an alternative remedy and the Supreme Court relied upon the mere availability of a state law cause of action to rebut the constitutional cause of action.[213]

5. Special Factors Counselling Hesitation

Primarily, special factors counselling hesitation have been military considerations. The military context in *Chappell v Wallace* was held to have prevented a *Bivens* action being available.[214] The Court considered that Congress did not intend to subject the government to tort actions brought by military soldiers for injuries suffered in service and other compensation existed. Further, a unique relationship existed between the government and military personnel which distinguished military from civilian life and had an equivalent effect on individual rights.[215] The Court concluded that these equated to special factors counselling hesitation: 'The special nature of military life—the need for unhesitating and decisive action by military officers and equally disciplined responses by enlisted personnel—would be undermined by a judicially created remedy exposing officers to personal liability at the hands of those they are charged to command.'[216]

A second case in which the military context provided special factors counselling hesitation was *US v Stanley*.[217] The Court held that the claim under the FTCA of a soldier who was given LSD in a military experiment failed because precedent was clear that there was no action arising out of active service. His *Bivens* claim also failed, as those same considerations equalled special factors counselling hesitation; no injury incidental to military service is able to support a *Bivens* claim.[218]

6. Immunities

Having determined an absence of both special factors counselling hesitation and alternative remedies in a *Bivens* case, the Supreme Court will then consider the best way in which the plaintiff's right to compen-

213 M Pastore, 'Running from the Law: Federal Contractors Escape *Bivens* Liability' [2002] *U Pa J Const L* 850, 872.

214 *Chappell v Wallace* 462 US 296, 103 S Ct 2362 (1983).

215 *Ibid*, pp 2365–67.

216 *Ibid*, p 2367.

217 *US v Stanley* 483 US 669, 107 S Ct 3054 (1987). Bandes (n 173 above) 297–98 suggests that this was a 'shocking governmental wrongdoing' and that the case illustrates the Court's movement towards emphasising deference to the legislature, rather than the need to remedy the victim.

218 *Stanley* (n 217 above) 3064.

sation is balanced with the need to protect the decision-making process; in other words, whether an immunity applies.[219]

In *Butz*, for example, the Supreme Court held that federal executive officers exercising discretion are entitled to a qualified immunity.[220] In exceptional circumstances such as those officials exercising functions akin to adjudicators and prosecutors, an absolute immunity would be available if it was essential to the conduct of business.[221] In essence, the Supreme Court has held that it is now impossible to distinguish between the immunities available in *Bivens* cases and those available in Section 1983 cases:

> in the absence of congressional direction to the contrary, there is no basis for according to federal officials a higher degree of immunity from liability when sued for a constitutional infringement as authorized by *Bivens* than is accorded state officials when sued for the identical violation under § 1983. The constitutional injuries made actionable by § 1983 are of no greater magnitude than those for which federal officials may be responsible. The pressures and uncertainties facing decision-makers in state government are little if at all different from those affecting federal officials.[222]

7. Potential Defendants

This leads into the question of whose actions may provide the basis of a *Bivens* cause of action. In *FDIC*, a *Bivens* action was brought against a federal agency, rather than federal agents; the Supreme Court refused to extend the *Bivens* cause of action to this situation on the basis that the *Bivens* logic itself forbade it.[223]

Having held that there was a waiver of sovereign immunity,[224] the Court noted its recent 'cautious' response to the extension of *Bivens* remedies.[225] The Court considered that *Bivens* contemplated official immunity and to circumvent official immunity by allowing this claim against the agency would be to 'eviscerate' the remedy: 'It must be remembered that the purpose of *Bivens* is to deter *the officer* … . If we were to imply a damages action directly against federal agencies, thereby permitting claimants to bypass qualified immunity, there would be no reason for aggrieved parties to bring damages actions against individual officers.'[226]

219 *Butz* (n 56 above) 2909.
220 *Ibid*, p 2911.
221 *Ibid*, pp 2912–16.
222 *Ibid*, pp 2907–8; repeated in *Harlow v Fitzgerald* (n 56 above) 2733.
223 *FDIC* (n 199 above).
224 *Ibid*, p 1004.
225 *Ibid*, p 1005.
226 *Ibid*. This analysis mirrors the analysis in *Will* (n 69 above) in relation to §1983 actions.

Finally, the Court noted that even if such a remedy were consistent with *Bivens*, the potentially enormous financial burden on the federal government was a special factor counselling hesitation and so a damages remedy would be inappropriate in any case.[227] Thus, the *Bivens* cause of action is actionable only against individual federal officers and not against either the United States or federal agencies. It is 'firmly established' that *Bivens* actions cannot be maintained against the United States government because of sovereign immunity.[228]

While it is not clear whether private actors acting under color of federal law or in concert with federal actors will be considered liable under *Bivens*,[229] it seems unlikely in the context of the Supreme Court's decision in *Malesko*.[230] In *Malesko*, the Supreme Court firmly refused to extend the *Bivens* cause of action against a private corporation operating a halfway house under contract with the Bureau of Prisons.[231] The Court held that the 'caution toward extending *Bivens* remedies into any new context ... forecloses such an extension' beyond individual federal officers.[232] It is possible, however, that *Bivens* applies to state actors implementing federal law: in *Chilicky*, the Court did not decide on this ground, thus leaving open that option.[233] It is unclear whether or not *Bivens* actions are available against municipalities.[234]

8. The Remedy

Rules relating to the calculation of damages are unique to the two causes of action.[235] This issue can, therefore, be considered as having been discussed in relation to Section 1983 except for the issue of attorney's fees: it seems likely that attorney's fees under Section 1988 are not available for prevailing plaintiffs in *Bivens* actions.[236] In *Bush v Lucas*, the Supreme Court decided not to address this point, leaving it open for further discussion.[237] While certain statutes could theoretically enable a court to

227 *FDIC* (n 199 above) 1005–6.

228 Speiser (n 187 above) 122. Although note that this is a somewhat disputed position: Chemerinsky (n 19 above) 539–40.

229 Chemerinsky (n 19 above) 544.

230 *Malesko* (n 210 above).

231 *Ibid*, p 517.

232 *Ibid*, p 523. Note that this differs from §1983 jurisprudence concerning action against contractors: See Mazefsky (n 212 above) and Pastore (n 213 above).

233 Davis and Pierce (n 14 above) 277.

234 Chemerinsky (n 19 above) 541–42. There were hopes that the *Bivens* cause of action may allow a way around the limitations on §1983 suits against municipalities: See Note, 'Damage Remedies Against Municipalities for Constitutional Violations' (1976) 89 *Harv L Rev* 922, 958.

235 Schwartz and Kirklin (n 21 above) 289.

236 Chemerinsky (n 19 above) 543.

237 *Bush* (n 198 above) 2408–9 (n 9).

award Section 1988 fees, the Supreme Court has not addressed this point and lower courts have assumed that fees awards under the federal statutes cannot be made.[238]

9. Summary

Thus, while the *Bivens* cause of action clearly exists within the Section 1983 context, many issues which have received attention in Section 1983 cases have not been conclusively determined in relation to the *Bivens* cause of action. This may be partially attributable to the relative newness of the *Bivens* cause of action and to the fact that it is used less frequently than the Section 1983 cause of action.[239] Further, as there is a substantial link between the two causes of action, much of the *Bivens* cause of action replicates the Section 1983 cause of action, despite the suggestion in *Malesko*[240] that the scope of the *Bivens* action will be curtailed in the future.

D. SUMMARY: THE CAUSES OF ACTION IN THE UNITED STATES

The monetary remedy for breach of constitutional rights is well-developed in the United States. This is perhaps unsurprising in a legal system which has had a constitution for a significant length of time, and which places a high priority on the protection of individual rights. The large potential for awards of a monetary remedy to the individual whose rights were breached, as well as the possibility of undesirable social impacts, has been considered in the United States jurisprudence, and many immunities and exceptions apply.

The initial wide application of these causes of action has subsequently receded. Since the 1970s, it has been suggested, Supreme Court opinions 'have become more hostile to individual rights claims, fragmented, contentious, impermanent, and methodologically simplistic'.[241] Nevertheless, the United States causes of action for breach of constitutional rights sounding in a monetary remedy are a central part of the United States legal system.

238 Chemerinsky (n 19 above) 543.

239 Davis and Pierce (n 14 above) 203 suggests that judge-made law under *Bivens* is a 'multiple-iteration, trial-and-error process... Perhaps it is capable of creating a sensible, stable, and coherent body of law if it continues the process for another century or two'.

240 *Malesko* (n 210 above).

241 Schuman (n 9 above) (n 1).

3

India: Article 32

A. INTRODUCTION

THE CONSTITUTION OF India was 50 years old in 1999. The half century of its existence has resulted in a highly developed tradition of constitutional and human rights law in India. This chapter analyses the Supreme Court of India's jurisprudence concerning the remedying of rights breaches by the payment of compensation or damages. The chapter will focus on the Court's approach to Article 32 of the Constitution, which creates a right to a remedy upon breach of the constitutional rights. The National Human Rights Commission, which has the power to grant compensation in relation to human rights breaches, will not be considered in this book as it is not a judicial body.

B. THE CONSTITUTION AND THE SUPREME COURT

Modern constitutional law in India is sourced in the sub-continent's colonisation by England.[1] In the move from Empire to self-government, legislative change notably included attempts at developing a Constitution.[2] The India ultimately created by the India Independence Act 1947 (UK) was a union of states; it was due to the large religious and social variety, and the perceived threat of discrimination and communal discord, that a constitution for the newly created state was considered necessary.

The current Indian Constitution remains largely the same in form and substance to that enacted in 1949 by the Indian Constituent Assembly. It is

1 For more detailed legal and constitutional history see eg D Agarwal, 'India' in A Allen, (ed), *International Encyclopedia of Laws: Constitutional Law* (Deventer, Kluwer, 1993); J Johari, *The Constitution of India: A Politico-legal Study* (New Delhi, Sterling Publishers, 1995); J Johari, *Indian Political System* (New Delhi, Anmol, 1996); G Joshi, *Aspects of Indian Constitutional Law: Sir Chimanlal Setalvad Lectures* (Bombay, University of Bombay Press, 1965); S Sen, *A Comparative Study of the Indian Constitution*, Vol 2 (New Delhi, Orient Longmans, 1966); H Saharay, *Indian Legal and Constitutional History* (Calcutta, Central, 1985).

2 See especially the Government of India Act 1935.

a federal constitution 'modified and adjusted to meet the particular circumstances, problems and needs of India'.[3]

The Supreme Court, at the apex of the judicial system and with original and appellate jurisdiction, 'is the supreme interpreter of the Constitution and the protector of the fundamental rights of the citizens'.[4] It has been activist in its interpretation of the Constitution, perceiving itself as having 'a sacred duty' to deter and condemn unconstitutional actions.[5] All articles of the Constitution have, thus, been interpreted according to 'the dynamic constitutional jurisprudence' evolved by the Supreme Court.[6]

The Supreme Court will interpret the Constitution according to indigenous rules of construction, and not by importing rules from the common law or the United States.[7] The Constitution will be granted a broad and liberal interpretation.[8] The Court has clearly held that it is bound to interpret meaning from the words of the Constitution and not to legislate, although it will go with the 'soul' of the Constitution if it is in conflict with the 'body'.[9]

The Constitution is regarded as the supreme law in Indian society. It is long, detailed and elaborate,[10] and includes, in Part III, a Bill of Rights (Articles 12–32A). The Part is divided into sections. The first section deals with general matters. Article 12 defines the 'state' to include the government, parliament and legislatures of the union and each of the states, in addition to the local or other authorities within India or 'under the control of the Government of India'. Article 13 states that all laws which are inconsistent with the Part are void and that legislation cannot take away rights. The following sections are the Bill of Rights proper, including equality rights[11]; freedoms, including those relating to criminal procedure[12]; rights against exploitation[13]; freedom of religion[14]; cultural

[3] Joshi (n 1 above) 1.

[4] Johari (1995) (n 1 above) 157.

[5] *Basu v West Bengal* (1996) 9 SCALE 298, 302.

[6] *Khatri v Bihar* (1981) 1 SCC 627, 630 re right to life and liberty.

[7] *Ibid*, p 10.

[8] *Ibid*.

[9] *CST v Parson Tools and Plants* AIR 1975 SC 1039 (re general legislation); *Janardhan Reddy v The State* AIR 1951 SC 124, 127.

[10] Joshi (n 1 above) 3. See also Johari (1995) (n 1 above) 12: 'The lengthiest written constitution in the world'.

[11] Art 14 is the classic equality right; Arts 15 and 16 relate to discrimination and equality of opportunity; Art 17 abolishes the concept of untouchability; and Art 18 prevents citizens from taking titles other than military or academic from foreign states.

[12] Art 19 is the right to freedom; Art 20 includes the criminal procedure rights; Art 21 is the right to life and liberty; and Art 22 includes the rights relating to arrest and detention.

[13] Art 23 prevents forced labour and traffic in people; Art 24 prevents child labour (under the age of 14 years old) in dangerous occupations.

[14] Art 25 guaranteed freedom of religion; Art 26 the right to religion; Art 27 relates to taxation with religious connotations; and Art 28 states that there shall be no religious instruction in schools.

and educational rights[15]; property rights[16]; and the right to a constitutional remedy.[17]

C. THE CENTRALITY OF ARTICLE 32

A remedy for breach of the rights is guaranteed in Article 32 of the Constitution:

> **Right to Constitutional Remedies**
>
> **32. Remedies for enforcement of rights conferred by this Part.**
>
> (1) The right to move the Supreme Court by appropriate proceedings for the enforcement of the rights conferred by this Part is guaranteed.
>
> (2) The Supreme Court shall have power to issue directions or orders or writs, including writs in the nature of *habeas corpus*, *mandamus*, prohibition, *quo warranto* and *certiorari*, whichever may be appropriate, for the enforcement of any of the rights conferred by this Part.
>
> (3) Without prejudice to the powers conferred on the Supreme Court by clauses (1) and (2), Parliament may by law empower any other court to exercise within the local limits of its jurisdiction all or any of the powers exercisable by the Supreme Court under clause (2).
>
> (4) The right guaranteed by this article shall not be suspended except as otherwise provided for by this Constitution.

The other relevant clause in relation to remedying breaches is Article 226 which allows claims to the High Court.[18] This article confers the power 'to issue to any person or authority, including in appropriate cases any Government ... orders or writs ... for the enforcement of any of the rights conferred by part III and for any other purpose'.[19] It does not derogate the power of the Supreme Court under Article 32.[20]

15 Art 29 creates a right to minority language and culture and a right to education; Art 30 allows minorities to establish educational institutions.

16 Art 31A relates to the acquisition of property; Art 31B relates to the validity of certain regulations; and Art 31C relates to the validity of laws to give effect to directive principles.

17 Art 32 creates a right to a constitutional remedy. Art 33 reserves the right for Parliament to decide which of these rights apply within the armed services; Art 34 allows restrictions on rights when there is a state of martial law; Art 35 allows parliament to legislate to give effect to the rights in the part; and Art 35A relates to the specific situation in the state of Jammu and Kashmir concerning permanent residency.

18 Except insofar as it relates to Art 32, this section will not be discussed in this book.

19 Art 226(1).

20 Art 226(4).

It is clear that Article 32 is an extremely wide provision which creates a right to bring an appropriate proceeding for one of an indefinite number of remedies available for the 'enforcement' of rights.[21] Article 32 has been described as a unique provision with 'no constitutional precedent'.[22] When discussing the draft Constitution's equivalent of Article 32 in the Constituent Assembly, Dr BR Ambedkar stated:

> If I was asked to name any particular article in this Constitution as the most important—an article without which this Constitution would be a nullity—I could not refer to any other article except this one. It is the very soul of the Constitution and the very heart of it and I am glad that the House has realised its importance.[23]

In the very earliest years of constitutional litigation, the Supreme Court stressed the fact that Article 32, while providing a remedy to rights breaches was, itself, a guaranteed fundamental right.[24] Thus, the existence of other adequate legal remedies could not be used by the Court to decline an Article 32 petition.[25] It is possible that the right extends to a right to obtain a writ when a petition establishes a case for it.[26]

The Supreme Court held that under Article 32 it not only had powers wider than prerogative writs,[27] but it was entitled to hear disputed questions of fact.[28] Thus, petitions for a remedy could be heard under Article 32, even without a first instance decision as to fact and with disputed facts. Such width was based on the Court's constitutional obligation to protect fundamental rights, necessarily resulting in 'the power to forge new remedies and fashion new strategies designed to enforce the fundamental rights'.[29] This was repeated when the Court began to grant the monetary remedy.[30] Other later decisions commented that the jurisdiction conferred on the Supreme Court by Article 32 was 'an important and integral part of the basic structure of the Constitution'[31] and the right guaranteed was 'highly cherished'.[32] This approach was

21 *Mehta v Union of India* AIR SC 1086, 1091: 'The power of the Court is not only injunctive in ambit, that is, preventing the infringement of a fundamental right, but it is also remedial in scope and provides relief against a breach of the fundamental right already committed'.

22 Sen (n 1 above) 160.

23 Constituent Assembly Debates, 9 December 1948, Vol VII, 953 cited in *Fertiliser Corporation Kamgar Union v Union of India* [1981] 1 SCC 568, 574–75; also reproduced (with slightly different wording) in Joshi (n 1 above) 127.

24 *Kochunni v State of Madras* AIR 1959 SC 725, 729.

25 *Ibid*, p 730.

26 *Masthan Sahib v Chief Commissioner, Pondicherry* AIR 1962 SC 797, 804 (minority).

27 *Rashid Ahmed v Municipal Board* AIR 1950 SC 163, 165 (minority).

28 *Kochunni* (n 24 above) 734–35.

29 *Mehta* (n 21 above) 1089.

30 *Ibid*, p 630: 'Forge new tools and devise new remedies'.

31 *Fertiliser Corporation* (n 23 above) 574.

32 *Ibid*, p 575.

reflected in the widening of the cause of action over the past 50 years, to gradually include the power to grant compensation.

D. THE RELATIONSHIP BETWEEN ARTICLES 32 AND 226

The question of *res judicata* and the relationship between Articles 32 and 226 illustrates early rhetorical pronouncements by the Supreme Court about the importance of Article 32. The issue was first heard in *Daryao v State of UP*.[33] The Court held that *res judicata* arguments can be pleaded in Article 32 cases, but provided such strong pronouncements of the right to Article 32 relief that the cause of action and remedy were hardly limited.

Specifically, the Court held that mere technical rules, which *res judicata* was not, would be inadmissible in Article 32 cases. Further, the Court held that where the High Court had decided an Article 226 application on the merits, the parties could not commence the same proceedings in the Supreme Court but, if the High Court's decision was not made on the merits of the case—for example, for reason of an alternative remedy—then it would not be a bar to an Article 32 hearing.[34]

The Court reiterated the importance of Article 32 in protecting the constitutional rights of citizens and the corresponding duty of the Supreme Court. Citizens were considered to be ordinarily entitled to appropriate relief under Article 32 once it was shown that a fundamental right had been violated. The Court held that under Article 32, a right existed to bring proceedings appropriate to the particular writ or order claimed.[35]

The width of this judgment echoed the Court's pronouncements in *Kochunni* in the 1950s: while hearing disputed questions of fact would encourage litigants to bring proceedings under Article 32 rather than by initiating proper proceedings, this was not a cogent reason for denying individuals the fundamental right to approach the Court by way of Article 32.[36]

The issue of the relationship between Articles 32 and 226 resurfaced in the 1980s in a series of decisions which may have reduced the scope of Article 32. *Fertiliser Corporation Kamgar Union v Union of India*[37] was a case brought by the employees of a government-controlled company, seeking to prevent the sale of its plant and equipment. The Court held that the petitioners' fundamental rights would not be infringed by the proposed sale and so it was not possible to utilise the Article 32 writ, which was

33 *Daryao v State of UP* AIR 1961 SC 1457.
34 *Ibid*, pp 1465–66.
35 *Ibid*, p 1461.
36 *Kochunni* (n 24 above) 734.
37 *Fertiliser Corporation* (n 23 above).

only available when a final right was breached. Yet despite this limitation, the Supreme Court stressed the importance of Article 32, 'one of the most highly cherished rights'.[38] The Court reserved judgment on the question of whether arbitrariness would have been sufficient for an Article 32 writ without injury to the fundamental right.[39]

In two cases in the early 1980s, the Court held that there was no right to relief under Article 32. In a tax assessment case, the Court held that it could not act on the documents, because they were still to be proved at first instance: 'The facts being controverted, the petitioners have no right to relief under Article 32 of the Constitution'.[40] In a customary rights case, it was held that usually Article 32 could not be used to determine title or rights, but only for the enforcement of existing or established rights.[41] In other words, the Court developed a requirement for the facts of a case to be determined at first instance, and not to be considered within Article 32 proceedings.

Two further cases falling within this theme can also be seen to have reduced the scope of Article 32. These cases expressed concern with the backlog of Article 32 cases awaiting hearing in the Supreme Court that existed by the 1980s and evinced a sense of relief in being able to refer some matters to the High Court for consideration in the first instance under Article 226.

The Court held that it was more appropriate for the petition in *PN Kumar v Municipal Corporation of Delhi* to be heard in the High Court under Article 226 than in the Supreme Court under Article 32.[42] The Supreme Court would thus be left with more time 'to dispose of old matters in which parties are crying for relief'.[43] The Court stressed that petitioners would not lose any rights by applying first to the High Court. In *Brahmbhatt v State of Gujarat*,[44] the Supreme Court noted that more than 9000 writ petitions were pending, some for more than ten years. The Court took the view that '[t]he time for imposing self-discipline has already come, even if it involves shedding of some amount of institutional-ego, or raising of some eyebrows' to ensure that matters in which the Supreme Court exercised exclusive jurisdiction under the Constitution were able to be dealt with in a timely manner.[45]

Thus, it seems clear that the contemporary jurisprudential picture is that there is a concurrent jurisdiction created by Articles 32 and 226.[46]

38 *Ibid*, p 575; also citing Dr Ambedkar's comments in the Parliamentary Debates.
39 *Ibid*, p 579.
40 *Mohan v State of UP* AIR 1982 SC 33, 48.
41 *Abbas v UP* AIR 1981 SC 2198, 2207.
42 *Kumar v Municipal Corporation of Delhi* (1987) 4 SCC 609.
43 *Ibid*, p 611.
44 *Brahmbhatt v State of Gujarat* AIR 1987 SC 1159.
45 *Ibid*, p 1160.
46 Joshi (n 1 above) 129.

Article 32 relates only to breaches of fundamental rights, while Article 226 applies also to 'other claims'. Whereas Article 226 is discretionary, Article 32 creates a guaranteed remedy for infringements of fundamental rights—'the jurisdiction is at once original, special and compulsive'.[47]

E. STANDING

A second theme evident in an analysis of the first fifty years of the remedy is the relaxation of the standing rules, resulting in the emergence of public interest litigation in the last two decades. The Court in *Gupta v President of India* stressed that it ought 'not be forgotten that procedure is but a handmaiden of justice and the cause of justice can never be allowed to be thwarted by any procedural technicalities'.[48] In *Morcha v Union of India*, a case concerning bonded labour, the Supreme Court held that the state should encourage public interest litigation.[49] The Court stated that public interest litigation was not adversarial; that Article 32 was the way to enforce such rights; and that there were no strict procedural requirements for public interest litigation pursuant to Article 32.[50] This extends to postcards and letters to Judges and media reports of breach.[51]

The Court made further pronouncements in *Gupta* that any member of the public could approach the Supreme Court for Article 32 relief on behalf of another, if acting in good faith 'with a view to vindicating the cause of justice'.[52] The claim must be on behalf of a person or class of persons who by reason of 'poverty, helplessness or disability or socially or economically disadvantaged position' would be 'unable to approach the Court for relief'.[53]

This incursion into what otherwise would be a severe restriction on the practical effect of Article 32 is perhaps especially significant in a country such as India, where the Constitution aims to protect the rights of those whose social or economic disadvantage renders them unable to pursue court proceedings for enforcement. It has had a huge impact upon the legal culture and upon Article 32, by relaxing the rules relating to standing and the procedural requirements for bringing a case.[54]

While the standing rules in Article 32 cases are undoubtedly wider now than 50 years ago, it is possible that the width discussed above may have

47 M Kagzi, *The Constitution of India*, 2nd edn, (Delhi, Metropolitan, 1967) 529.
48 *Gupta v President of India* AIR 1982 SC 149, 189.
49 *Morcha v Union of India* AIR 1984 SC 802.
50 *Ibid*, pp 811–13.
51 *Mehta* (n 21 above) 1089.
52 *Gupta* (n 48 above) 188.
53 *Ibid*, p 189.
54 C Cunningham, 'Public Interest Litigation in India: In Light of the United States Experience' (1987) 29 *JILI* 494, 498.

narrowed somewhat in recent years.[55] In *Narmada*, the Supreme Court seems to have adopted a significantly more cautious approach to public interest litigation in a case concerning the building of a dam.[56] The Court held that 'ordinary principles applicable to litigation' will apply even if a petition is 'termed as a PIL'.[57] The Court set out the intention of public interest litigation as the safeguarding and protection of human rights of people who are unable to do so themselves; and warned against the burgeoning of petitions to encompass wider subject areas: 'Public Interest Litigation should not be allowed to degenerate to becoming Publicity Interest Litigation or Private Inquisitive Litigation'.[58]

F. THE DEVELOPMENT OF A MONETARY REMEDY

In recent years, public interest litigation has become closely intertwined with the development of the monetary remedy.[59] Many of the following cases were commenced and brought as public interest litigation.

Khatri, concerning the systematic blinding of prisoners in a state prison, was one of the first of a group of decisions in the 1980s in which the concept of compensation was raised and considered to be of 'the gravest constitutional importance': 'Why should the court not be prepared to forge new tools and devise new remedies for the purpose of vindicating the most precious of the precious fundamental right to life and personal liberty.'[60]

In two further cases in the 1980s, monetary compensation was sought under Article 32 and denied without any meaningful discussion.[61] It took the shocking fact situation in *Rudul Sah v State of Bihar* for compensation to be granted.[62] In that case, the petitioner was acquitted but not released

55 Further, the wide concept of public interest litigation may not have been wholly followed by the lower courts: Eg in *Manoharan v DIG of Police, Special Task Force* 1994 (3) Cri LJ 2591, the High Court commented that the unlawful detainment claim was better brought by the person concerned than as a public interest litigation; and in *Jain v State of Rajasthan* AIR 1993 Raj 149, 155–56, the Chief Justice of the High Court dismissed a public interest litigation claim on the basis that claiming damages for third parties was not allowed, suggesting that the appropriate process was for the victims to commence civil suits.

56 *Narmada Bachao Andolan v Union of India* AIR 2000 SC 3751.

57 *Ibid*, p 3827.

58 *Ibid.*

59 Eg *Supreme Court Legal Aid Committee v State of Bihar* (1991) 3 SCC 482. See further P Singh, 'PIL' (1993) XXIX *ASIL* 245, 253: 'One of the positive achievements of PIL has been to provide monetary relief to the victims of governmental lawlessness'.

60 *Khatri* (n 6 above) 630.

61 *Kochar v Union of India* AIR 1983 SC 1107; *Chaturvedi v MP* 1983 (2) Cr LJ 1928 (SC).

62 *Rudul Sah v State of Bihar* AIR 1983 SC 1086. For general discussion of the early monetary remedy cases, see eg B Dwivedi, 'From *Sah* to *SAHELI*: A New Dimension to Government Liability' (1994) 36 *JILI* 99; S Jain, 'Money Compensation for Administrative Wrongs Through Article 32' (1983) 25 *JILI* 118; K Joshi 'Compensation Through Writs: *Rudul Sah* to *Mehta*' (1988) 30 *JILI* 69; P Rao 'Retrogressive Step in Compensatory Jurisprudence: A Critique of *State of Maharashtra v Ravikant S Patil*' (1992) 34 *JILI* 472; S Sathe, 'Constitutional Law—I (Fundamental Rights)' (1986) XXII *ASIL* 359, 397.

from custody until 14 years later. The Court noted that Article 32 was no substitute for the enforcement of rights through the ordinary courts when that would be efficacious: '[a] money claim has therefore to be agitated in and adjudicated upon in a suit instituted in a court of lowest grade competent to try it'.[63] This case was, however, considered to be illustrative of cases in which under Article 32 the Supreme Court can order compensation to be paid consequent upon the deprivation of a fundamental right.

The Court centred the discussion of constitutional compensation around civil law compensation. As the Court was convinced that the petitioner would be entitled to compensation in a civil case, to refuse to grant such compensation in the constitutional case was considered to do 'mere lip-service to his fundamental right to liberty'.[64] Emphasising the democratic principles at the basis of their opinion and couching those interests in strong rhetorical language, the Court considered that one of the best ways in which violations of rights could be prevented would be:

> to mulct its violators in the payment of monetary compensation. Administrative sclerosis leading to flagrant infringements of fundamental rights cannot be corrected by any other method open to the judiciary to adopt. The right to compensation is some palliative for the unlawful acts of instrumentalities which act in the name of public interest and which present for their protection the powers of the State as a shield. If civilisation is not to perish in this country as it has perished in some others too well-known to suffer mention, it is necessary to educate ourselves into accepting that, respect for the rights of individuals is the true bastion of democracy. Therefore, the State must repair the damage done by its officers to the petitioner's rights. It may have recourse against those officers.[65]

Thus, while an order for constitutional compensation would not preclude a civil suit against the state and officials for appropriate damages, the compensation granted under Article 32 was to ensure that the petitioner would not be left penniless until the end of the civil legal process:

> A full-dressed debate on the nice points of fact and law which takes place leisurely in compensation suits will have to await the filing of such a suit by the poor Rudul Sah. The Leviathan will have liberty to raise those points in that suit. Until then, we hope, there will be no more Rudul Sahs in Bihar or elsewhere.[66]

63 *Rudul Sah* (n 62 above) 1089.

64 *Ibid.*

65 *Ibid.*

66 *Ibid.* In addition, note *Peoples' Union for Democratic Rights v Police Commissioner, Delhi* (1989) 4 SCC 730, 731 which further suggests that petitioners could also bring a proceeding at tort law subsequent to the constitutional proceedings.

Two further cases in the 1980s completed a triumvirate of cases which established the right to a monetary remedy under Article 32. In *Hongray v Union of India*, 'as a measure of exemplary costs as is permissible in such cases', the state was ordered to compensate the widows of men who had been unlawfully killed by the army.[67] The Ministry of Defence was held to have committed civil contempt in a *habeus corpus* application by implying that the men in question had left the camp when in fact it seemed most likely that they had 'met an unnatural death'.[68] In *Bhim Singh v State of Jammu and Kashmir*,[69] the Court considered that it had the right to award monetary compensation 'by way of exemplary costs or otherwise' to a member of the state legislature who was arrested by the police and secretly detained without charge. The Court noted that in illegal detention cases, 'the mischief or malice and the invasion may not be washed away or wished away by his being set free'.[70]

These early 'appropriate cases' in which monetary compensation was awarded[71] concerned, therefore, unlawful death or illegal detention, involving the more basic of human rights and indisputable breaches. Further, the Court reasoned by analogy to civil law damages, to some extent predicting civil law damages, rather than truly awarding constitutional damages: 'it would not make any difference to the outcome just because a civil suit for damages or compensation was filed'.[72] Making such awards in constitutional proceedings without detailed argument on civil liability was justified by the Supreme Court by rhetorical pronouncements concerning the role of the Constitution and Article 32 in maintaining civilisation and democracy. The imposition of a monetary remedy was justified as no other remedy would correct the infringements.

The jurisdiction was summed up in *Mehta v Union of India*, a petition in the late 1980s seeking compensation for victims of a gas leak:

> The power of the court to grant such remedial relief may include the power to award compensation in appropriate cases. We are deliberately using the words 'in appropriate cases' because we must make it clear that it is not in every case where there is a breach of a fundamental right committed by the violator that compensation would be awarded by the Court in a petition under Article 32. The infringement of the fundamental right must be gross and patent, that is, incontrovertible and ex facie glaring and either such infringement should be on a large scale affecting the fundamental rights of a large number of persons or it should appear unjust or unduly harsh or oppressive on account of their poverty or disability or socially or economically disadvantaged position to require the

67 *Hongray v Union of India* [1984] 3 SCR 544, 548–49.
68 *Ibid*, p 549.
69 *Bhim Singh v State of Jammu and Kashmir* AIR 1986 SC 494.
70 *Ibid*, p 499.
71 *Ibid.*
72 S Sathe, 'Constitutional Law—I (Fundamental Rights)' (2000) XXXVI *ASIL* 97, 114.

> persons or persons affected by such infringement to initiate and pursue action in the civil Courts. Ordinarily, of course, a petition under Article 32 should not be used as a substitute for enforcement of the right to claim compensation for infringement of a fundamental right through the ordinary process of civil Court. It is only in exceptional cases of the nature indicated by us above, that compensation may be awarded in a petition under Article 32 ... . If we make a fact analysis of the cases where compensation has been awarded by this Court, we will find that in all the cases, the fact of infringement was patent and incontrovertible, the violation was gross and its magnitude was such as to shock the conscience of the Court and it would have been gravely unjust to the person whose fundamental right was violated, to require him to go to the civil Court for claiming compensation.[73]

Thus, by this time, the Supreme Court clearly perceived the ability to award monetary damages or compensation under Article 32 as a way for petitioners to avoid unnecessary proceedings to obtain money to which the Court considered them to be undeniably entitled. In this way, the scope of Article 32 was increased to overlap the ambit of civil law proceedings, to provide both compensation and exemplary damages, without requiring petitioners to bring collateral proceedings in the civil courts. The Court emphasised the limited nature of this extension to Article 32, by referring to the requirement for the fact situation to be grave, the breach incontrovertible, the injury obvious and the personal situation of the petitioner such that it would be unjust to require them to bring other proceedings. Once again, rhetoric concerning the protection of fundamental rights was considered ample justification for the increased width of Article 32 to allow the monetary remedy.

The development of the monetary remedy continued in the 1990s. In *SAHELI, a Women's Resources Centre v Commissioner of Police, Delhi*[74] the Court considered a claim on behalf of two women and their children who, in a tenancy dispute, were beaten up by off-duty police officers, resulting in the death of one child and the detention of one woman in jail for two days. It was held that it was 'well settled now that the State is responsible for the tortious acts of its employees', but was entitled to take appropriate steps for recovery of the compensation from any officers found responsible for the actions.[75] Thus, the state was liable *vis-à-vis* the petitioners, but may be able to bring indemnity actions against the individuals actually responsible for the breach. Again, the Supreme Court stressed the tortious nature of the remedy, rather than the constitutional element.

[73] *Mehta* (n 21 above) 1091. Like many claims for monetary compensation under Art 32, it was brought as a public interest litigation. In this way, the increase in scope by one theme allowed a corresponding increase in the growth of another theme.

[74] *SAHELI, a Women's Resources Centre v Commissioner of Police, Delhi* AIR 1990 SC 513.

[75] *Ibid*, p 516.

Nilabati Behera v State of Orissa[76] was one of a series of constitutional decisions in which the Court held that liability to pay compensation for 'custodial death' could not be doubted. The mother of a man who died in custody sought compensation from the state for contravention of his fundamental right to life. The Court emphasised the public law nature of the remedy, which made it distinct from civil law. Thus, it was based on strict liability and was not controlled by the principle of sovereign immunity: '[t]his is a distinction between the two remedies to be borne in mind which also indicates the basis on which compensation is awarded in such proceedings'.[77] Further, this public law remedy must 'be more readily available when invoked by the havenots, who are not possessed of the wherewithal for enforcement of their rights in private law, even though its exercise is to be tempered by judicial restraint to avoid circumvention of private law remedies, were more appropriate'.[78]

Despite the Court's clear statement about the public law nature of the cause of action, commentators still submit that in Article 32 cases involving the monetary remedy, the Supreme Court acts as a civil court, hearing questions of fact, liability, damage and compensation.[79]

Similar statements as to the ability to award compensation, and the distinction from civil suit in terms of the need to mount detailed arguments, were made in relation to further cases in which in addition to the actions of prison officers and the police,[80] the actions of the armed forces formed the basis of the breach.[81] The distinction between civil and public law compensation for a constitutional breach was of great significance in relation to whether common limitations within civil law liability should be imported to the constitutional law.

Basu v State of West Bengal[82] was public interest litigation in response to reports of widespread torture and death in police lock-ups further to the earlier case of *Nilabati*.[83] The Supreme Court noted its own role 'as custodian and protector of the fundamental and the basic human rights of the citizens'[84] and considered that the victim of a crime which involved breach of the Constitution needed to be compensated monetarily in addition to criminal charges being brought against the wrongdoer: '[t]o

76 *Nilabati Behera v State of Orissa* [1993] Cri LJ 2899.

77 *Ibid*, p 2905.

78 *Ibid*, p 2909.

79 P Singh, 'PIL' (1993) XXIX *ASIL* 245, 256.

80 *Re Death of Sawinder Singh Grover*, [1995] Supp (4) SCC 450 re custodial death. See also *PUDR* (n 66 above) re forced unpaid labour and beatings at a police station of innocent people.

81 *Charanjit Kaur v Union of India* AIR 1994 SC 1491, 1495: A finding that the death of the petitioner's husband was attributable to and aggravated by the military meant that the Supreme Court held that the petitioner was entitled to the relevant pensions in addition to compensation under the Constitution.

82 *Basu* (n 5 above).

83 *Nilabati* (n 76 above).

84 *Basu* (n 5 above) 302.

repair the wrong done and give judicial redress for legal injury is compulsion of judicial consequence'.[85] This was at public law and not private law, 'due to breach of public duty by the Sate of not protecting the fundamental right to life of the citizen'.[86]

The Court once again stressed not only that this meant that sovereign immunity did not apply and the claim was based on strict liability, but also that the remedy was in addition to, and not instead of, criminal and civil cases: punishment of the offender would not provide solace to the family of a victim and civil action for damages is a cumbersome process.[87] The Court repeated earlier comments that constitutional damages for breach of the right to life was, therefore, sometimes the only effective remedy for the family,[88] but that it would be without prejudice to any civil action for damages legally available for the same matter.[89]

While noting that the proper aim was compensation and not punishment,[90] the Court felt that 'the purpose of public law is not only to civilise public power but also to assure the citizens that they live under a legal system wherein their rights and interests shall be protected and preserved'.[91] Quantum will be a matter for individual cases and 'no strait jacket formula can be evolved in that behalf'.[92] The state, while primarily liable, may be indemnified by the wrongdoer.[93]

Clearly, the Supreme Court has established a rule that a monetary remedy is available in cases of custodial death. This will be so whether the prison authorities could reasonably be assumed to have caused the death, through torture or otherwise,[94] or where they are found simply to have failed to protect prisoners in custody.[95] It has been pointed out that making the state liable for the failure of its servants to act imposes a 'positive obligation upon the state to protect peoples' freedoms'.[96]

G. EXPANSION OF THE REMEDY

At the beginning of 2000, the Supreme Court decided the important appeal in *Chairman Railway Board v Chandrima Das*, in which an advocate filed a public interest litigation petition in relation to the gang

85 *Ibid*, p 313.
86 *Ibid*, p 313.
87 *Ibid*, p 314.
88 *Ibid*.
89 *Ibid*, p 318.
90 *Ibid*, pp 317–18.
91 *Ibid*, p 314.
92 *Ibid*, p 318.
93 *Ibid*, p 317.
94 Eg *Ajab Singh v UP* AIR 2000 SC (Supp) 3421.
95 Eg *Andhra Pradesh v Reddy* AIR 2000 SC 2083.
96 Sathe (n 72 above) 114–15.

rape of a foreign national by employees of the Indian Railways.[97] This decision made 'more manifest' the principle that where a state employee is guilty of a crime, 'the state must pay compensation for its failure to protect the human beings'.[98] The Supreme Court restated much of the law relating to the Articles 226 and 32 jurisdiction to grant a monetary remedy for breach of fundamental rights. The Court considered the submission that this was, in truth, a claim in private law and not in public law, and held that it was a public law case:

> The Public Law remedies have also been extended to the realm of tort. This Court, in its various decisions has entertained petitions under Article 32 of the Constitution on a number of occasions and has awarded compensation to the petitioners who had suffered personal injuries at the hands of the officers of the Government. The causing of injuries, which amounted to tortuous act, was compensated by this Court in many of its decisions beginning from *Rudul Sah*.[99]

The Supreme Court made it clear that it was beyond doubt that the remedy was available under public law despite the availability of a suit for damages at private law, '[w]here public functionaries are involved and the matter relates to the violation of Fundamental Rights or the enforcement of public duties'.[100] The Court then considered the submission that the advocate had no *locus standi* to bring the claim. The Court held that the case was public interest litigation and reiterated the scope of *locus standi* in that area.[101] Third, the Court held that, excepting those rights which explicitly referred to 'citizens', the fundamental rights in the Indian Constitution are also guaranteed to other persons within the borders.[102] The final submission concerned the vicarious liability of the State for the employees' illegal actions. The Court held that the state was vicariously liable for its employees' actions in this commercial state enterprise, and sovereign immunity could not be pleaded.[103]

In the 1990s, the scope of cases under Article 32 in which a monetary remedy was granted extended to different subject matters from the more usual life and liberty cases. First, the scope of what constitutes a rights breach was extended greatly, in particular in relation to life and liberty. In relation to the decision of the Court in *Neelu Sarin v Union of India*,[104] it

[97] *Chairman Railway Board v Chandrima Das* AIR 2000 SC 988.

[98] Sathe (n 72 above) 115.

[99] *Chandrima Das* (n 97 above) 993–94.

[100] *Ibid*, p 994.

[101] *Ibid*, p 995.

[102] *Ibid*, p 998.

[103] *Ibid*, pp 999–1000.

[104] *Neelu Sarin v India* (1991) 1 Supp SCC 300 re allegations of medical negligence. The Court refused the application for Art 32 compensation, stating that the petitioner would better claim at civil law.

has been submitted that the Court should have held that no fundamental right was involved: 'The court did not do so because in recent years it has given such a wide meaning to the right to life that any claim can now come within the scope of Article 32.'[105]

Second, there has been a significant increase in cases in which the monetary remedy is available, from custodial crimes and atrocities by the police and army towards a 'general theory' that damages may be awarded.[106] In *Rural Litigation and Entitlement Kendra, Dehradun v UP*, for example, when a mining licence was breached, the Supreme Court ordered monetary compensation to be paid by the breaching corporation pursuant to an Article 32 writ brought by the monitoring committee.[107]

Gautam v Chakraborty[108] was a decision extending monetary compensation beyond actions of the state. This case arose from a 'secret marriage' between a young woman and her former teacher which despite the impression given to her by the man, was not a complete marriage. The Supreme Court held that the man could be ordered under Article 32 to pay 'maintenance' to the woman until criminal charges of rape against him were decided. The Court stated that 'Fundamental Rights can be enforced even against private bodies and individuals' and the Court's powers include the ability to award compensation.[109] The Court extended the right to life to include freedom from rape[110] and noted that a victim may receive compensation from an offender on conviction in a criminal court.[111] The Court considered that this ought to be extended to interim compensation as part of the overall jurisdiction of the courts trying offences of rape.[112]

In contrast with most other decisions of the Court,[113] *Gautam* clearly applied the fundamental rights to the actions of private individuals. This decision has probably been over-ruled to the extent that there was no state involvement in the breach. Although the *Railway Board* case also concerns a rape, the Court identified the state's involvement in that rape.[114]

Other decisions in which the defendant's identity was at issue likewise concerned the scope of the state. In *Mehta v Union of India*, for example,

105 S Sathe, 'Constitutional Law—I (Fundamental Rights)' (1991) XXVII *ASIL* 203.

106 R Dhavan, 'Promises, Promises ...: Human Rights in India' (1997) 39 *JILI* 149, 184.

107 *Rural Litigation and Entitlement Kendra, Dehradun v UP* AIR 1991 SC 2216.

108 *Gautam v Chakraborty* (1996) 1 SCC 490.

109 *Ibid*, p 499.

110 *Ibid*, p 500.

111 *Ibid*, p 501.

112 *Ibid*, p 503.

113 *Kochunni* (n 24 above) 730 assumed that a claim must have the actions of the state at its basis. See further, eg R Hingorani, *Human Rights in India* (Delhi, IBH Publishing, 1985) 97; S Kulshreshtha, *Fundamental Rights and the Supreme Court: With Special Reference to Articles 14 to 22* (Jaipur, Rawat, 1995) 53; N Kumar, *Constitutional Law of India* (Faridabad, Pioneer Publications, 1999) 54.

114 *Chandrima Das* (n 97 above) 992: 'The rape was committed at the building ... belonging to the Railways and was perpetuated by the Railway employees'.

the Court had considered the scope of the Constitution in relation to corporations, holding that certain corporate functions, at the least, will be subject to the Constitution in certain cases.[115] Similarly, the Court held that, among other *quasi*-state agencies, a governmental company was required to adhere to the fundamental rights,[116] as were a mining company[117] and match factories.[118]

In one way this restricts the ambit of the cause of action, although as the sort of entities that have been included is so wide, it could be argued that the impact is minimal beyond those cases involving purely private defendants. The *Railway Board* decision is particularly clear in this regard as the Supreme Court held that it was sufficient that the actions were undertaken by employees within the commercial arm of the State.[119]

Early constitutional jurisprudence held that practical difficulties in enforcing a writ were not relevant to the Supreme Court, if such a writ was the appropriate response.[120] In modern cases, the Court has increased the width and possibilities of orders made under Article 32 as adjuncts to the monetary remedy. For example, the Court in *Grover* directed 'that all the persons named in the report ... and others who are accused as a result of the investigation, be prosecuted for the appropriate offences under the law' in addition to the compensation ordered.[121]

In *MC Mehta v State of Tamil Nadu*,[122] the width of directions is especially clear. There, the Supreme Court directed that child workers in match factories could continue to pack matches, but only in areas away from their manufacture. The Court ordered a minimum wage; the provision of education, recreation and socialisation facilities; state enforcement of statutory requirements for medical and recreation facilities at match factories; and the establishment of compulsory insurance for both children and adult workers. Finally, directions were made as to how to fund these orders and the composition of a committee to oversee enforcement of the judgment.

In other compensation awards under Article 32, this imaginative approach to relief can be seen in orders as to where a compensation award must be invested.[123] In public interest litigation where it might not be clear

115 *Mehta* (n 21 above) 1097.

116 *Workers of M/s Rohtas Industries Ltd v M/s Rohtas Industries Ltd* AIR 1990 SC 481.

117 *Rural Litigation* (n 107 above).

118 *MC Mehta v State of Tamil Nadu* AIR 1991 SC 417.

119 *Chandrima Das* (n 97 above) 994, 1000.

120 Eg *N Masthan Sahib v Chief Commissioner, Pondicherry* AIR 1962 SC 797, 805 (minority): Practicalities in the enforcement of the writ should not be allowed to defeat fundamental rights.

121 *Grover* (n 80 above) 450.

122 *Mehta v Tamil Nadu* (n 118 above).

123 *PUDR* (n 66 above): Order that compensation should be invested in a scheme under the Life Insurance Corporation 'so that the destitute family may get some amount monthly and the money may also be kept secure'; and *Nilabati Behera* (n 76 above) 2909: A term deposit for three years during which time the wife would receive the interest.

to whom the award should be paid, the Court has ordered the payment of compensation to be deposited with a District Judge, who in turn was directed to inquire into the identity of the appropriate heirs and then to pay the quantum into a long-term fixed deposit in their favour, if he felt that was the optimal course of action.[124]

H. SUMMARY

The remedial jurisdiction of the Supreme Court under Article 32 of the Constitution has greatly developed in the first 50 years of the Constitution. Remedies awarded by the Supreme Court under Article 32 are of immense width and imagination. A monetary remedy has been inferred in the Constitution with a large scope. Public interest litigation has allowed many cases to be brought before the Supreme Court which would not otherwise have been heard and, although it has perhaps decreased in scope recently, it has been of great importance in the development of remedies. The cause of action and remedy is continually evolving, responding to developments in international and national jurisprudence as well as changing social conditions and expectations. The latest monetary remedy cases make it clear that the Supreme Court is not reducing the scope of these cases.

124 *Supreme Court Legal Aid Committee* (n 59 above) 483.

4

New Zealand: Baigent's *Case*

A. INTRODUCTION

CONSTITUTIONAL RIGHTS IN New Zealand are statutorily guaranteed by the New Zealand Bill of Rights Act 1990. The Act was declaratory, and neither entrenched nor supreme law.[1] The rights protected are classic constitutional rights. While the Act is silent on the question of remedies, New Zealand courts have given it a force beyond that which many critics had considered it to have.[2] A monetary remedy for breach of the guaranteed rights was implied by the Court of Appeal in the decision *Baigent's Case* in 1994.[3]

The jurisprudence discussed below includes cases decided by the High Court of New Zealand, as the number of appellate level decisions on this matter is rather limited.

B. NEW ZEALAND BILL OF RIGHTS ACT 1990

Section 3 of the Bill of Rights states that it applies to acts of the legislative, executive and judicial branches of government and to persons performing public functions, powers or duties conferred by law. The Bill of Rights preserves inconsistent statutes: pursuant to Section 4, courts are not able to hold legislation invalid merely because of inconsistency with the Bill of Rights. The rights are not absolute and, according to Section 5, are subject to such reasonable limitations prescribed by law as are demonstrably justifiable in a free and democratic society. Section 6 provides that

[1] It was not possible to constitutionally entrench the Bill of Rights when there was neither the parliamentary nor public passion and support for any form of a Bill of Rights. See P Joseph, *Constitutional and Administrative Law in New Zealand* (Sydney, Law Book, 1993) 847: The Bill not only did not have the support of the Opposition, but also was opposed by most government members of Parliament.

[2] Joseph (n 1 above) 848. Note that the judicial development of a monetary remedy in *Baigent's Case* has been the subject of 'widespread academic criticism' on the basis that it was granted despite a proposed remedies clause being omitted from the Bill of Rights Act at Select Committee stage: See *Brown v Attorney-General* [2003] 3 NZLR 335, 345.

[3] *Simpson v Attorney-General (Baigent's Case)* [1994] 3 NZLR 667.

where a statute may be given a meaning consistent with the Bill of Rights, that interpretation is to be preferred. Pursuant to Section 7, the Attorney-General must bring any bill that is inconsistent with the Bill of Rights to the attention of parliament. This section replaces the stronger judicial review of legislation and 'exacts political accountability for government legislation that would flout the rights and freedoms proclaimed'.[4]

It is now settled that a broad and purposive approach is taken to interpretation of the Bill of Rights.[5] In relation to remedies, courts have applied the general principle that where there is a breach there will be a remedy.[6] These doctrines have steadily evolved, courts taking a strongly comparative angle.[7]

One decision of importance to the issue of remedies prior to *Baigent's Case* was *Noort*, which confirmed the rule[8] that where evidence has been obtained in breach of the Bill of Rights, the *prima facie* remedy is its exclusion.[9] Procedurally, the Court could not consider the appellants' suggestion of compensation for breaches of the Bill of Rights in the instant case. Despite that, Cooke P commented that the conduct of the appellants was such that the Act would 'fall into disrepute if they were entitled to compensation as well' as their avoidance of conviction.[10]

In *R v Goodwin*, the Court of Appeal further discussed remedies. The Court noted that:

> A statement of fundamental human rights would be a hollow shell and the enactment of a Bill of Rights an elaborate charade if remedies were not available for breach. On the contrary the premise underlying the Bill is that the courts will affirmatively protect those fundamental rights and freedoms by recourse to appropriate remedies within their jurisdictions.[11]

It is within this context that the cause of action sounding in damages was developed.

[4] Joseph (n 1 above) 869.

[5] Eg *Flickinger v Hong Kong* [1991] 1 NZLR 439.

[6] Eg *Noort v Ministry of Transport* [1992] 3 NZLR 260.

[7] Eg *Noort* (n 6 above) 268–69; *R v Goodwin (1)* [1993] 2 NZLR 153, 191–92; *Dunlea v Attorney-General* [2000] 3 NZLR 136, 150–51.

[8] From *R v Kirifi* [1992] 2 NZLR 8, 12, now over-ruled by *R v Shaheed* [2002] 2 NZLR 377.

[9] See especially *Noort* (n 6 above) 285: 'The prima facie rule is that a violation of rights protected by the Bill of Rights should result in the rejection of evidence obtained in breach of those rights. In the present case I can see no justification for admitting [the evidence]'.

[10] *Ibid*, p 275.

[11] *Goodwin (1)* (n 7 above) 191–92. In this case, the Court held that there was no breach of s 23. In *R v Goodwin (2)* [1993] 2 NZLR 390, the Court of Appeal held that there was a breach of s 22. As the Crown did not prove that the breach did not cause or contribute to the inculpatory statement, the evidence was excluded and the manslaughter conviction quashed.

C. THE CAUSE OF ACTION

A monetary remedy for breach of the Bill of Rights was developed in the seminal decision of the New Zealand Court of Appeal in *Baigent's Case*.[12] As a later judgment described it, 'what *Baigent's Case* did was to establish the existence of a remedial jurisdiction'.[13] Both *Baigent's Case* and its partner case, *Auckland Unemployed Workers' Rights Centre*, were settled out of court following the Court of Appeal decisions and before proceeding to trial on matters of substance or quantum.

1. *Baigent's Case*

The police in *Baigent's Case* executed a search warrant for what was thought to be the home of a suspected drug dealer but which, in fact, was for an unrelated address as the warrant named the wrong street. The police continued with the search, despite advice from the homeowner's son and a neighbour that the named person did not live there, and discrepancies in the description of the house. It is alleged that the police officer in charge of the search stated that 'we often get it wrong, but while we are here we will have a look around anyway'.

The plaintiff pleaded, *inter alia*, breach of Section 21, which created the right to be secure against unreasonable search or seizure. The Court of Appeal, Gault J dissenting, refused to strike out the cause of action in relation to the breach of the Bill of Rights. The four majority judgments were extremely similar in conclusions and reasoning. The decision was a very strong and authoritative pronouncement that the monetary remedy lies for breaches of the Bill of Rights Act.

Despite the absence of a remedies provision, the Court held that the rights in the Bill of Rights should not be allowed to become empty words; the Court would develop appropriate remedies to ensure the enforcement of those rights and freedoms. The Court utilised various extrinsic aids to statutory interpretation as well as referring to international jurisprudence in the human rights area, including the Court's important role in ensuring the effectiveness of the International Covenant on Civil and Political Rights. The Court drew heavily on the House of Lords' decision in *Maharaj v Attorney-General of Trinidad and Tobago*.[14]

It was held that the appropriate cause of action to read into the statute was a cause of action sounding in public law compensation or damages as this will often be the only effective remedy in cases not involving the exclusion of evidence. Jurisprudence from other jurisdictions supported

12 *Baigent's Case* (n 3 above).

13 *Manga v Attorney-General* [2000] 2 NZLR 65, 80.

14 *Maharaj v Attorney-General of Trinidad and Tobago* [1979] AC 385.

both the need for, and the effectiveness of, a monetary remedy. Their Honours considered that the legislature intended the rights in the Bill of Rights to be enforced, and so must have contemplated monetary relief in those cases where there is no more appropriate remedy.

The new cause of action was at public law, actionable only against the Crown and only in relation to breaches of the Bill of Rights. This public law cause of action was not based upon vicarious responsibility but upon the direct actions of the Crown. Thus, the statutory Crown immunities from suit in relation to actions of Crown agents and employees did not apply.[15]

Various procedural points were made. The new public law cause of action would most properly be heard by a Judge alone as the damages claimed were not 'pecuniary damages' within the meaning of the Judicature Act 1908. If these damages had been pecuniary damages, then the applicants would have had the right to seek a trial by Judge with jury. Should other causes of action succeed in addition to a Bill of Rights cause of action, the Court considered that the amount of damages awarded should avoid double recovery. There were indications that damages under the new cause of action should not be extravagant; in the instant case, 'an award of somewhat less than $NZ70,000 would be sufficient vindication'.

Auckland Unemployed Workers' Rights Centre Inc v Attorney General was a companion case to *Baigent's Case* and the President stated that the two cases should be read together.[16] The pleadings once again revolved around police use of a search warrant. The New Zealand Court of Appeal reinstated the causes of action pleaded pursuant to the Bill of Rights, both in relation to monetary compensation and to declarations. It made no difference in principle which right or freedom was the basis of the cause of action.[17] The necessity of a remedy was stressed, as were the public law nature and novelty of the cause of action.[18]

The cause of action has developed since those two decisions, although the number of total decisions has not been large. A number of themes has emerged.

[15] See especially s 6 of the Crown Proceedings Act, that includes: No proceedings shall lie against the Crown by virtue of this section in respect of anything done or omitted to be done by any person while discharging or purporting to discharge any responsibilities of a judicial nature vested in him, or any responsibilities which he has in connection with the execution of judicial process.

[16] *Auckland Unemployed Workers' Rights Centre Inc v Attorney-General* [1994] 3 NZLR 720, 724.

[17] *Ibid.*

[18] See eg *ibid*, p 729.

2. Which Acts and Actors are Covered?

The introductory phrase of Section 3 indicates that the Bill of Rights Act applies to a limited class of acts: matters of government or the public sector. Membership of Paragraph (a) is determined by the status of the body or individual; all acts done by sufficiently 'public' persons are included. It is generally assumed that agents and employees are included;[19] as are divisions and branches.[20] In comparison, Paragraph (b) defines the nature of the acts, so that only acts with the appropriate 'public' status are covered; all bodies or individuals performing such functions, powers or duties will be covered, in relation to those acts.

Three themes are raised here: first, the inclusion of the judiciary; second, whether state owned enterprises are covered; and, third, whether private actors are covered.

(a) Is the Judiciary Included?

It seems clear that the *Baigent's Case* cause of action can be invoked in relation to the actions of the judiciary.[21] As this is a direct public law action against the Crown, rather than a personal action in tort against the individual judge, immunities that would prevent, for example, tort law claims, do not apply.

In *Upton*, the High Court upheld a claim for Crown liability under the Bill of Rights for actions of a District Court judge in a pure *Baigent's Case* claim.[22] Tompkins J considered that *Baigent's Case* made it clear that in actions for compensation under the Bill of Rights, the Bill of Rights clearly applied to acts of the courts and, further, that immunities for judicial actions did not apply.

At approximately the same time, the Court of Appeal held in *Harvey v Derrick* that the statutory immunity for District Court judges acting within jurisdiction did not prevent a tort action being brought against a judge for gross negligence.[23] Interestingly, in the course of his judgment in *Harvey*, Cooke P suggested that 'mere judicial error in interpretation of the law'

19 P Hogg, *Liability of the Crown*, 2nd edn, (Toronto, Carswell, 1989) 12; *Baigent's Case* (n 3 above) 677. See *M v Palmerston North Boys' High School* [1997] 2 NZLR 60, 70–71: For agency to exist, a 'close and direct relationship' with the Crown is required. The appropriate test is the 'control' test. In that case, there was no agency as the statute in question did not expressly provide for governmental control over the particular functions.

20 Public Finance Act s 2.

21 Joseph (n 1 above) 855; R Harrison, 'The Remedial Jurisdiction for Breach of the Bill of Rights' in G Huscroft and P Rishworth, (eds), *Rights and Freedoms: The New Zealand Bill of Rights Act 1990 and the Human Rights Act 1993* (Wellington, Brookers, 1996) 401, 433.

22 *Upton v Green and Attorney-General (2)* (Unrep, HC Chch Registry, Tompkins J, 10 October 1996) 19, 20.

23 *Harvey v Derrick* [1995] 1 NZLR 314.

would not give rise to an action for breach of the Bill of Rights.[24] Further, he noted that such an action would not lie against the individual judicial officer, nor would it be based on vicarious liability. Richardson J agreed that no immunity would exist, but seemed to envisage the fact that the defendant was a judge becoming relevant in a Section 5 analysis.[25] It is possible that such a judicial error would be in accordance with law[26] and may be reasonable. These comments were pure obiter, but indicated the future approach.

Thus, *Baigent's Case* circumvents common law and statutory immunities for judges, much like *Maharaj*, the Privy Council decision upon which *Baigent's Case* rested. In that case, it was held that public law damages existed to remedy a breach of natural justice by a high court judge in Trinidad and Tobago.[27] The Privy Council emphasized the public law nature of the remedy:

> … no change is involved in the rule that a judge cannot be made personally liable for what he has done when acting or purporting to act in a judicial capacity. The claim for redress under section 6(1) for what has been done by a judge is a claim against the state for what has been done in the exercise of the judicial power of the state. This is not vicarious liability; it is a liability of the state itself. It is not a liability in tort at all; it is a liability in the public law of the state, not of the judge himself … .[28]

While the early jurisprudence makes it clear that Section 3 of the Bill of Rights Act as currently drafted applies to judges,[29] there have been recommendations that this be changed.[30]

(b) Is the Common Law Included?

While an argument has been made that the phrase 'acts done by the judiciary' encompasses the common law so that the Bill of Rights Act

24 *Ibid*, p 322.

25 This is the analysis of Harrison (n 21 above) 434.

26 High Court and Court of Appeal judges cannot exceed jurisdiction; as the Court has the authority to determine its own jurisdiction, an erroneous conclusion as to the ambit of jurisdiction is merely a mistake within jurisdiction rather than an act outside jurisdiction: *Nakhla v McCarthy* [1978] 1 NZLR 291, 304.

27 *Maharaj* (n 14 above).

28 *Ibid*, p 399.

29 Judges will be protected in an individual capacity from suits under the Bill of Rights Act per *Nakhla* (n 26 above) (High Court and Court of Appeal Judges) and *Harvey* (n 23 above) (District Court Judges).

30 New Zealand Law Commission, *Crown Liability and Judicial Immunity: A Response to* Baigent's Case *and* Harvey v Derrick (Wellington, NZLC r37, 1997). The Commission concluded that legislation preventing a remedy against the Crown for breaches of the Bill of Rights by judges ought to be enacted.

applies to private acts and actors,[31] it seems that the courts have considered the Bill of Rights Act to have a purely public application only. Thus, a *Baigent's Case* cause of action should only be based on a claim with a private element if the conduct or the body is sufficiently public. The point has been addressed most explicitly in *Grayson*, in which the Court of Appeal considered application of the Act to the actions of a police informer who had carried out an illegal search of a neighbour's property: 'Wholly private conduct is left to be controlled by the law of the land. But a search and seizure actually carried out by an informer or other private individual will be governmental in character and subject to the Bill of Rights Act protections if there is governmental instigation or involvement in the search.'[32]

Despite that, the common law will be affected by the Bill of Rights whether or not there is a direct application. For example, when statutes are pleaded in private litigation, they must be interpreted in a manner consistent with the Bill of Rights insofar as that is possible. Further, the Courts are likely to use the standards set by the Bill of Rights by analogy to develop the common law.[33] For example, in *TVNZ Ltd v Newsmonitor Services Ltd*, Blanchard J considered: 'that it would be undesirable for a Court to make a decision inconsistent with those rights and freedoms [in the Bill of Rights] … . In this indirect way the Bill of Rights Act is always present in the background to judicial decision making.'[34]

The Court noted that had parliament intended the Bill of Rights to apply to each substantive judicial decision, it 'might have been expected to so enact in plain terms'.[35]

It seems, in summary, that the Bill of Rights Act in New Zealand will directly apply only to such common law as is called into disputes between the Crown and individuals, yet will continue to exert a background influence, thus indirectly changing the common law and affecting relationships between individuals. The Bill of Rights will not directly affect the common law in purely private litigation.

31 Each of the two opposing views has received academic support in New Zealand. A Butler, 'The New Zealand Bill of Rights and Private Common Law Litigation' [1991] *NZLJ* 261 took the view that by referring to 'acts done by the judicial branch', the section intended the common law to be subject to the Bill of Rights even in purely private litigation. He considered that the development of the common law is 'a paradigmatically judicial act' drawing it within the s 3 definition and meaning that the public or private identity of parties to the litigation is irrelevant. Rishworth and Paciocco, on the other hand, have argued that the Bill of Rights controls the common law only when the Crown or a public authority seeks to rely upon it to its advantage: P Rishworth, 'The Potential of the New Zealand Bill of Rights' [1990] *NZLJ* 68, 71; D Paccioco, 'The New Zealand Bill of Rights Act 1990: Curial Cures for a Debilitated Bill' [1990] *NZ Rec L* 353, 357.

32 *R v Grayson and Taylor* [1997] 1 NZLR 399, 407.

33 J Burrows, *Statute Law in New Zealand* (Wellington, Butterworths, 1992) 334.

34 *TVNZ Ltd v Newsmonitor Services Ltd* [1994] 2 NZLR 91, 95.

35 *Ibid.*

(c) What does Public Mean?

In Section 3(b), the focus is shifted from the nature of the actors (the branches of government) to the nature of the acts. Paragraph (b) requires a 'public' element. In post-devolution New Zealand, the true constitutional position of individual bodies is often a vexed question. As Joseph has noted, 'this limb also imports all the ambiguity that infects the public/private distinction'.[36] In essence, the jurisprudence has been concerned with whether or not state owned enterprises ('SOEs'), hybrids of pure commerciality and Crown entity,[37] are subject to the Bill of Rights.

In the *Palmerston North Boys' High School* case,[38] Goddard J concluded that the school board of trustees had exercised neither a statutory power of decision, nor a statutory function, and so there was no public function conferred by law. In her Honour's opinion, the function of administering a boarding school was an essentially private one, based upon a private commercial contract. She considered that 'the reference to "public" function reflects the principle that the Bill of Rights applies only to public and governmental action and not to private actions'.[39] She seemed to assume that 'statutory authority' equated to 'public function'.

In *Television New Zealand Ltd v Newsmonitor Services Ltd*, Section 3(b) of the Bill of Rights was considered in relation to TVNZ.[40] Blanchard J held that TVNZ's trading activities and control of its copyrights did not fall within the purview of Section 3(b) of the Bill of Rights Act as in those aspects, the SOE was in truth a trading company.[41]

In *Federated Farmers v NZ Post*, Section 3(b) was considered in relation to the postal service reformed in 1987 under the State Owned Enterprises Act.[42] McGechan J was called to consider NZ Post's ('NZP') provision of a rural mail service. His Honour addressed Section 3 as a threshold question:

> The Bill of Rights is to be interpreted in a suitably generous and purposive way, consistent with its aims … . It would not be in that spirit to shut a major vehicle of communication out from obligations under s 14 as to freedom of expression. I have no difficulty regarding mail handling as a 'public function'. It is carried out for the public, in the public interest, and moreover by a company which

36 Joseph (n 1 above) 855.
37 *Lawson v Housing New Zealand* (1996) 3 HRNZ 285, 328.
38 *Palmerston North Boys'* (n 19 above) 71.
39 *Ibid.*
40 *TVNZ* (n 34 above).
41 *Ibid*, p 96.
42 *Federated Farmers of New Zealand Inc v New Zealand Post Ltd* [1990–92] 3 NZBORR 339.

> while technically a separate entity presently is wholly owned and ultimately controlled by the Crown: a 'State-Owned Enterprise'. For Bill of Rights purposes and as an ordinary use of language NZP can and should be regarded as exercising 'public functions'. I do not encourage fine distinctions amongst those functions. Its public functions—mail handling, in the broad sense—are both conferred and imposed by law ... . NZP activity does not have its genesis in whim, or voluntary decision.[43]

McGechan J held that the claim, despite involving an example of 'public functions', failed on the Section 5 reasonableness test.[44] In this way, the cause of action and right were not limited at the threshold stage, and those factors which may have been limiting (ie SOE status) were brought into consideration later.

In *Lawson v Housing New Zealand*, the High Court considered Section 3(b) in relation to Housing New Zealand ('HNZ'), a state-owned corporation.[45] HNZ was set up in a manner similar to a SOE.[46] The submission that the implementation of a market rental policy is a private function merely because there is no statutory reference to it was rejected: 'the wording of s 3(b) does not require that a function must be explicitly mentioned in legislation for it to be "public".'[47] It was held that HNZ's actions fell within Section 3: 'the fact that a particular body is essentially private in nature does not of itself obviate compliance with the New Zealand Bill of Rights Act 1990 ... . Pursuant to s 3 the act done, the increasing of rent, does not need to be public provided it is done in the performance of a public function power or duty.'[48]

Thus, the court appeared to focus upon the functions carried out, rather than either the nature of the particular body or the particular acts in question. This approach means that it is most likely that SOEs will, *prima facie*, fall within Section 3(b), with the final decision determined by an examination of whether the particular functions in question are sufficiently public.

In summary, it seems that Paragraph (b) has a meaning allied to the bodies which fall within 'the branches of government' in Paragraph (a) as each subsection must give context to the other.[49] It seems reasonable for Section 3(b) to apply to bodies excluded from the definition of 'Crown' by recent public restructuring as such bodies must have been within the legis-

43 *Ibid*, p 394.
44 *Ibid*, p 395 et seq.
45 *Lawson* (n 37 above) 328–29.
46 Housing Restructuring Act 1992 s 4.
47 *Lawson* (n 37 above) 328.
48 *Ibid*, p 329. Note that this was not a concluded view, in light of the later finding that the substantive rights section did not apply here.
49 *Federated Farmers* (n 42 above) 394.

lature's contemplation when the distinction in Section 3 was drafted.[50] It is appropriate that individuals should be protected from the actions of bodies and individuals who are acting with the state's tacit backing or support, as much as bodies with direct state power.[51]

3. Protections from Suit

(a) Immunities

The Bill of Rights sets out neither the standard of liability required for a cause of action brought pursuant to it to be established, nor the immunities which will apply.

In the pre-*Baigent's Case* decision of *Goodwin*, Cooke P noted that 'Bill of Rights violations do not depend on a kind of *mens rea* on the part of the officer ... . It is primarily from the point of view of the actual effect of what is done that a Bill of Rights issue has to be approached. The right is the starting point.'[52]

There is a convincing consensus in post-*Baigent's Case* jurisprudence that there is neither a good faith defence nor a judicial immunity from liability under the *Baigent's Case* cause of action. At the most, there has been an indication that liability for judges' breaches will require more than 'mere judicial error', denoting a partial fault element at least in relation to actions of the judiciary.[53] This is a strict liability cause of action, with limited protections from suit.[54]

In *Whithair*, the Chief Justice authoritatively decided that no proof of fault was required when arguing a *Baigent's Case* claim.[55] The Chief Justice considered that there was no principled basis for Court-proscribed limits on the remedies in the absence of legislative intention.[56] As both the *Baigent's Case* decision and the statute are quiet on the matter, His Honour considered that to hold that bad faith was an element of the cause of action would be to circumscribe the remedy by imposing an additional requirement.[57]

[50] P Radich and R Best, 'Section 3 of the Bill of Rights' [1997] *NZLJ* 251, 254 suggest that by encompassing both governmental and public acts, s 3 'is consistent with the devolution of the state in New Zealand'.

[51] *Grayson* (n 32 above).

[52] *Goodwin (1)* (n 7 above) 172.

[53] *Harvey* (n 23 above) 322.

[54] This has echoes in the context of the exclusion of evidence: The Court in *Shaheed* noted that while evidence of bad faith will require the exclusion of evidence, 'good faith will in itself often be merely a neutral factor': *Shaheed* (n 8 above) 125.

[55] *Whithair v Attorney-General* [1996] 2 NZLR 45.

[56] *Ibid*, p 57.

[57] The District Court in *Kerr v Attorney-General* (Unrep, NP 233/95, DC, Timaru Judge Ryan, 7 August 1996) 9 felt bound to 'accept that it is not necessary to allege bad faith' in *Baigent's Case* pleadings.

Cooke P's comment in *Goodwin (1)* that Bill of Rights cases require no *mens rea* was repeated in *Manga.*[58] There, it was again held that good faith was irrelevant 'at least with respect to liability'.[59]

There are, of course, other immunities that may apply to the cause of action. The interplay of Sections 4–6 of the New Zealand Act makes it clear that the Bill of Rights will not be subject to common law, as opposed to statutory, immunities. In New Zealand, there are numerous statutory provisions providing protection from liability in relation to the exercise of statutory powers, some of which may provide at least a partial protection from suit under the *Baigent's Case* cause of action.[60]

(b) What Injury is Required?

While it has been suggested that the Bill of Rights claim for damages should be actionable *per se*,[61] the case law suggests the need for proof of some loss, in a wide sense. In *Kerr*, the Court noted that there was no measurable loss, but focussed on damage to the applicant's reputation.[62] *Baigent's Case* itself indicated that intangible harm such as distress and injured feelings may be compensated[63] and *J v Attorney-General* held that economic and projected economic loss are compensable.[64] *Upton*[65] and *Lewis*[66] suggest that some sort of consequential result is required, although it has been argued that this approach is inconsistent with *Baigent's Case*, which emphasises the difference between damages and public law compensation, and the rights-centred approach.[67]

While the matter was not directly raised in *Dunlea*, the majority's suggestion that the appropriate remedial approach for Bill of Rights cases was the same as for tort cases,[68] makes it highly likely that the injury requirement of civil law will be imported into *Baigent's Case* jurisprudence. The minority judgment, which emphasised the difference between private law and public law remedies, perhaps shows that the question is still somewhat open:

> Compensation for a breach of the Bill of Rights therefore embraces the extra dimension of vindicating the plaintiff's right, a right which has been vested with

58 *Goodwin (1)* (n 7 above) 172.
59 *Manga v Attorney-General* (n 13 above) 70.
60 See NZLC r37 (n 30 above) for a gathering together of all the immunities and an initial analysis of their applicability here.
61 Harrison (n 21 above) 427.
62 *Kerr* (n 57 above) 13.
63 *Baigent's Case* (n 3 above) 678.
64 *J v AG* (1995) 2 HRNZ 311, 316–18.
65 *Upton (2)* (n 22 above) 20.
66 *R v Lewis* (1995) 2 HRNZ 45, 49.
67 R Harrison, 'Public Law and Private Redress' [1996] *NZ Rec L Rev* 478, 484–85.
68 *Dunlea* (n 7 above).

> an intrinsic value, and it is that intrinsic value to the plaintiff for which he or she must be compensated over and above the damages which the common law torts have traditionally attracted.[69]

Nevertheless, it is most likely, given the majority judgment, that injury to the 'intrinsic value' of a right will not be sufficient for monetary relief to be awarded, but may be relevant at the point that quantum is determined.

4. The Remedy

A final set of themes surround the New Zealand approach to awarding the remedy being developed by the courts. This is despite the tendency for parties to settle cases, at least once liability has been established.[70] It is difficult to know whether the remedial approach developed so far is the result of what will develop into a pattern or is the disproportionate effect of the small number of early cases. Either way, at present the New Zealand approach to awarding monetary relief under *Baigent's Case* is flexible, discretionary, and linked with private law damages, even if only in juxtaposition.

(a) Remedial Discretion

It seems clear from the jurisprudence that the Court considers itself to have a remedial discretion. This is a defining feature of the case law.

The Courts have created a pool of potential remedies for the Bill of Rights. Although there have been suggestions of presumptive remedial rules, such an approach has lost its ascendancy.[71] In *Grayson*, the Court of Appeal made strong obiter statements suggesting a more flexible remedial approach than a classic exclusionary rule, while reiterating a robust and rights-centred approach to individual rights.[72] The Court emphasized that remedies ought to be appropriate to all the circumstances, including the

[69] *Ibid*, p 157.

[70] Eg *Baigent's Case* (n 3 above) and *AUWRC* (n 16 above). The High Court in *Brown* (n 2 above) 345 noted that in only five cases to date had a monetary remedy been awarded, although in relation to other cases, out of court settlements were reached and common law damages had been awarded concerning the same matters. In *Manga* (n 13 above) 82, the Court commented on the risk of a disproportionate effect of individual cases in a small democracy like New Zealand; this effect is obviously accentuated when in only a small subset of cases the court is called upon to determine quantum.

[71] Eg the presumptive exclusionary rule in relation to evidence tainted by a Bill of Rights breach: See *Noort* (n 6 above) and *Kirifi* (n 8 above) for the development of the rule. There has been the suggestion in *Martin v Tauranga District Council* [1995] 2 NZLR 419, 427–28 the standard setting decision for delay cases, that there may be a presumption in favour of monetary compensation. For criticisms of the presumptive approach to evidence, see C Walker, 'Wilkes and Liberty: A Critique of the Prima Facie Exclusionary Rule' (1996) 17 *NZULR* 69.

[72] *Grayson* (n 32 above) 412.

nature and seriousness of the breach: a remedy should be 'appropriate to the circumstances of the breach rather than a remedy inflexibly applied in respect of all breaches'.[73] The Court was concerned that the remedy should be 'fashioned to bear some relationship to the nature and seriousness of the breach'.[74]

The majority judgments in *Baigent's Case* suggest that the idea of tailoring the remedy to best fit the circumstances of the breach is embedded in the concept of an effective and appropriate remedy.[75] This is consistent with the Court's approach in earlier cases such as *Noort*, where Cooke P noted that the New Zealand courts were obliged to give practical effect to the Bill of Rights. As practical effect is 'a question of fact dependant on the particular circumstances', this must prohibit detailed rules being laid down in advance.[76]

The tailoring approach to remedy seems to work by the court taking into account at that time all the factors that the New Zealand decisions have determined do not affect liability, such as good faith, intention, plaintiff's conduct, the seriousness of the breach, and the wider circumstances. In *Hewitt*, the Full Court considered that 'the Courts ought to take a flexible approach to do justice and to meet the circumstances of the particular case, especially in the early stages of exploring and developing the ways in which the rights afforded by the Act should be vindicated or made effective.'[77] In that case, the Court considered that damages at common law would not be different from 'a proper award of compensation for breach of the NZBORA'.[78] Thus, there was no need for a separate award of Bill of Rights compensation in addition to the global sum already awarded.

In *Manga*, the High Court held that 'the question of the degree of culpability of a defendant is much better addressed in a remedial context' than in relation to liability.[79] His Honour commented that taking such remedial choices 'is a complex and difficult area of the law of remedies', but that the sort of relevant factors influencing remedial choice in *Baigent's Case* cases are both wider than those governing private law damages, and differing in character.[80] The Court suggested starting with a declaration of the violation of rights; '[w]hether a Court should move to

73 *Ibid.*

74 *Ibid.*

75 *Baigent's Case* (n 3 above) 692; 718. See M Pilkington, 'Damages as a Remedy for Infringement of the Canadian Charter of Rights and Freedoms' (1984) 62 *Can Bar Rev* 517, 535 who suggests that 'the elements of a remedy in damages for constitutional wrongs can be tailored to meet [the various] objectives'.

76 *Noort* (n 6 above) 270–71.

77 *Attorney-General v Hewitt* [2000] 2 NZLR 111, 127.

78 *Hewitt* (n 77 above) 127.

79 *Manga* (n 13 above) 72.

80 *Ibid*, p 81.

monetary relief surely depends on whether there is anything which is not (appropriately) covered by an existing or collateral cause of action'.[81] Remedial powers should be exercised with restraint because the Court should look for voluntary compliance rather than confrontation whenever possible, and the 'real power' of Courts is 'moral persuasion'.[82] In this case, nothing outside compensatory civil law damages was necessary to vindicate the rights breach.

Dunlea was a Court of Appeal decision decided shortly after *Manga* and *Hewitt*. The majority refrained from commenting on the most desirable approach to remedying breaches of the Bill of Rights, but indicated that they favoured an approach that would be the same as that for determining damages for torts arising from similar facts.[83] The common law approach, the Court considered, indicates the importance of assessing all the circumstances of the unlawful act, including the value of the right infringed.[84]

Thomas J, in dissent, chose to comment on his view of the proper approach to remedy in Bill of Rights cases. He vigorously rejected the ideas that a declaration alone would vindicate rights and that monetary relief should only be awarded where an equivalent common law cause of action also exists.[85] He considered that the vindication of rights is an 'extra dimension' to private law claims; and that the amount will vary dependant on such matters as the nature of the right and the gravity of the breach.[86]

In *Upton (2)*, Tompkins J utilised this approach to some extent. He held that compensation would be available if the plaintiff could 'demonstrate that the events that occurred, resulting from the denial of his right, justify an award of compensation'.[87] Holding that there was 'a reasonable possibility'[88] that the result may have been different if there had been no breach, the Court made the first discretionary decision: the nature of the remedy, in this case, the monetary remedy. His Honour then exercised the second discretion, of quantum. Noting that there was no magical or mathematical reasoning leading to his conclusion, Tompkins J assessed all the factors surrounding the breach and concluded a figure as appropriate compensation in the case.[89]

The later cases clearly support the highly flexible and discretionary approach to remedy suggested in the earlier cases. In *R v Shaheed*, the

[81] *Ibid*, p 82.
[82] *Ibid*.
[83] *Dunlea* (n 7 above) 149.
[84] *Ibid*, p 151.
[85] *Ibid*, p 153.
[86] *Ibid*, p 157.
[87] *Upton (2)* (n 22 above) 20.
[88] *Ibid*, p 23.
[89] *Ibid*.

majority of the Court of Appeal expressly stated that, rather than a *prima facie* exclusionary rule, 'the proper approach is to conduct a balancing exercise in which the fact that there has been a breach of the accused's guaranteed right is a very important but not necessarily determinative factor'.[90] The Court commented that, in certain situations, the exercise of the alternative remedy of *Baigent's Case* damages may be a relevant factor to take into account in the balancing exercise.[91]

In *Brown*, the High Court noted with approval that such an approach would ensure that there was no distortion of the rights themselves, as judges could determine that although a right had been breached, no remedy should be awarded in the particular circumstances.[92] In that case, the Court held that monetary compensation was not available but stated that, even if it had been available, compensation would not have been awarded: 'compensation is a discretionary remedy and must be seen as only available in exceptional circumstances'.[93]

As the *Baigent's Case* monetary remedy is awarded in the exercise of a judicial discretion, in *Sugrue* it was likened to compensation awards in equity, so allowing the courts flexibility to, for example, refuse monetary relief in the case of significant delay.[94]

(b) Calculation of Remedy

Determining quantum in these cases will be part of the discretionary and flexible approach. The early decisions illustrate the way in which the court has reached a decision as to the amount of an award. *Baigent's Case* clearly stated that awards should not be 'extravagent'.[95] Further, Cooke P envisaged the award of a global sum and pointed out that courts needed to be astute to avoid double recovery in Bill of Rights cases for monetary relief gained in tort cases.[96]

In *J v Attorney-General*, Tompkins J held that any compensation awarded pursuant to the *Baigent's Case* cause of action could properly include loss of earnings. The assessment would involve a calculation of earnings lost until the date of the eventual hearing and a projection of lost earnings after it. On the other hand, it was accepted that a claim for exemplary damages could not stand. The Court reached that conclusion on the basis of the discussion in *Baigent's Case*, without expressing any

90 *Shaheed* (n 8 above) 122.
91 *Ibid*, pp 129–130.
92 *Brown* (n 2 above) 349.
93 *Ibid*, p 359.
94 *PF Sugrue Ltd v Attorney-General* [2004] 1 NZLR 207.
95 *Baigent's Case* (n 3 above).
96 *Ibid*.

conclusion as to whether the cause of action requires an approach similar to or different from that of tort actions.[97]

In *Upton (2)*, Tompkins J considered *Baigent's Case* to be authority that a monetary payment by way of compensation may be, but not necessarily will be, the appropriate remedy.[98] His Honour observed that actual injury did not need to be proved, but that it was sufficient that there was a risk of it.[99] Fair compensation was determined to be $NZ 15,000: 'I do not arrive at this figure by any mathematical process. Rather it is a broad assessment of an appropriate amount for the loss of the chance.'[100]

The distinction between private law and public law monetary relief has been influential in determining the calculation of quantum in New Zealand. The High Court in *Hewitt* and *Manga* considered that the fact that *Baigent's Case* established a public law remedy meant that different rules applied to the awarding of compensation or damages for breach of the Bill of Rights from those that applied to tort law awards.[101] The human rights context of Bill of Rights Act cases was considered determinative.

A Court of Appeal decision of the same year potentially overruled this. In *Dunlea*, the majority refrained from deciding the matter, but strongly suggested that no different approach was required[102]; the minority preferred to emphasise the difference between private law and public law remedies.[103] As a result, any award of monetary relief would reflect more than the expected loss, and would include vindication for the intrinsic value of the right.

The idea that tort law rules will operate as a basis for determining Bill of Rights quantum seems to have received further support in *Wilding*, where the Court of Appeal held that the statutory bar to damages for personal injury applied equally to *Baigent's Case* claims, as what mattered was that an effective remedy was available for the breach of the Bill of Rights, and not that it was ordered under the Bill of Rights itself.[104]

In that case, the fact that Parliament had deemed the amount of compensation recoverable under the relevant law to be effective for personal injury, barring all claims at tort law for personal injury in New Zealand, meant that the statutory compensation would be an effective remedy for Bill of Rights breaches also. The Court noted that in such cases

97 *J v Attorney-General (1)* (1995) 2 HRNZ 311, 317–18. The substantive claim failed on the facts, Morris J finding that no breach had occurred: *J v Attorney-General (2)* (Unrep, HC Akld Registry, Morris J, 26 November 1996, CP 82/95).
98 *Upton (2)* (n 22 above) 19.
99 *Ibid*, pp 22–23.
100 *Ibid*, p 23.
101 *Hewitt* (n 77 above); *Manga* (n 13 above).
102 *Dunlea* (n 7 above).
103 *Ibid*, p 157.
104 *Wilding v Attorney-General* [2003] 3 NZLR 787, 792–93.

declaratory relief under the Bill of Rights might be issued contemporaneously. The Court could 'see no need for direct recourse to the Bill of Rights Act in a civil claim where an effective remedy can be provided by other means'.[105]

Nevertheless, the Court noted that it did not consider 'that the breach of a guaranteed right which results in physical injury cannot be marked out by an award of *Baigent* damages, merely that the award is not to be quantified so as to provide compensation for the injury itself'.[106] The Court observed that, dependent on the facts determined at trial, it might be that the High Court could award *Baigent's Case* compensation for the affront to the plaintiff's rights, rather than for the injury actually suffered.

(c) Who Pays?

The first option, that the relevant individual is liable, was dismissed in *Innes v Wong*.[107] In that case, the claim against a Board's Chief Executive was struck out as he had done nothing outside the scope of his employment; a claim against the Board or Attorney-General was sufficient and an individual claim was inappropriate in a case involving public law damages. The Judge considered that the state had responsibilities both under the Bill of Rights and generally to prevent human rights abuses.[108]

The second option, that the liability for monetary compensation should lie with the public body that caused it, emphasizes the devolution of Crown responsibilities to many public bodies. Such clear governmental intent ought not to be subverted, it is argued, by holding the Crown and not the individual entity responsible under the Bill of Rights.[109] Devolution has reduced Crown control over many of the bodies which are subject to the Bill of Rights.[110] A Crown guarantor liability for breaches of the Bill of Rights by such bodies would emasculate the remedy as the Crown cannot influence the behaviour of the body beyond legislation. In such a context, courts may be wary of awarding the remedy.[111]

105 *Ibid*, p 792.

106 *Ibid*, p 793.

107 *Innes v Wong* [1996] 2 HRNZ 618.

108 *Ibid*, p 624.

109 NZLC r37 (n 30 above) 33–35. The Law Commission recommended this second option, in preference to the third, although noting that the concept of a residual Crown liability for situations in which there would otherwise be no effective remedy warranted further consideration.

110 Eg the boards of trustees which run schools in New Zealand are undoubtedly subject to the Bill of Rights: *Palmerston North Boys High School* (n 19 above). At the same time, the Crown—in this case, the central Ministry of Education—has no direct effect upon the actions of the board. Likewise, New Zealand Post and Housing New Zealand are subject to the Bill of Rights but, pursuant to the State Owned Enterprises Act, are subject to only minor control by central government: SOEs are accountable to the Minister as shareholder: *Mercury Energy Ltd v Electricity Corporation of New Zealand* [1994] 2 NZLR 385.

111 Harrison (n 21 above) 421.

The third option is the opposite of the second: that, despite the criticisms above, the Crown ought to retain a guarantor-type liability for all claims under the Bill of Rights. The Crown would always be the appropriate defendant and would always be responsible for the payment of any monetary compensation awarded in relation to breaches by all Crown agents and public bodies which fall within Section 3.[112] This option is based on the public nature of the Bill of Rights and *Baigent's Case*. Protection and enforcement of the rights in the Bill of Rights is the responsibility of the Crown. The long title refers to New Zealand's international law commitments; these commitments are imposed on the Crown, the entity recognised at international law.

In *Baigent's Case*, McKay J suggested that the remedy must be against the Crown.[113] The remainder of the majority judges held that the Crown was an appropriate defendant without considering whether it was the only appropriate defendant. In relying upon *Maharaj*, however, the Court seems to have assumed that the Crown operated as guarantor.[114]

The most explicit post-*Baigent's Case* jurisprudence on the issue is found in *Hobson v Harding*.[115] The plaintiffs alleged that a subsidiary of the Regional Health Authority had breached the Bill of Rights in an audit of medical records. Thorp J accepted a Crown argument that in any Bill of Rights claim, the Crown is the proper defendant as it would be responsible to meet any judgment obtained on that claim. The Bill of Rights claims against the other defendants were consequently struck out.

The point was raised less directly in *Innes*, where Cartwright J seemed to assume a primary responsibility existed in the Crown:

> ... [I]t is arguable that under the New Zealand Bill of Rights Act an action against an individual, even one with responsibilities under the relevant legislation, is inappropriate when the State has primary liability or responsibility. That being so the State must provide any remedy which might be considered appropriate. Moreover, the remedy sought by the plaintiffs is for a sum of money by way of public law compensation. That is consistent with an acknowledgment that these proceedings are not private law in the nature of a tort claim but a public law action brought directly against the state.[116]

112 Eg the central Ministry of Education budget may be responsible for breaches of the Bill of Rights by the Minister, employees and agents of the Ministry, the various agencies run at governmental level (such as the Education Review Office), school boards of trustees, teachers and other employees.

113 *Baigent's Case* (n 3 above) 718.

114 *Maharaj* (n 14 above) 395: The redress claimed was 'redress from the Crown (now the state) for a contravention of the appellant's constitutional rights by the judicial arm of the state'. For reliance upon *Maharaj* in *Baigent's Case*, see eg (n 3 above) 677 (Cooke P).

115 *Hobson v Harding* (1995) 1 HRNZ 342. See Harrison (n 21 above) 421 for criticism of this decision.

116 *Innes* (n 107 above) 624.

The suggestion is, therefore, that the New Zealand Crown will operate as a guarantor for the *Baigent's Case* remedy.

(d) Procedural Issues

Four procedural issues, in particular, have arisen. First, the plaintiff's statement of claim was appended to the judgment of Cooke P in *Baigent's Case*.[117] This will be the model for statements of claim in cases seeking monetary relief.

Second, the issue of whether the trial as to Bill of Rights issues should be before a judge and jury or before a judge alone has been a matter for pre-trial determination. In *Upton v Green (1)*, Blanchard J accepted that a monetary claim under the *Baigent's Case* jurisdiction 'ordinarily will not be heard by a jury'.[118] In *M and E v Attorney-General*, the Master held that following *Baigent's Case* and *Upton (1)*, there was no right to have Bill of Rights claims held before a jury.[119]

Third, the Court has held that the proper defendant in *Baigent's Case* cases is the Attorney-General. In *Hobson*, the Attorney-General was substituted for the other defendants, at the Court's instigation.[120] Thus, a properly pleaded *Baigent's Case* statement of claim will name as defendant the Attorney-General in respect of the particular public entity alleged to have breached the Bill of Rights. *Hobson* suggests that obviously if a matter is improperly pleaded, it will not fail, but the pleadings will be amended by the Court.

Finally, it seems that while the Limitation Act does not apply to Bill of Rights Act cases, an excessive delay in bringing a claim may result in a refusal by the court to provide a monetary remedy.[121]

D. SUMMARY

The principal lesson from this survey is the youth of the *Baigent's Case* cause of action. There has been neither the time nor the concentration of cases to create one certain approach. The cause of action will continue to develop incrementally in response to facts and legal questions as they arise.

Two final points may be made from the cases that have been decided so far. First, the cause of action is very wide. Second, the jurisprudence has been very comparative, with much reference to foreign decisions. This will inevitably affect the way that the cause of action develops, and the results.

117 *Baigent's Case* (n 3 above) 678–83.
118 *Upton v Green (1)* (1995) 2 HRNZ 305, 308.
119 *M and E v Attorney-General* [1997] 2 NZLR 746.
120 *Hobson* (n 115 above).
121 *Sugrue* (n 94 above) 236.

PART II

COMPARATIVE ANALYSIS

5

Structure of the Cause of Action

A. INTRODUCTION

IN THIS PART of the book, the focus turns from the jurisdictions individually to a comparative analysis of the 'facts' set out in the previous chapters. If the first part was a vertical analysis, then this part of the book is horizontal. It attempts to determine the essence of the cause of action, by utilizing insights gained from a comparison.

The following structure of a generic cause of action is common to the causes of action in the United States, India and New Zealand. It is presented as four questions, which roughly correspond to the determinants of tort.[1] First, what does the cause of action protect? In other words, the issues falling within this question concern the basis of the cause of action. The second question asks who the cause of action protects. In practice, this amounts to issues surrounding the identity of the plaintiff. Third, who is the cause of action directed against? This question relates to the issues concerning the identity of the defendant. Fourth, what does the Court order? This question concerns the remedial part of the cause of action and, in particular, considers how quantum is determined. Within each of these questions, many aspects of the cause of action are raised.

The four questions are sometimes asked in different ways in the jurisdictions, and are often answered differently. Nevertheless, the underlying issues are the same. Each cause of action addressed issues falling within these four questions during the development of the monetary remedy. Presenting them in this generic structure allows them to be seen more clearly and highlights the similarities between the causes of action in the United States, India and New Zealand.

This chapter illustrates both the commonality of constitutional rights litigation and—perhaps in contradiction—the choices that were available to jurisdictions in fashioning the cause of action and remedy. In other words, by highlighting the similarities between the causes of action, the

1 Most causes of action seem to be built on the 'framework of tort law': D Shelton, *Remedies in International Human Rights Law* (Oxford, OUP, 1999) 57.

structure puts into stark relief the differences in the way each jurisdiction has addressed and answered the questions.

What follows, therefore, paints a picture of the cause of action by providing an initial set of questions to be asked that structure the cause of action in a generic way. This chapter is concerned with the similarities. The differences will be considered in chapter 6.

B. WHAT DOES THE CAUSE OF ACTION PROTECT?

1. Introduction

While this starting point might appear self-evident, it has been a relevant issue in all three jurisdictions. In essence, this question concerns the basis of the cause of action: the rights. I should begin by making clear what this section does not address. First, having indicated that a jurisprudential discussion of what is meant by 'rights' is beyond the scope of this book, rights are assumed to be anything given that appellation in constitutional-type documents. Second, this book is concerned with remedy, and not with what is required to fulfil a particular right. This section considers, therefore, the practicalities of determining what are rights for the purposes of the cause of action. The features that are raised involve determining which rights are amenable to suit.

2. Is a Constitutional Right Required?

The first feature raised in this respect seems obvious: a constitutional right is needed to found any claim. In other words, unsurprisingly, causes of action for breach of constitutional rights sounding in a monetary remedy will require a constitutional right to be breached.[2] Nevertheless, this is a live feature in a consideration of the cause of action. This question has, primarily, been raised in relation to the distinction between tort causes of action and fundamental rights causes of action, as jurisdictions have been faced with determining whether actions amounting to a breach in civil law were sufficient to found a constitutional claim.

In the United States, it was held that mere tort breaches were not sufficient to found a Section 1983 cause of action; it was necessary for a constitutional right to be breached before the remedy was available.[3] The

[2] The obvious exception is the United States, where statutory rights may be sufficient in certain circumstances.

[3] *Paul v Davis* 424 US 693, 96 S Ct 1155: It was necessary to show that the defamation in question breached a constitutional guarantee, as well as tort law.

remedy under Section 1983 was held to concern the protection of rights, while tort law protected interests.[4] This makes it clear that in the United States, it is necessary for the action complained of to be phrased as a recognised breach of a recognised constitutional right.

In New Zealand, the Court in *Baigent's Case* also stressed the distinction between tort law and Bill of Rights' breaches.[5] The cause of action was clearly positioned within public law with tort claims considered parallel, suggesting that something extra would be needed to convert a tort action into a constitutional claim. In this jurisdiction it has been assumed that a claim must be based on one of the rights listed in the Bill of Rights Act, underlined by the differentiation of the cause of action from tort. In fact, the cause of action was explicitly developed in opposition to tort law.[6]

In India, the cause of action based on constitutional rights overlaps significantly with tort breaches. It is the similarities between the two causes of action which are stressed in India, rather than the differences, which are emphasized in the United States or New Zealand. In fact, the Indian cause of action was explicitly created out of tort law causes of action and so the link is unsurprising. Early cases justified awards of a constitutional monetary remedy for breaches of rights by stressing the tortious nature of the breach. Judgments explained the development of the remedy on practical grounds, holding that it would be wrong to require the petitioner to pursue a long and expensive civil action when it was certain that civil compensation would eventually be granted; in such circumstances, damages or compensation should be awarded under Article 32 of the Constitution.[7] Nevertheless, it was never suggested that the impugned actions could be expressed in any way other than the language of constitutional rights for this to succeed.

Later Indian cases suggest an approach more similar to that of the United States and New Zealand, with emphasis being laid on the distinction between civil and constitutional claims. For example, a claim for Article 32 compensation for breach of the right to life by medical negligence was refused on the basis of the claim being better made at civil law.[8] On the other hand, recent Indian decisions in which a constitutional

[4] *Ibid*, p 1165.

[5] Eg *Simpson v Attorney-General (Baigent's Case)* [1994] 3 NZLR 667, 677. Especially followed in *Hobson v Harding* (1995) 1 HRNZ 342, 356; and *Manga v Attorney-General* [2000] 2 NZLR 65, 79–82.

[6] This was to avoid the immunities that applied to civil suits and which otherwise would have defeated the claim.

[7] Eg *Rudul Sah v State of Bihar* AIR 1983 SC 1086; *Hongray v Union of India* [1984] 3 SCR 544; *Bhim Singh v State of Jammu and Kashmir* AIR 1986 SC 494; and *Mehta v Union of India* AIR 1987 SC 1086.

[8] *Neelu Sarin v India* [1991] Supp 1 SCC 300. See S Sathe, 'Constitutional Law—I (Fundamental Rights)' (1991) XXVII *ASIL* 203 who suggests that cases have gone too wide in allowing every claim to fall within the right to life.

remedy has been granted could perhaps have been dealt with adequately within the employment context, suggesting that the Indian courts do not require the actions to be exclusively constitutional breaches.[9] It may be that when the Supreme Court declines to grant a petition that could be analysed as a tort, the distinction between civil and constitutional rights is more likely to be cited.

In the development of the constitutional cause of action, therefore, the question of its scope and how it fits with other causes of action was addressed by the three jurisdictions. The relationship with tort law has been crucial in all three jurisdictions: either to differentiate the cause of action from tort law, as in the United States and New Zealand, or to emphasise the power of the fundamental rights cause of action to cover all aspects of civil law, as in India. The monetary aspect of the remedy means that this cause of action is very similar to tort law and so the fact that the issue has arisen is not unexpected. Constitutional causes of action cover subject matter that could fit within many areas of law and the subject boundaries are likely to be considered in early cases.

3. Upon which Right was the Cause of Action Originally Based?

The second feature of this question relates to the effect on the remedy of the right upon which the cause of action was originally based. While none of the causes of action are specific to one particular right, issues exist concerning the relevance of which right has been breached. These issues concern the subject matter of claims.

In the United States, the Section 1983 cause of action was enacted to combat breaches of racial equality but in 1972 was held to cover property rights as well as personal rights.[10] Following that clear indication that all constitutional rights could found the cause of action, the Section 1983 cause of action was later held to be potentially available for breach of federal statutory rights as well as constitutional rights,[11] although the statute in question must confer substantive rights and contain non-exclusive remedies.[12] This is based on the wording of Section 1983, which creates a remedy for breaches of the federal Constitution 'and laws'.

[9] Eg *Chandra v All India Institute of Medical Sciences* AIR 1990 SC 1670; and *Dooradarshan Cameramen's Welfare Association v India* AIR 1990 SC 1387.

[10] *Lynch v Household Finance Corporation* 405 US 538, 92 S Ct 1113 (1972).

[11] *Maine v Thiboutot* 448 US 1, 100 S Ct 2502 (1980).

[12] *Pennhurst State School and Hospital v Halderman* 451 US 1, 101 S Ct 1531 (1981); *Middlesex County Sewerage Authority v National Sea Clammers Association* 453 US 1, 100 S Ct 2615 (1981).

Despite being originally involved with racial equality, the remedy has, in the United States, been closely associated with search and seizure.[13] *Monroe v Pape*, in which the cause of action under Section 1983 was given a wider effect,[14] and *Bivens*, in which the Courts established the other cause of action,[15] both concerned search and seizure. The subject matter of both causes of action was extended through later cases.[16] It is clear that the Section 1983 remedy is available in relation to most constitutional rights at least.[17]

In New Zealand, the remedy in *Baigent's Case* was also established in relation to a breach of rights relating to search and seizure.[18] The companion case to *Baigent's Case*, *AUWRC*, which also related to a search and seizure, explicitly stated that the remedy would apply no matter which right was at the base of the claim.[19] It is, as a result, used no matter which right from the New Zealand Bill of Rights Act is cited as the basis.

In India, by contrast, the potential for the granting of compensation was cited with approval in a case which concerned the systematic blinding of prisoners.[20] The remedy was granted for the first time in *Rudul Sah*, which concerned a particularly heinous illegal detention.[21] In the subsequent early cases in which the remedy was discussed, the Court held that compensation would be available only in 'appropriate' cases.[22] Clearly, appropriate cases were those most likely to equate to personal torts and involving life and liberty rights, most usually illegal detention and unlawful death. Despite that, there seems to have been no explicit expression of such a requirement and, in later cases, it became clear that the scope was significantly wider.[23]

It is clear that the cause of action may develop out of a variety of subject areas and rights, and yet will probably extend to cover all. It is striking that all three jurisdictions consider it necessary to consider the ambit of the cause of action in this way—and yet all three jurisdictions

13 C Walker, 'Wilkes and Liberty: A Critique of the Prima Facie Exclusionary Rule' (1996) 17 *NZULR* 69.

14 *Monroe v Pape* 365 US 167, 81 S Ct 473 (1961).

15 *Bivens v Six Unknown Named Agents of Federal Bureau of Narcotics* 403 US 388, 91 S Ct 1999 (1971).

16 *Davis v Passman* 442 US 228, 995 S Ct 2264 (1979); *Lynch* (n 10 above).

17 It may not be available in relation to the breach of all rights, as certain federal statutes have been held to exclude the cause of action: M Schwartz and J Kirklin, *Section 1983 Litigation: Claims, Defences and Fees* (New York, NY, Wiley Law Publications, 1986) 37.

18 *Baigent's Case* (n 5 above).

19 *Auckland Unemployed Workers' Rights Centre Inc v Attorney-General* [1994] 3 NZLR 720, 724.

20 *Khatri v State of Bihar* (1981) 1 SCC 627.

21 *Rudul Sah* (n 7 above).

22 *Bhim Singh* (n 7 above) 499; *Mehta* (n 7 above) 1091.

23 Eg *Rural Litigation and Entitlement Kendra, Dehradun v UP* AIR 1991 SC 2216. See further *Narmada Bachao Andolan v Union of India* AIR 2000 SC 3751 in which the Supreme Court expressed concern with the increased width in relation to public interest litigation.

allow an almost unfettered scope in relation to which rights and which fact situations may form the basis of the cause of action. The different fact situations and rights about which a particular case is concerned appear more likely to become relevant for the determination of later aspects of the cause of action, and not as threshold issues.

4. Is the Breach of a Right Sufficient for the Cause of Action?

The following features are related to, but distinct from, the first two. Having seen that, in general, a constitutional right must be breached for the cause of action to apply, and that this may be any right, one must consider the nature of the breach of that right. The third feature concerns the question of whether any breach of those rights will be sufficient to found the cause of action. The short answer is no; while a breach of a right will be a necessary precondition for the cause of action, it will not always be sufficient.

This is particularly clear in the United States. The *Bivens* cause of action has distinguished between compensable breaches of constitutional rights and breaches made within employment, social security and military relationships, for which the constitutional remedy will not be available.[24] The Court held that breaches of constitutional rights made within contexts for which the *Bivens* remedy was not intended cannot be compensated through the constitutional cause of action. This means that the fact that the impugned actions amounted to a constitutional breach would be irrelevant, as the actions should be categorized and considered in the legal context within which they arise. In other words, for the *Bivens* cause of action to apply, a constitutional right will need to be breached in a context to which the constitutional remedy relates. Thus, a constitutional right will be a necessary precondition to the *Bivens* cause of action, but will not always be sufficient. In comparison, it seems that in general the Indian jurisprudence considers that Article 32 of the Constitution requires the Supreme Court to adjudicate any actions shown to be a breach of a right guaranteed in the Constitution.[25] It will not usually be relevant that an alternative legal remedy is available.

The jurisprudence in New Zealand is rather split on this point. While there are suggestions that an approach similar to that of the Indian courts is evolving,[26] it should be noted that the development of a pragmatic

24 *Bush* 462 US 367, 103 S Ct 2402 (1983) re employment relationship; *Schweiker v Chilicky* 487 US 412, 108 S Ct 2460 (1988) re social security scheme; *Chappell v Wallace* 462 US 296, 103 S Ct 2362 (1983) re military.

25 *Kochunni v State of Madras* AIR 1959 SC 725.

26 *Baigent's Case* (n 5 above); and *Noort v Ministry of Transport* [1992] 3 NZLR 260 suggest that the Court of Appeal believes it to have a duty to provide a remedy for any breach of the Bill of Rights.

approach to the awarding of remedy suggests the opposite conclusion.[27] In fact, *Dunlea* states that sometimes it may not be necessary to award any remedy as a declaration may be sufficient to vindicate rights[28] and *Shaheed* indicates that the balancing act precludes any *prima facie* rule.[29] In *Brown*, the High Court stated that *Baigent's Case* could not be taken as authority for the proposition that compensation will always be awarded for a breach of the Bill of Rights Act, or even that it will often be the appropriate remedy; in fact 'the remedy is reserved for exceptional cases'.[30] This suggests that some breaches may be insufficient to form the basis of the cause of action in New Zealand.

5. What amounts to the Breach of a Right?

The fourth feature is also concerned, in a general sense, with breach. There are suggestions of a broadening of the cause of action by allowing wider definitions of what constitutes a breach of a right. This is exemplified by the fact that the cause of action can apply in the United States even where the action of the state official was unlawful, in contrast to the previous postition which was that the cause of action could only apply where a lawful action breached a constitutional right.[31] In India, rape has been considered to be a breach of the right to life and liberty, thus constitutionalising the crime and rendering the victim entitled to the constitutional monetary remedy.[32] The result is a larger number of cases being brought, in relation to an extensive set of rights, subject matter and breaches in both the United States and India.[33]

At the same time, there is also evidence of a—perhaps corresponding—narrowing in what is held to amount to a constitutional rights breach. The link between the broadening and narrowing can be seen especially clearly in India. There, the problems caused by the increased scope of what constitutes a breach has been a matter for judicial notice: judgments refer to the impossibility of resolving all the matters expeditiously.[34] The Supreme Court has, therefore, referred cases back to the

27 *R v Grayson and Taylor* [1997] 1 NZLR 399.

28 *Dunlea v Attorney-General* [2000] 3 NZLR 136, 149–51.

29 *R v Shaheed* [2002] 2 NZLR 377.

30 *Brown v Attorney-General* [2003] 3 NZLR 335, 345.

31 *Monroe* (n 14 above). Note that the causes of action in India and New Zealand were developed in relation to illegal actions.

32 Eg *Gautam v Chakraborty* (1996) 1 SCC 490 in which compensation was given in a rape case.

33 30,000 §1983 were filed in 1981 compared to 270 in 1961: Schwartz and Kirklin (n 17 above). In 1987, over 9,000 Art 32 writs were pending before the Indian Supreme Court: *Brahmbhatt v State of Gujarat* AIR 1987 SC 1159.

34 *Brahmbhatt* (n 33 above); *Kumar v Municipal Corporation of Delhi* (1987) 4 SCC 609.

High Court for decision, retaining the width of allowable cases by solving the matter by choice of forum.

In comparison, in the United States, the Supreme Court has introduced limitations on the type of case that may be brought. As was discussed earlier in this part, not all rights, nor all breaches, will serve as sufficient basis for a Section 1983 or *Bivens* cause of action in the United States. Further, the courts require the actions at the base of the cause of action to be state actions and for the breach to have been part of official conduct.[35] This emphasizes the constitutional nature of the cause of action by requiring the breach to be one that is of a public nature. Many cases, it seems, fail on this basis in the United States.

While the United States concern that *Bivens* would lead to an 'avalanche' of cases was noted in *Manga*,[36] the New Zealand High Court was not overly worried about an increasing width. In *Manga*, Hammond J seemed to consider that the *Bivens* floodgates concern was adequately countered by the fact that the number of *Bivens* cases has been small: 'as with most slippery slope arguments, the anticipated landslide has not occured' in the United States.[37] Nevertheless, as was discussed above, there are indications that the New Zealand courts may limit the availability of the monetary remedy to 'exceptional cases'.[38]

6. Does it matter which Right was Breached?

The final feature meriting discussion concerns the effect that the particular right alleged to have been breached has on the cause of action and remedy in individual cases. The New Zealand approach seems to be that both the particular right at the base of the cause of action and the nature of the breach influence remedy and, in particular, quantum, but that the cause of action itself is not affected.[39] Thus, the remedy will be affected by the right at the basis of the cause of action, and tailored to the particular circumstances.

In India, likewise, it seems that the right at the basis will affect the remedy granted, at least insofar as the court is more likely to grant a meaningful remedy if a personal right has been breached. Further, in developing the cause of action, the Indian Supreme Court stressed the importance of the right to life and liberty that was breached and held that

[35] Eg *Lugar v Edmondson Oil Co* 457 US 922, 102 S Ct 2744 (1982).
[36] *Manga* (n 5 above) 80.
[37] *Ibid.*
[38] *Brown* (n 30 above) 345.
[39] *Grayson* (n 27 above); *Manga* (n 5 above); *Brown* (n 30 above).

a remedy was necessary because the facts 'shocked the conscience of the Court'.[40]

In the United States, the issue of different rights has affected the cause of action itself, in the manner discussed previously in this section. Thus, in the United States, the particular right may prevent the existence of a valid cause of action or affect the relevance of immunities and other potentially limiting aspects of the cause of action.

7. Summary

The rights at the basis of the cause of action have, therefore, impacted upon the remedy in each of the three jurisdictions. The issues discussed concern the impetus for the entire cause of action: what should be protected by the monetary remedy? The answers differ between the jurisdictions, as does the importance of the questions and the nature of the discussion. It seems clear, however, that the cause of action in any jurisdiction will be required to address these questions. While causes of action are likely to be right-independant, the individual right breached and the nature of the breach may either impact upon individual cases more than upon the cause of action as a whole, or may be considered to be relevant to the cause of action in general. The effect of the solution to the issues raised under this heading will relate to the width of the application of the cause of action.

C. WHO DOES THE CAUSE OF ACTION PROTECT?

1. Introduction

In relation to administrative law, it has been said that decisions as to standing will reflect 'something more' than the fact that a person can bring a claim; they will express 'assumptions about the nature of administrative law'.[41] If anything, this is accentuated in the highly political context of constitutional human rights law. Decisions as to standing to bring constitutional rights claims under this cause of action highlight important assumptions about the cause of action itself.

This question involves the relevance and identity of the plaintiff.[42] In practice, it primarily concerns *locus standi*[43] and questions relating to

40 *Mehta* (n 7 above) 1091.

41 P Craig, *Administrative Law*, 3rd edn, (London, Sweet & Maxwell, 1994) 479.

42 Although the term 'plaintiff' is used here, the person who brings the cause of action could equally be the applicant, appellant or petitioner.

43 The cause of action is a mixture of public and private law and so it is not clear that the focus should be on public law doctrines such as *locus standi*, rather than private law conceptions.

public interest litigation.[44] The issue can be approached in two ways. The first is to ask who the cause of action aims to protect; the second is to ask who is entitled to bring the cause of action. While conceptually distinct, these will usually be the same for all practical purposes, as it is expected that an individual who the cause of action aims to protect will be entitled to rely upon the cause of action. In the context of constitutional rights, however, it seems that people other than those who the cause of action aims to protect may also be entitled to rely upon the cause of action. In other words, the group of individuals who the cause of action protects may be a subset of a larger group who can bring the cause of action.

2. What is the Statutory Basis?

The principal source for determining both who the cause of action aims to protect and who is best suited to bring claims is, of course, the constitutional document itself. Different documents reflect the different approaches taken. Article 32 of the Indian Constitution guarantees the right to move the Court by proceedings 'for the enforcement of the rights'; it does not refer to standing. The jurisprudence in this jurisdiction suggests that the identification of the person enforcing the rights will be less relevant than ensuring that the rights are enforced no matter by whom. The Supreme Court has shied away from the establishment of many procedural rules and emphasised its own duty to enforce the constitutional rights through Article 32.[45]

Section 1983, setting out the cause of action in the United States, contains certain indications as to standing. The section states that a person 'injured' by the 'deprivation' of any rights may bring the action. Further, Article III(2) of the United States Constitution relates to standing under the Constitution. It refers to the Court's power to hear 'cases' and 'controversies'. It is no surprise that a set of procedural rules has been developed here based on the constitutional restrictions. As a complement, the Court has developed prudential grounds governing standing.

The *Bivens* cause of action in the United States and the *Baigent's Case* cause of action in New Zealand are not based on any explicit statutory provision and so it is necessary to look at the context to answer the

Despite that, the issues surrounding the identity of the plaintiff are those associated with *locus standi* and so approaching this on the basis of public law is consonant with the case law. The terms *locus standi* and standing are used interchangeably.

44 Class actions will not be considered as they are merely a matter of procedure and each member of a class action must, in general, have standing in their own right: L Stein, (ed), *Locus Standi* (Sydney, Law Book, 1979) 21–22.

45 Eg *Daryao v State of UP* AIR 1961 SC 1457: 'Mere technical rules' should not defeat Art 32 cases; *Rudul Sah* (n 7 above): A 'full-dressed debate on the nice points of fact and law' would have to wait for something other than the Art 32 cause of action.

questions surrounding the identity of the plaintiff. In relation to *Bivens*, this includes judicial decisions taken in connection with the Section 1983 cause of action.[46] This is due to both the close links between the two causes of action, as well as the fact that the *Bivens* cause of action was inferred from the Constitution. Thus, the Article III(2) restriction to 'cases' or 'controversies' must apply.[47]

Section 29 of the New Zealand Bill of Rights Act states that: 'Except where the provisions of this Bill of Rights otherwise provide, the provisions of this Bill of Rights apply, so far as practicable, for the benefit of all legal persons as well as for the benefit of all natural persons.' Most provisions refer to 'everyone', thus suggesting that only a few of the guarantees will have a limited application.[48]

In all three jurisdictions, much of the jurisprudence and literature emphasises the vindication of rights, with compensation and deterrence expressed as secondary purposes of the cause of action.[49] Thus, the focus is on the rights rather than the identity of the person whose rights are breached. It seems that standing is essentially dependant upon first being a rights-holder and, second, having suffered a constitutional rights breach.[50] Other aspects of the person may not be of importance in determining standing.

In other words, it seems that the cause of action aims first to protect the rights contained in the constitutional documents and, almost incidentally, to protect the rights-holder. The relationship with the rights contained in the constitutional document will be of primary importance to questions of standing. Determining the group of individuals entitled to bring a claim will be based on the primacy of the rights.

[46] *Butz v Economou* 438 US 478, 98 S Ct 2894 (1978): The same immunities apply to *Bivens* and §1983 cases. It is likely that this will extend beyond immunities to all procedural rules.

[47] There is no reason why the prudential, as well as the constitutional, grounds for standing in the §1983 cause of action should not be relevant here as well.

[48] Eg s 12 is guaranteed to 'every New Zealand citizen'.

[49] Re New Zealand: *Baigent's Case* (n 5 above) 692. Re India: *Khatri* (n 20 above) 630 (first case to discuss monetary remedy which refers to vindication of rights as the purpose) and *Basu v West Bengal* 1996 (9) SCALE 298, 317–18, although note the Indian Supreme Court's tendency to award exemplary damages and to attempt to 'civilise' society. Re the United States: *Owen v City of Independence Missouri* 445 US 622, 100 S Ct 1398 (1980); *Robertson v Wegmann* 436 US 584, 98 S Ct 1991 (1978); *Carey v Piphus* 435 US 247, 98 S Ct 1042 (1978); *Bell v Hood* 327 US 678, 66 S Ct 773 (1946). Shelton (n 1 above) 55 provides an international discussion of the purposes of remedy and argues for restitution as a primary aim; S Sturm, 'A Normative Theory of Public Law Remedies' [1991] 79 *Geo LJ* 1355, 1378: 'The widely accepted principle that rights should find vindication in an effective remedy'.

[50] *Fertiliser Corporation Kamgar Union v Union of India* [1981] 1 SCC 568, 579–80: 'The question whether a person has the locus to file a proceeding depends mostly and often on whether he possesses a legal right and that right is violated'.

3. Who is a Rights-holder?

Thus, it is necessary to consider who has the capacity to be a rights-holder. The class of potential plaintiffs is unlikely to be limited by rules of capacity. It seems that generally the rights will be available for residents within a country's borders[51]; for minors and those with disabilities[52]; for companies and other legal persons[53]; for those convicted of criminal offences[54]; and to the estate of deceased persons.[55] Further, in India, plaintiffs may be able to bring these claims despite issues still requiring determination at first instance.[56] Such issues of capacity have had little impact in the United States, India or New Zealand, suggesting a very wide interpretation of who is protected by the cause of action.

The category of rights-holder may be even wider than that. Constitutional rights are often presented as being for the benefit of the entire community, with the particular plaintiff bringing the cause of action for breach as almost a mouthpiece for the community:

> If society as a whole is injured by human rights violations, so also may society as a whole benefit from public remedies. Any action the state is required to take to remedy human rights violations will likely have effects beyond the individual plaintiff. Remedies for public wrongs must be seen, then, as serving not only private redress but public policy, as an important means of promoting compliance with the human rights norm.[57]

This is especially obvious in India, where the rights are seen as constitutive of a better society.[58] In New Zealand and the United States, the approach has perhaps been more individualistic, although the impact of the case and remedy beyond the individual plaintiff will often be acknowledged.[59]

[51] In the United States, permanent residents and illegal immigrants fall within the wording of §1983: Schwartz and Kirklin (n 17 above) 21–22 (cf *US v Verdugo-Urquidez* 494 US 259, 110 S Ct 1056 (1990)). In India, non-citizens are entitled to Art 32 protection: *Narmada* (n 23 above). S 29 of the New Zealand Bill of Rights Act is not limited to New Zealand citizens or residents.

[52] *Mehta v Tamil Nadu* AIR 1991 SC 417; *DeShaney v Winnebago County Department of Social Services* 489 US 189, 109 S Ct 998 (1989); *Re J (An Infant)* [1996] 2 NZLR 134.

[53] Eg New Zealand Bill of Rights Act s 29 includes legal persons as well as natural persons.

[54] Eg *Martinez v California* 444 US 277, 100 S Ct 553 (1980); *Khatri* (n 20 above); *R v Goodwin (1)* [1993] 2 NZLR 153.

[55] Eg *Baigent's Case* (n 5 above); *Nilabati Behera v State of Orissa* [1993] Cri LJ 2899.

[56] *Kochunni* (n 25 above) 734–35.

[57] Shelton (n 1 above) 52. See further J Raz, *The Morality of Freedom* (Oxford, OUP, 1986) 256: 'One reason for affording special protection to individual rights is that thereby one also protects a collective good, an aspect of public culture'.

[58] Eg *Rudul Sah* (n 7 above) and *Mehta* (n 7 above).

[59] This is especially clear in *City of Riverside v Rivera* 477 US 561, 106 S Ct 2686 (1986) 2694: By bringing a §1983 claim, an individual 'secures important social benefits' to the wider community. See also *Manga* (n 5 above) 81.

Thus, although the general rule is that an individual may be a plaintiff if he or she 'has a vested interest in the subject matter of the claim',[60] the nature of the constitutional cause of action may create a wide set of 'vested interests', resulting in a wide set of potential plaintiffs. It is possible that members of the community who are not directly affected by a rights breach may be considered to have a vested interest in its vindication as all members of the community will be considered to have suffered when any right is breached. It may be, therefore, that an expansive definition of rights-holder exists for the purpose of this cause of action, so that a large number of people will be entitled to bring claims in their own right.

4. Is Public Interest Litigation Available?

These considerations are perhaps the reason that public interest litigation has been relevant in enforcing fundamental rights. Public interest litigation has been described as illustrating an increased use of the courts to 'enforc[e] laws to the benefit of the general community', recognising benefits to people beyond the individual rights-holder.[61]

The need for public interest litigation in constitutional rights law is perhaps compounded by the problem that the rights that are breached are often those of rights-holders who are least able to pursue their vindication through the legal system. Public interest litigation aims to combat this problem by both allowing a large group of people to bring claims on behalf of other individuals and enlarging the concept of breach.[62] A working definition has been suggested to be 'the use of litigation ... to advance the cause of minority or disadvantaged groups, and individuals, or the public interest'.[63] In other words, as victims will, almost by definition, be in a vulnerable position and will often be unable to enforce the rights, other people may be entitled to bring a claim for enforcement of the rights.

Some commentators in India have argued that the proper term should be 'social action litigation', rather than 'public interest litigation', the term

60 *Halsbury's Laws of England: Practice and Procedure*, vol 37, 4th edn, Reissue, (London, Butterworths, 2001) para 252.

61 Australian Law Reform Commission, *Beyond the Door-keeper: Standing to Sue for Public Remedies* (ARLC r 78, 1996) 22.

62 These two categories are 'representative' standing and 'citizen' standing: C Cunningham, 'Public Interest Litigation in India: In light of the United States Experience' (1987) 29 *JILI* 494.

63 J Cooper and R Dhavan, 'Introduction' in J Cooper and R Dhavan, (eds), *Public Interest Law* (London, Basil Blackwell, 1986) 3, 5. The difficulties with definition are discussed in R Dhavan, 'Whose Law? Whose Interest?' in J Cooper and R Dhavan, (eds), *Public Interest Law* (London, Basil Blackwell, 1986) 17, 38: 'Public interest law was a culture-specific phenomenon which was developed in America and confidently exported to the rest of the world'.

used in the United States.[64] The distinction illustrates the different agendas in the United States and India. In India, social action litigation has been an 'integral part of the poverty jurisprudence of the Supreme Court',[65] an example of the 'democratisation' of constitutional justice,[66] and 'a catalyst in the process of social transformation'.[67] It has been suggested that an examination of writs 'reveals the lawlessness of the Indian State as the basic source of social action litigation'.[68] Clearly, the legal community, at the least, perceives the extension of standing as being about social action, rather than the more politically subtle (and less influential) public interest approach developed in the United States Courts.[69]

Social action litigation in India has been intrinsically linked with the expansion of the cause of action sounding in a monetary remedy[70] and the development of a constitutional right to 'compensation and rehabilitation'.[71] The Courts have proclaimed that the state should encourage public interest litigation of rights breaches through Article 32.[72] To bring a case under the public interest litigation rules, a person must be acting in good faith on behalf of people who, for valid reasons, are not able to bring the action themselves.[73] Valid reasons, the Court has held, include 'poverty, helplessness, disability, or social or economic disadvantage'; public interest litigation allows 'the portals of the court ... [to be] thrown open to the poor and the downtrodden, the ignorant and the illiterate'.[74] At the basis of the petition there must be concerns shared by a large number of people, rather than more usual individualistic concerns.[75]

Public interest litigation in India has involved a relaxation of *locus standi*, by allowing 'representative standing'[76] and 'citizen

64 U Baxi, 'Forward' in M Mridul, *Public Interest Litigation—A Profile* (Jaipur, Bharat Law House, 1986); U Baxi, 'Judicial Discourse: The Dialectics of the Face and the Mask' (1993) 35 *JILI* 1; S Sathe, 'Preface' in S Ahuja, *People, Law and Justice: Casebook on Public Interest Law*, Vol I (London, Sangam, 1997). See also *Mehta* (n 7 above) 1091.

65 Sathe (n 64 above) xxxv.

66 Baxi (1993) (n 64 above) 7.

67 Sathe (n 64 above) xliv.

68 Baxi (1986) (n 64 above) iii.

69 Dhavan (n 63 above) 21 argues that the United States public interest law has moved away from issues of poverty to be used by more advantaged groups and suggests that the ideal is better encapsulated by 'social action litigation'. Further, Cunningham (n 62 above) argues that while public interest litigation declined in the United States in the 1980s, it flourished in India. The idea that public interest litigation is part of a revolution is shared by judges: *Gupta* AIR 1982 SC 149, 189: 'A vast revolution is taking place in the judicial process'.

70 Baxi (1993) (n 64 above) 7.

71 *Ibid*; S Ahuja, *People, Law and Justice: Casebook on PIL*, Vol II (London, Sangam, 1997) 789.

72 *Morcha v Union of India* AIR 1984 SC 802, 811.

73 *Gupta* (n 69 above) 189.

74 *PUDR v Union of India* AIR 1982 SC 1473, 1478; *Gupta* (n 69 above) 189: 'The theatre of the law is fast changing and the problems of the poor are coming to the forefront'.

75 Sathe (n 64 above) xliii.

76 In other words, the petitioner is accorded *locus standi* as a representative of the person or persons whose rights have been breached: Cunningham (n 62 above) 498–500.

standing'.[77] Equally, the Court has developed an 'epistolary jurisdiction',[78] relaxing procedural rules in response to the notion that 'procedure is but a handmaiden of justice and the cause of justice can never be allowed to be thwarted by any procedural technicalities'.[79] As public interest litigation is not adversarial and does not allow for fact-finding, the Supreme Court appoints commissions of inquiry to elicit facts first and submit representations to the Court.[80]

In the United States, most plaintiffs will have to meet the prudential grounds which basically ensure that the plaintiff is the proper person to bring the claim.[81] Prudential grounds were developed by the Supreme Court as a parallel set of requirements to those developed in relation to the constitutional standing rules. In general, organizational standing is allowed only if an 'actionable causal relationship' is established.[82] Third parties can have standing if they can show a relationship with the person whose rights have been breached and where there are practical reasons preventing the victim from bringing the cause of action.[83] The concept of public interest litigation was extremely important in the United States legal system in the 1960s–1970s where it was sourced in the fight against poverty and grew to the aim of contributing 'to the representation of the under-represented'.[84] These laudable aims seem not to have been fulfilled, and the public interest litigation model has not been extensively developed by the Supreme Court.[85] Interestingly, it has been suggested that: '[o]ver the years, America has witnessed a "take-over" of the public interest law movement by diverse groups in a way that has altered and transformed the initial impetus that inspired it.'[86]

Equally interestingly, the Indian Lawyers' Collective has suggested that an indefinite expansion of the standing rules in India 'could lead to public interest law for the rich, with the powerful resisting change through the use of expanded standing'.[87] This fear may be borne out by certain of the

77 The petitioner sues in his or her own right, as a citizen 'to whom a public duty is owed': Cunningham (n 62 above) 500–2.

78 *Mehta* (n 7 above) 1089; *Gupta* (n 69 above) 189.

79 *Gupta* (n 69 above) 189.

80 R Dhavan, 'Law as Struggle: Public Interest Law in India' (1994) 36 *JILI* 302, 310.

81 *Warth v Seldin* 422 US 490, 95 S Ct 2197 (1975); *Singleton v Wulff* 428 US 106, 96 S Ct 2868 (1976).

82 *Arlington Heights v Metropolitan Housing Corporation* 429 US 252, 97 S Ct 555 (1977).

83 *Singleton* (n 81 above) 114–16.

84 Dhavan (n 63 above) 18–19.

85 Cunningham (n 62 above) 495; A Chayes, 'The Role of Judges in Public Law Litigation' (1976) 89 *Harv L Rev* 1281; cf A Chayes, 'The Supreme Court 1981 Term Forward: Public Law Litigation and the Burger Court' (1982) 96 *Harv L Rev* 4.

86 Dhavan (n 63 above) 20.

87 J Chambers, *et al*, (eds), *Public Interest Litigation Around the World—Report of a Symposium held at Columbia University in May 1991 with Descriptions of Participating Legal Organizations from Twenty Countries* (New York, NY, Columbia Human Rights Law Review, 1992) 8.

recent public interest law cases which suggest that it has been 'appropriated'.[88] The 1991 Annual Survey of Indian Law suggested that it had become: 'painfully apparent that the original commitment of PIL activism to combat state repression, social oppression and victimisation of the poor has been to a large extent been diffused. PIL is now being employed more and more for remedying all critical ills in the body politic and in the governance of the country.'[89]

This critical conclusion has been reflected in the more recent Supreme Court decisions, which illustrate a judicial concern with the extension of public interest litigation.[90] The suggestion is that the growth in public interest litigation in India may be slowing.

In any event, in the United States there has been an increasingly restrictive interpretation of the standing rules by the Supreme Court,[91] and the nature of decisions is intensely discretionary and pragmatic.[92] The limited importance of public interest litigation in the development of the cause of action, however, may be mostly attributable to the different social structure and subject matters which come to the courts.

One conclusion of a symposium of international public interest litigation centres was that '[w]hereas public interest litigation in the North is a minor issue, in the South public interest litigation is a major issue'.[93] It is at least arguable that the rules of standing may assume less importance in the United States constitutional rights jurisprudence if the Supreme Court were faced with similar allegations of 14-year illegal detentions[94]; unlawful deaths by the armed forces[95]; the systematic blinding of prisoners[96]; and beating of women and children by the police.[97]

Conversely, it seems likely that if the Indian Supreme Court were not faced with a 'lawlessness' in Indian society, and it was called upon to adjudicate such matters as those that come before the United States Supreme Court, then rules that limit standing might be perceived as more pressing. This is not to suggest that human rights breaches should be ranked; rather, it seems clear that the different levels of urgency illustrated by different fact situations call for different approaches to procedure.[98]

88 Dhavan (1994) (n 80 above) 311. Although note that the author believes that public interest litigation still fulfils its intention in India.

89 P Singh, 'PIL' (1991) XXVII *ASIL* 35, 36.

90 *Narmada* (n 23 above).

91 L Casdorph, 'The Constitution and Reconstitution of the Standing Doctrine' [1999] *St Mary's LJ* 471.

92 K Ripple, *Constitutional Litigation* (Virginia, MD, Michie, 1984) 208–9.

93 Chambers (n 87 above) 5.

94 *Rudul Sah* (n 7 above).

95 *Hongray* (n 7 above).

96 *Khatri* (n 20 above).

97 *SAHELI, a Women's Resources Centre v Commissioner of Police, Delhi* AIR 1990 SC 513.

98 This is reminiscent of the concept of a 'hierarchy of needs', where Indian society's constitutional rights needs would be seen as more pressing than those with which the United

Further, it is possible that culture has also been relevant. It has been argued that, historically, Indians saw themselves as members of communities and not as individuals.[99] This has been somewhat reflected in the Constitution which, although it guarantees individual rights, also refers to groups: a majority of the categories of protected people are in fact groups.[100] This cultural—and perhaps constitutional—expectation of group rights may account for the ease with which public interest litigation was accepted and developed by the Indian courts. In comparison, fundamental rights in the United States largely concern guarantees of individual freedoms.

As a final point, it should be mentioned that none of the questions of *locus standi* have been considered in New Zealand in Bill of Rights Act cases; and there is no clear indication whether innovative *locus standi* doctrines will be developed in the future. While the fact situations in New Zealand are more akin to those heard by the United States courts, the cases heard so far suggest that an approach somewhat more similar to that of the Indian courts is possible. In particular, it has been held that the courts should not proscribe limits on the Bill of Rights Act remedies in the absence of legislative intent.[101] Further, Chayes' article defining public law litigation was referred to with approval in *Manga*, suggesting that such submissions would be looked upon with favour by the Court.[102]

Mindful of the fact that there is nothing in the Bill of Rights that suggests a narrow approach to standing, it seems likely that in the 'absence of legislative intent', the New Zealand approach to standing and rules of procedure would be wide. Nevertheless, the demands on the Courts are likely to be less from a social action perspective than those in India, and so it is unlikely that the extreme width of the Indian model will be replicated.

Finally, it should be noted that an expansive approach to standing in New Zealand would be consistent with the evolution of both of the two older causes of action studied. The recent decrease in standing in the United States occurred only after earlier widening.[103] Having said that, an examination of the public interest law model in India suggests that,

States Supreme Court is faced. In this context, Clapham has noted that the lower United States federal courts 'have constructed a sort of hierarchy of rights' (in this case, referring to state action) in which racial discrimination is at the top and breach of procedural due process is at the bottom: A Clapham, *Human Rights in the Private Sphere* (Oxford, Clarendon Press, 1993) 159 (n 36).

99 J Derrett, 'Human Rights and Fundamental Freedoms in India' in Recueils de la Société Jean Bodin Pour L'Histoire Comparative des Institutions *XLVII: L'Individu Face au Pouvoir Deuxième Partie: Afrique, Asie, Amérique* (Paris, Dessain et Tolra, 1988) 159, 163.

100 Derrett (n 99 above) 167: The 'five recognised categories of focus of constitutional rights' in India are the individual, the citizen, the religious denomination, the cultural minority and the Scheduled Caste or Tribe.

101 *Whithair v Attorney-General* [1996] 2 NZLR 45, 57.

102 *Manga* (n 5 above) 82; Chayes (1976) (n 85 above).

103 Cunningham (n 62 above); Chayes (n 81 above).

although the rules relating to *locus standi* may be somewhat narrowed in recent cases,[104] the way in which it is embedded into the legal system means that it is unlikely to atrophy to the extent that it has in the United States.

5. Is Injury Required?

The final aspect to consider is the meaning and relevance of injury in determining who is entitled to be a plaintiff. In all three jurisdictions, it seems that the rights-holder must prove that a right has been breached to pass the threshold test for the cause of action; proving actual injury is usually relevant later, at the stage of determining quantum.[105] This is, of course, not always a clear differentiation, particularly as the threshold test of injury to the right will usually involve some level of causality between that injury and the plaintiff.

In India and New Zealand, such procedural rules have not been developed explicitly. In India, the Supreme Court has not discussed injury or causation in these sorts of cases; this may be because the breaches, and resulting injury, have often been so profound as to render this unnecessary. In fact, as early as 1967, it had been commented that no damage, material or pecuniary loss, or bodily injury need be proven to bring a claim under Article 32; it was necessary only to prove the existence of a right and its infringement or that it was in imminent threat of infringement.[106] The maxim '*damnum sine injuria*' was suggested to apply, when '*injuria*' meant injury-infringement of a fundamental right.[107] Other more recent comment seems likewise to assume that injury to a right is sufficient.[108]

In New Zealand, there has been some suggestion in the case law that a degree of causation or consequential result is required.[109] It should be noted that this approach has been categorized as contrary to the rights-centred approach which was considered more desirable and consistent with *Baigent's Case*.[110] That no indepth body of jurisprudence has developed around these points is probably attributable to the youth of

104 Eg *Simranjit Singh Mann v Union of India* AIR 1993 SC 280 (public interest litigation is not available in criminal law cases); *Krishna Swami v Union of India* AIR 1993 SC 1407 (public interest litigation cannot be used to review an earlier judicial decision in which they were not a party); and *Narmada* (n 23 above).

105 At this point, I focus on injury to the right, and leave to the discussion on quantum the issue of whether something more in the way of actual injury to the rights-holder is required for the cause of action.

106 M Kagzi, *The Constitution of India*, 2nd edn, (Delhi, Metropolitan, 1967) 528.

107 Kagzi (n 106 above) 528.

108 M Jain, *Indian Constitutional Law*, 4th edn, (Bombay, Tripathi Private, 1987) 710.

109 *Upton v Green and Attorney-General (2)* (Unrep, HC Chch Registry, Tompkins J, 10 October 1996) 20; *Lewis* (1995) 2 HRNZ 45, 49.

110 R Harrison, 'Public Law and Private Redress' [1996] *NZ Rec L Rev* 478, 484–85.

the cause of action; it is difficult to predict future developments. Previous comments about the likely approach of the Courts to allow a wide application of the Bill of Rights Act may be of equal importance here.

In the United States, the requirement for injury is statutory, raising the question of what this means in these cases. The United States has developed an 'amazing, complex, intricate web' of standing rules including those related to injury.[111] The case and controversy requirement has three components. First, it is necessary to show an 'injury in fact' which means 'a concrete and particularized personal injury that is imminent and not speculative, conjectural, or hypothetical'.[112] Second, it is necessary to show that the injury was caused by the defendant's conduct.[113] Third, the injury must be able to be redressed by the Court.[114] There must be a connection between the injury and the conduct.

Distinctions between the jurisdictions studied thus become pronounced at this point. Clearly, the issues of standing, injury and causation have received a great deal of legislative as well as judicial scrutiny in the United States; they have been formalized and the courts have considered it necessary to exercise some restraint on who may be a plaintiff. The threshold level inquiry of whether the particular individual is the most appropriate person to bring the case is very different from that in India, where the focus has been more resolutely on the right and its breach and not the means by which it has been brought to the court's attention. It is unclear which approach will be followed in New Zealand.

6. Summary

By way of summary, it is clear that the question of who is eligible to be protected by the cause of action generally equates to rights-holders whose rights have been breached. The question of who can use the cause of action includes that group of people, but extends wider as, due to public interest litigation, third parties may use the cause of action to vindicate the rights of other rights-holders. The Indian Supreme Court has not required much in the way of any formal standing requirements. In the United States, in comparison, the Supreme Court has interpreted a constitutional limit to standing, as well as established its own prudential grounds, so as to restrict suits at this threshold point. It will be interesting to see how the New Zealand jurisprudence on this point develops.

111 Casdorph (n 91 above) 472 (quoting Colloquia, 'Group Discussion on the Supreme Court's Recent Administrative Jurisprudence' (1993) 7 *Admin LJ Am U* 287, 288).

112 Casdorph (n 91 above) 475.

113 *Allen v Wright* 468 US 737, 104 S Ct 3315 (1984) 3324; *Warth* (n 81 above).

114 *Simon v Eastern Kentucky Welfare Rights Organization* 426 US 26, 96 S Ct 1917 (1976) 38.

Finally, it should be noted that public interest litigation organizations from other countries look to India as a desirable model for standing rules.[115] Interestingly, public interest litigation in India has politicised the law, so that many of the cases are brought by lawyers, or lawyers' groups, who make the claims on behalf of the wider society.[116] In particular, *Rudul Sah*, the case in which the first award of a monetary remedy was made under the Constitution, was initially brought to the High Court by a law student on the basis of a newspaper report; an experienced New Delhi lawyer filed the writ in the Supreme Court.[117] It is questionable whether this case would have been litigated had the Indian Supreme Court not developed its wide, non-procedural approach to *locus standi*.

Thus, the cause of action is in some ways influential on both the social and legal reality of India: '[p]ossibly the most remarkable effect of public interest litigation has been upon the judicial process itself'.[118] This illustrates the very wide impact of the question of who can use the cause of action. Correspondingly, it is also illustrative of the wider legal and social influences evident on the Courts when answering this question.

D. AGAINST WHOM IS THE CAUSE OF ACTION DIRECTED?

This part of the structure concerns the defendant. There are two conceptually distinct aspects to this question. The first set of issues arises from the public side of the cause of action: whether it is mandatory for the defendant to be a public entity or official; whether *quasi*-public bodies are amenable to suit under this cause of action; whether the cause of action should be brought against individual state officials or against the state itself; and whether immunities apply. The second set of issues reflects the private side of the cause of action: the relevance of fault and intention to the cause of action.

1. Does the Cause of Action Apply to Private as well as Public Entities?

The first issue, whether the cause of action is actionable only against entities with some public element, has been extremely important not only in the three jurisdictions discussed in this book, but also inter-

115 Chambers (n 87 above) 7.

116 Eg *Mehta* (n 7 above): Writ petition filed by the Legal Aid and Advice Board and Bar Association; *Supreme Court Legal Aid Committee v State of Bihar* (1991) 3 SCC 482: Petition filed on the basis of a newspaper report of a death in police custody.

117 *Rudul Sah* (n 7 above).

118 Ahuja (Vol II) (n 71 above) 766. See also Dhavan (1994) (n 80 above).

nationally.[119] This debate is referred to as either 'public/private application' or 'vertical/horizontal effect', and has involved considering whether the cause of action is available when rights are breached by private individuals, or only when breached by a state entity.

One classic article, in relation to the likely direction of the courts in the United Kingdom to the question of the horizontal or vertical application of the Human Rights Act, sets out the various approaches.[120] The vertical approach argues that the fundamental rights have application only to the state, and do not govern relations between private individuals except when a statutory instrument is in question.[121] The horizontal approach is the opposite, arguing that the fundamental rights are directly applicable to analysis of the common law in disputes between purely private individuals.[122]

Hunt argues that two approaches exist between those two extremes. According to the indirect horizontal approach, the fundamental rights will found actions only against the state, but will indirectly affect the common law. In this way, the fundamental rights will indirectly affect cases involving private individuals but will not be able to be the subject of litigation. The final approach Hunt identifies (and favours) is 'the application to all law' approach which focuses on the involvement of the law, rather than the public or private nature of the defendant. This approach falls between indirect horizontal effect and a pure horizontal effect.

The United States is cited as an example of purely vertical—or public—application.[123] The general rule is that 'an act attributable to government' is necessary to found a constitutional violation in the United States.[124] The Court has held that 'under color of law' equates to a requirement of state action and thus obviously requires a state component

119 There is a large set of writings on this subject. See eg A Butler, 'Constitutional Rights in Private Litigation: A Critique and Comparative Analysis' (1993) 22 *Anglo–American L Rev* 1 re North America and Ireland; Clapham (n 98 above); R McCorquodale and R Fairbrother, 'Globalization and Human Rights' (1999) 21 *HRQ* 735; and C Jochnick, 'Confronting the Impunity of Non-state Actors: New Fields for the Promotion of Human Rights' (1999) 21 *HRQ* 56 re international law; A Butler, 'The New Zealand Bill of Rights and Private Common Law Litigation' [1991] *NZLJ* 261; P Rishworth, 'The Potential of the New Zealand Bill of Rights' [1990] *NZLJ* 68; and D Paccioco, 'The New Zealand Bill of Rights Act 1990: Curial Cures for a Debilitated Bill' [1990] *NZ Rec L* 353 re New Zealand; B Markesinis, 'Privacy, Freedom of Expression, and the Horizontal Effect of the Human Rights Bill: Lessons from Germany' (1999) 115 *LQR* 47; R Buxton, 'Horizons of Horizontality' (2000) 116 *LQR* 217; M Hunt, 'The "Horizontal Effect" of the Human Rights Act' [1998] *PL* 423; G Phillipson, 'The Human Rights Act, "Horizontal Effect" and the Common Law: A Bang or a Whimper?' (1999) 62 *MLR* 824; and D Oliver, 'The Human Rights Act and Public Law/Private Law Divides' [2000] *EHRLR* 343 re the United Kingdom.

120 Hunt (n 119 above).

121 Eg Buxton (n 119 above)

122 Eg Butler (n 119 above).

123 Hunt (n 119 above) 427.

124 T Blumoff, 'Some Moral Implications of Finding No State Action' (1994) 70 *Notre Dame L Rev* 95 97.

to the cause of action.[125] Nonetheless, the simplicity of this is deceptive: the United States Supreme Court has engaged 'in a confusing and convoluted exercise, which attempts to identify whether particular individuals or bodies can be fairly said to represent the face of governmental action'.[126] The various procedural categories relating to the application of the United States Bill of Rights have been suggested to mask 'an ideological resistance to state intrusion into a "private sphere"'.[127]

Since the 1880s, this issue has been of great importance in the United States. The *Civil Rights Cases* held that legislation preventing racial discrimination in hotels, theatres and public transport was unconstitutional as it breached the freedoms of those institutions.[128] The Court held that the breach must rely 'upon some state law or state authority for its excuse and perpetration' and must be 'corrective in nature, adapted to counteract and redress the operation of such prohibited state laws or proceedings of state officers'.[129] Thus, the Constitution was used by private individuals to prevent the state from delimiting private freedoms by enacting a non-discrimination statute.

DeShaney activated a heated debate.[130] The case concerned the responsibilities of the Department of Social Services which was aware, it seemed, that a child was being abused by his father, and yet took no real action. Eventually, the father beat the child so severely that he caused permanent brain injury. The case was brought by the mother and child. The Supreme Court held that fundamental rights should be to 'protect the people from the State, not to ensure that the State protected them from one another'.[131] Thus, there was 'no affirmative obligation on the State to prevent that beating, no matter what the State agents knew, or how easily the beating could have been prevented'.[132]

Generally, therefore, the defendant in the United States must be a state actor and the breach must be caused by the exercise of a public right or privilege or a state-imposed rule of conduct, or by a person for whom the state is responsible.[133] Two often cited examples are *Sullivan*[134] and *Shelley v Kraemer.*[135] In the *New York Times* case, defamation was held to be subject to the constitutional guarantee of free speech. In that case, the defamed individual was a public official who had brought the action against critics of his official conduct. The Court held that, despite the fact

125 *Lugar* (n 35 above).
126 Butler (n 119 above) 6.
127 Clapham (n 98 above) 157.
128 *The Civil Rights Cases* 109 US 3, 3 S Ct 18 (1883).
129 *Ibid.*
130 *DeShaney* (n 52 above).
131 *Ibid.*
132 Blumoff (n 124 above) 98.
133 *Lugar* (n 35 above).
134 *Sullivan v New York Times* 376 US 254, 84 S Ct 710 (1964).
135 *Shelley v Kraemer* 334 US 1, 68 S Ct 836 (1948).

that the dispute was between private individuals, the constitutional guarantees applied because the state court had applied a state rule of law that the petitioners alleged breached their constitutional freedoms: 'The test is not the form in which state power has been applied but, whatever the form, whether such power has in fact been exercised.'[136]

In *Shelley*, the Supreme Court held that state-level judicial enforcement of racist restrictive covenants was unconstitutional. Despite the clearly private nature of the agreements, they were held to be subject to the Constitution because the judiciary enforced them, and this amounted to a state action.[137] These two cases illustrate that although the general rule is that a defendant must be public, the various definitions mean that some individuals or actions which may intuitively seem to be substantively private, will be held to be subject to the constitutional guarantees.

There is significant jurisprudence in the United States determining whether a particular entity is governmental in character.[138] Certain private entities have been held to be governmental through the 'public functions' test: an entity or person may be amenable to suit under the Constitution in relation to particular functions 'encouraged' by the state.[139] Usually the function should be historically governmental.[140] This is mirrored by the Supreme Court's rules in relation to municipalities, which will be liable for their policies, laws or customs.[141] This amounts to a requirement that the action be governmental in nature: the mere employment of a tortfeasor will not be sufficient to found a claim.

The opposite statement must also be made: the actions of officials made in a personal, rather than official, capacity will not be subject to the fundamental rights.[142] Further, private individuals will only be defendants if they are co-conspirators—in other words, because of their relationship with state actors, acting under color of law.[143] This exception (if it is that) again emphasises the pre-eminence of the general rule that the defendant must have a public element.

Thus, it is clear that a state involvement is required in the causes of action in the United States. The boundaries of what is considered to be governmental or to amount to a public element have changed in response,

136 *Sullivan* (n 134 above) 718.

137 *Shelley* (n 135 above) 845.

138 See Butler (n 119 above) 4 for general discussion.

139 A state's 'mere acquiescence in a private action' does not convert the action into a state action: *Flagg Bros v Brooks* 436 US 149, 98 S Ct 1729 (1978) 164.

140 Schwartz and Kirklin (n 17 above) 103.

141 *Monell v Department of Social Services of the City of New York* 436 US 658, 98 S Ct 2018 (1978).

142 *Polk County v Dodson* 454 US 312, 102 S Ct 445 (1981). This should not be confused with the way in which pleadings are framed to avoid the application of immunities available for officials sued in their official capacity. The suit must be against officials named in their personal capacity, but be in relation to actions made in their official capacity.

143 *Dennis v Sparks* 449 US 24, 101 S Ct 183 (1980) 186.

perhaps, to a changing institutional context. The United States jurisprudence has expanded the boundary of the restrictions on who may be a defendant, but by doing so has emphasised the public/private distinction.

This issue has also generated much jurisprudence in India. Article 12 of the Indian Constitution defines 'the state': '"the State" includes the Government and Parliament of India and the Government and Legislature of each of the States and all local or other authorities within the territory of India or under the control of the Government of India.'

The fundamental rights set out in the Constitution are state-focussed at the least and, occasionally, state-specific.[144] Rights which amount to 'essentially negative obligations of the state towards social revolution, primarily protect the individual and the minority groups from arbitrary, prejudicial state action and thereby put limitations on state power'.[145] These rights 'are enforceable only against the State'.[146]

There is an interesting exception: certain of the articles 'have been designed to protect the individuals against the action of other private citizens'.[147] Such articles 'are enforceable against the whole world' and relate primarily to untouchability and forced labour.[148] The Supreme Court has commented in relation to forced labour that the reason for these articles was the socio-economic condition of the people at the time the Constitution was enacted: forced labour was an 'ugly and shameful' feature of Indian life.[149] The Court noted that:

> whenever any fundamental right which is enforceable against private individuals ... is being violated, it is the constitutional obligation of the State to take the necessary steps for the purpose of interdicting such violation and ensuring observance of the fundamental right by the private individual who is transgressing the same. Of course, the person whose fundamental right is violated can always approach the Court for the purpose of enforcement of his fundamental right, but that cannot absolve the State from its constitutional obligation to see that there is no violation of the fundamental right of such person.[150]

Thus, it seems that certain of the rights are enforceable against private individuals, without a state component to the breach, but that most are enforceable only against the state. Further, the Supreme Court has indicated that the state will not be able to escape liability in relation to the

144 Eg Arts 14 and 15(1) cf Art 19.

145 K Vibhute, 'Social Justice: Constitutional Scheme and Spirit' in K Vibhute, (ed), *Dr Ambedkar and Empowerment: Constitutional Vicissitudes* (Pune, University of Poona Press, 1995) 126.

146 *PUDR* (n 74 above) 1485.

147 Vibhute (n 145 above) 126.

148 *PUDR* (n 74 above) 1485.

149 *Ibid*, pp 1485–86.

150 *PUDR* (n 74 above) 1490–91.

privately enforceable rights—it has a duty to ensure they are not breached by individuals.

Early cases emphasised the need for a state action as a prerequisite to the cause of action. In *Kochunni*, the constititional requirement for a state action was made out as the enactment of a statute by a state legislature was considered to be sufficient state involvement. The Court held that 'it cannot certainly be said that the subject-matters of the present petitions comprise disputes between two sets of private individuals unconnected with any State action'.[151] Interestingly, while the Court assumed the need for state involvement, this did not seem to reduce the scope of the Article 32 writ.

Clearly, the Supreme Court considers that Article 32 primarily relates to the state's actions. Unsurprisingly in this context, most defendants have either been public officials or have had some state involvement. In addition, most of the cases decided under this cause of action have involved serious misuse of governmental power, and the judiciary has seen it as a duty to negotiate the balance of power between the state and its officials, and the ordinary person.[152]

Contemporary Indian jurisprudence assumes that only entities falling within the definition of 'state' can be liable for breach of fundamental rights.[153] Having said that, the Supreme Court's interpretation of the definition section in the constitution has extensively extended the scope of the word beyond its ordinary meaning.[154] Over time, it seems that the scope of 'other authorities' has expanded, so that most entities with some public element will fall within the definition.[155]

151 *Kochunni* (n 25 above) 730.

152 Eg *Rudul Sah* (n 7 above) 1089: Compensation is 'some palliative for the unlawful acts of instrumentalities which act in the name of public interest and which present for their protection the powers of the State as a shield'. See also *SAHELI* (n 97 above) 516 in which the Court held that it was 'well settled' that the state was responsible.

153 Commentators have likewise assumed that the rights are enforceable only against the state eg N Kumar, *Constitutional Law of India* (Faridabad, Pioneer Publications, 1999) 54: 'Conceptually the fundamental rights are available only against the State'; S Kulshreshtha, *Fundamental Rights and the Supreme Court: With Special Reference to Articles 14 to 22* (Jaipur, Rawat, 1995) 53: 'Meant to protect persons against the wrong doings of the State, certainly not against the condition of private persons. Private actions are sufficiently protected by the ordinary law of the land'; Jain (n 108 above) 11; R Hingorani, *Human Rights in India* (Delhi, IBH Publishing, 1985) 97.

154 *Central Inland Water Transport Corporation Ltd v Brojo Nath Gaguly* AIR 1986 SC 1571, 1583.

155 See especially *Ajay Hasia v Khalid Mujib Sehravardi* AIR 1981 SC 487 (a Regional Engineering College was an instrument of the state); *Som Prakash Rekhi v Union of India* AIR 1981 SC 212 (Bharat Petroleum Corporation was part of the state); and *Shetty v International Airport Authority of India* AIR 1979 SC 1628 (Airport Authority was part of the state). Further examples held to fall within the definition include: *Minhas v Indian Statistical Institute* AIR 1984 SC 363 (statistical institute); *AL Kalra v P & E Corporation of India* Ltd AIR 1984 SC 1361 (a Government of India Undertaking); *Manmohan Singh v Commissioner, Union Territory, Chandigarh* AIR 1985 SC 364 (a private but aided school); *Chandra v All Indian Institute of Medical Sciences* AIR 1990 SC 1670 (research institute).

The Court has held that even non-statutory authorities may fall within the ambit of 'state'. For example, even a corporation has been held to be the state for the purposes of Article 12: 'one must necessarily see through the corporate veil to ascertain whether behind that veil is the face of an instrumentality or agency of the State'.[156] It seems that any entity which 'in one form or the other' is an instrumentality or agency of the government, will be considered to fall within the definition,[157] in relation to the particular 'functional context'.[158] Pronouncements emphasising the importance of fundamental rights explain the judicial decisions: 'this Court has throughout the last few years expanded the horizon of Article 32 primarily to inject respect human rights and social conscience in our corporate structure. The purpose of expansion has not been to destroy the *raison d'etre* of creating corporations but to advance the human rights jurisprudence.'[159]

While these cases were, for the most part, decided prior to the development of the monetary remedy, there is no indication that different approaches will be taken in monetary remedy cases.[160] The first cases under the cause of action seem to have continued the focus on the state, but with a wide interpretation of what constitutes 'state'. In particular, a fertiliser company was held to be the state,[161] as was the Railway Board.[162] The classic suit was somewhat reversed in *Rural Litigation*, where the plaintiff was a *quasi*-public committee and the defendant a corporation who had breached a mining licence.[163] Even here, the Supreme Court allowed the use of the constitutional cause of action to enforce the order.

Further, it should be noted that the burgeoning of public interest litigation in India contributed to the expansion in the sorts of entities held to fall within Article 12. In fact, it was suggested that the combination of the two developments meant that public interest litigation was being used to remedy 'all critical ills in the body politic and in the governance of the country'.[164] It seems that the broadening of one aspect of the cause of action has led to corresponding broadenings in relation to other aspects.

156 *Central Inland* (n 154 above) 1601.

157 M Hidayatullah, (ed), *Constitutional Law of India*, Vol I (Liverpool, Lucas, 1986) 156. See in particular, *Ajay Hasia* (n 155 above) and *Som Prakash* (n 155 above).

158 *Mehta* (n 7 above) 1097.

159 *Ibid*.

160 Although doubts have been expressed that it would be possible for the monetary remedy to be available for breaches by entities falling within the wider ambit of Art 12 as defined by the Supreme Court: S Sathe, 'Constitutional Law—I (Fundamental Rights)' (1986) XXII *ASIL* 359. The statement is made without support in a generally sceptical annual survey of the rapid expansion of Arts 32 and 12 and is not repeated in later surveys.

161 *Mehta* (n 7 above).

162 *Chairman Railway Board v Chandrima Das* AIR 2000 SC 988.

163 *Rural Litigation* (n 23 above).

164 Singh (n 89 above) 36.

More recently at least one purely private individual, without any link to public law, has been held liable to pay a monetary remedy through an Article 32 fundamental rights writ. In *Gautam*, the Court awarded a monetary remedy under the Constitution against a man who was to be tried for inducing an abortion and conducting a fraudulent marriage ceremony.[165] The case was justified as providing 'interim compensation', as it was believed to be inevitable that a monetary remedy would be granted through civil or criminal law. Nevertheless, the constitutional cause of action was used to provide a monetary remedy for a woman raped by an individual who could in no way be held to be a state actor. That the Indian courts consider that the application of the cause of action to be secondary to the protection of rights is clear from the judgment, which mentions the non-governmental aspect of the defendant and his actions only to state that 'Fundamental Rights can be enforced even against private bodies and individuals'.[166] Indications are that this case will not be followed.[167]

The situation is not clear in New Zealand. At first glance, the New Zealand Bill of Rights Act seems to be limited to public sector entities. The argument has been made, however, that it applies to the actions of private individuals through its application to the judiciary: it is argued that the development of the common law is necessarily included.[168] Thus, the Courts would have recourse to the Bill of Rights Act when called upon to take any decision on a common law rule, including purely private matters arising between purely private parties. This argument of pure vertical application does not seem to have been accepted by the courts. Judgments emphasise the public nature of the cause of action and the Crown's duties in relation to the Bill of Rights, suggesting that the Court has assumed that one party will be the Crown or have some nexus with the Crown.[169]

In *Grayson*, the matter was considered directly.[170] The Court of Appeal in that case held that 'wholly private conduct is left to be controlled by the law of the land' and considered what was required for an individual to be acting as a state actor for the purposes of the cause of action.[171] In that case, if the person involved had not been held to be carrying out a 'public' function, then the cause of action would have failed.

A similar approach is illustrated by the jurisprudence surrounding

165 *Gautam v Chakraborty* (1996) 1 SCC 490.

166 *Ibid*, p 499.

167 Eg *Vishaka v State of Rajasthan* AIR 1997 SC 3011 in which the Supreme Court refused compensation without comment. See K Vibhute, 'Victims of Rape and Their Right to Live with Human Dignity and to be Compensated: Legislative and Judicial Responses in India' (1999) 41 *JILI* 222.

168 Butler (n 119 above) cf Paccioco (n 119 above) and Rishworth (n 119 above).

169 In particular, see *Hobson* (n 5 above) in which the Court accepted that it was the appropriate defendant in Bill of Rights cases.

170 *Grayson* (n 27 above).

171 *Ibid*, p 407.

quasi-public entities with mixed public and private functions. New Zealand courts have assessed individual state-owned enterprises, to determine whether the particular actions were public and so subject to the rights arising from the Bill of Rights.[172] In other words, the New Zealand jurisprudence looks at the particular functions of *quasi*-public entities to decide on a pragmatic basis whether organisations are liable under *Baigent's Case*. Thus, the focus is moved from the nature of the entity or the official, to whether the particular actions of an entity or official are public. Once again, the expectation is that there will be a state element to the cause of action and the focus of the case law is on defining the boundaries, rather than questioning that assumption.

Thus, it seems that while the scope of application of the cause of action differs from jurisdiction to jurisdiction, a 'state-centric paradigm' exists.[173] Private actors held to be appropriate defendants under the cause of action are the exceptions that prove the general rule. Even in India, where there is less limitation on application, most cases involve the use or misuse of governmental powers; the extension of the cause of action to non-state entities is usually by analogy to those public entities.

2. What Immunities Apply?

The immunity doctrine excludes liability for certain public entities and officials who would otherwise be liable by virtue of their relationship with the state. Immunities are linked to the public nature of the defendants. This is an issue that has the potential to limit greatly the width of the cause of action and availability of the remedy.

In the United States, immunities have somewhat overtaken the general rule, so that not only do most cases concern the application of immunities, but almost all public entities and officials will be immune. An absolute immunity applies for officials performing legislative, judicial and prosecutorial functions,[174] as well as for state governments and state officials acting in their official capacity.[175] These absolute immunities are based on the sovereign immunity of the states and policy considerations relating to public administration.

[172] *TVNZ Ltd v Newsmonitor Services Ltd* [1994] 2 NZLR 91 (TVNZ's trading activities and control of copyrights were not a public function); *Federated Farmers of New Zealand Inc v New Zealand Post Ltd* [1990–92] 3 NZBORR 339 (provision of a rural service by New Zealand Post was a public function); and *Lawson v Housing New Zealand* (1996) 3 HRNZ 285 (implementation of a market rental policy by Housing New Zealand was a public function).

[173] Jochnick (n 119 above) 57: Re international human rights law.

[174] *Pierson v Ray* 386 US 547, 87 S Ct 1213 (1967); *Imbler v Pachtman* 424 US 409, 96 S Ct 984 (1976).

[175] *Will v Michigan Department of State Police* 491 US 58, 109 S Ct 2304 (1989).

A good faith immunity exists in the United States for governmental officials sued in their official capacity.[176] The standard against which good faith is judged is so low that it is basically equivalent to an absolute immunity.[177] Immunities do not exist for co-conspirators,[178] or for officials sued in their personal, rather than official, capacity[179] or for the policies, laws or customs of municipalities.[180] In *Mt Healthy*, the Supreme Court distinguished between municipalities, on the one hand, and state entities on the other which, as arms of state, were entitled to the immunity.[181] This reinforces the rule that there must be a state involvement in a particular action for liability to attach.[182] In practice, cases in the United States can be brought only against co-conspirators, officials in their personal capacity, or municipalities on the basis of policies, laws and customs.

In New Zealand and India, in comparison, no immunities exist for officials. Good faith will not be relevant in determining liability in New Zealand.[183] Sovereign immunity has no relevance as the cause of action was explicitly held to be at public law, so avoiding immunities.[184] In India, the Supreme Court held that the cause of action was strict liability and so no good faith immunity applied.[185] Sovereign immunity will not apply due to the public law nature of the remedy.[186] Absolute immunities based on the public nature of the defendants have not been introduced in either jurisdiction. Significantly, there is no immunity for judicial officers.[187]

The complex and comprehensive set of rules surrounding the defendant developed in the United States jurisprudence has not been followed in the other two jurisdictions. The issue has, nevertheless, received much discussion in those two jurisdictions. The decision to allow no immunities is a departure from the expected approach in a common law jurisdiction. As a final aside, it could be observed that the strong element of immunity

176 *Scheuer v Rhodes* 416 US 232, 94 S Ct 1683 (1974); *Butz* (n 46 above).

177 A Burris, 'Qualifying Immunity in §1983 and *Bivens* Actions' (1992) 71 *Texas L Rev* 123; *Malley* 475 US 335, 106 S Ct 1092 (1986).

178 *Dennis* (n 143 above).

179 *Kentucky v Graham* 473 US 159, 105 S Ct 3099 (1985), although note that the impugned conduct must still have been made in an official capacity; this is a matter of pleadings.

180 *Monell* (n 141 above).

181 *Mt Healthy City School District Board of Education v Doyle* 429 US 274, 97 S Ct 568 (1977).

182 *Lugar* (n 35 above).

183 *Whithair* (n 101 above). Note that the existence of good faith might, however, be relevant in determining quantum in New Zealand: *Grayson* (n 27 above) and *Manga* (n 5 above).

184 *Baigent's Case* (n 5 above).

185 *Nilabati* (n 55 above); *Basu* (n 49 above).

186 *Basu* (n 49 above) 314; *Nilabati* (n 55 above) 2905.

187 In *Upton (2)* (n 109 above), a claim was considered in relation to a New Zealand District Court Judge and in *Baigent's Case* itself (n 5 above), the Court referred to *Maharaj v Attorney-General of Trinidad and Tobago* [1979] AC 385 which involved a fundamental rights claim against a judge. In India, the judiciary falls within the scope of Art 12 in relation to its 'rule-making' or administrative powers and not 'when it discharges judicial functions': Jain (n 108 above) 168.

in the United States mirrors the absolute requirement of state involvement in that jurisdiction. This could be considered as classic common law: a public defendant to whom immunities attach for reasons of policy.

3. Is the Nature of the Pleadings Important?

While the previous discussion has concerned the question of whose actions form the basis of the claim, this aspect involves identifying who should be named as the defendant—in other words, how the cause of action should be pleaded. In practice, this has involved considering whether individual officers or the state should be named as defendant.

In India, the Article 32 writ is usually brought against the state: the Union of India, an individual state or one of the 'other authorities'. Certain environmental public interest litigation cases, which have to all intents and purposes been against companies, have cited the Union of India or one of the states as a co-respondent, thus avoiding the general prohibition against non-state entities being named as defendants.[188] As the cause of action was explicitly based on vicarious liability,[189] the state will be liable for the acts and defaults of government officials.[190] The Court has indicated, however, that the state can seek indemnification from the individual or individuals responsible if the impugned actions exceeded the performance of official duties.[191] This may avoid the criticism that by ordering payments to come from a state exchequer, rather than the wrongdoer, there was no real deterrent effect and the result was not fair for taxpayers.[192]

All that is relatively unimportant in light of the 'epistolary jurisdiction' developed by the Supreme Court. The Court has definitively determined that public interest pleadings in India will not have to conform to any prescribed pattern: the epistolary jurisdiction means that even a letter addressed to an individual judge will be sufficient.[193] The Indian Supreme Court will not allow procedural matters to defeat the cause of action. The issue of pleadings is, therefore, very different in India from that in the United States.

188 U Rai, 'Reach of Fundamental Rights' (1994) 36 *JILI* 292, 300. An example is *Mehta* (n 7 above).

189 *SAHELI* (n 97 above) 516.

190 B Dwivedi, 'From *Sah* to *SAHELI*: A New Dimension to Government Liability' (1994) 36 *JILI* 99, 110.

191 *State of Maharastra v Christian Community Welfare Council of India* [2003] 4 LRI 299, 305. See also *SAHELI* (n 97 above) 516 and *Basu* (n 49 above) 317.

192 K Joshi 'Compensation Through Writs: *Rudul Sah* to *Mehta*' (1988) 30 *JILI* 69, 76; P Rao 'Retrogressive Step in Compensatory Jurisprudence: A Critique of *State of Maharashtra v Ravikant S Patil*' (1992) 34 *JILI* 472, 473–74.

193 *Mehta* (n 7 above) 1090; *Gupta* (n 69 above).

In New Zealand, the traditional idea that the Attorney-General will be the 'guardian of the public interest'[194] is enhanced to the extent that the Attorney-General must be a defendant in all cases. In *Hobson*, the Court held that the proper defendant in Bill of Rights Act cases was the Attorney-General; the defendants named in the pleadings were replaced by the Attorney-General.[195] This is perhaps especially remarkable as this was at the request of the Attorney-General's representative, seemingly in recognition of Crown responsibilities for all breaches of the Bill of Rights and to ensure consistency in the way in which cases are defended.

Thus, the cause of action in New Zealand will properly be brought against the Attorney-General—the state—and not the individual officer or even the individual entity. In other words, regardless of whether the breach concerned the actions of the police,[196] the Court,[197] or a crown health authority,[198] the pleadings would name the Attorney-General as defendant, sued in respect of the relevant entities or officials. The liability of individual state agents responsible for a breach 'remains confined to tort and subject to common law limitations and statutory immunities'.[199]

In the United States, the way in which the pleadings are framed is crucial: it will determine whether the cause of action will be viable or not. Entities will, in effect, be immune from suit for breaches of rights by their agents or employees, as will officials sued in their official capacity.[200] Bringing a suit against individual officers in their personal capacity, therefore, is the only way for a case to be brought in relation to such breaches. The difference is merely one of form, however, and not of substance, as the actions at the basis of the claim are the same as for a claim to which the immunity would apply.[201]

Thus, whereas the conventions that apply to pleadings in India and New Zealand are unlikely to cause the case to fail, should there be a mistake in the pleadings, in the United States the framing of the pleadings will determine the success of the plea. Further, in India and New Zealand the pleadings most appropriately name the entity, or in the case of New Zealand the abstract state, as the defendant while, in the United States, the pleadings must name the individual wrongdoer. It is arguable whether these differences result in differences in the sort of cases brought.

This raises the question of who should pay any remedy eventually

194 Australian Law Reform Commission (n 61 above) 23.
195 *Hobson* (n 5 above).
196 *Baigent's Case* (n 5 above).
197 *Upton (2)* (n 109 above).
198 *Hobson* (n 5 above).
199 J Smillie, 'The Allure of "Rights Talk": *Baigent's Case* in the Court of Appeal' (1994) 8 *Otago L Rev* 188, 199.
200 *Will* (n 175 above).
201 J Jeffries, 'In Praise of the Eleventh Amendment and Section 1983' (1998) 84 *Virg L Rev* 47, 62.

ordered. The three jurisdictions once again illustrate three different options. In India, it is clear that the courts usually order a remedy against the state or entity, but consider that the wrongdoer may be personally liable to the state through an indemnity.[202] The responsibility for the payment of a monetary remedy will rest with the state which may seek reimbursement from the individual erring officers. In the United States, the indemnity operates the other way around as the state will provide an indemnity for any individual against whom a remedy is awarded.[203] In other words, a suit will only succeed if the pleadings name an individual as defendant, and yet any remedy ordered will usually be paid by the immune state. In New Zealand, the courts have suggested that the Attorney-General, and not the individual official, nor even the individual entity, should pay any monetary remedy.[204] This matter is by no means settled and has been the subject of some dispute in the secondary sources.[205] Clearly, it is unlikely that officials would ever be held individually liable in New Zealand, in light of the fact that it is unlikely that even individual entities will be liable.

Thus, there is a distinction between the situation in India, where it is considered appropriate that individual wrongdoers should pay, and the situation in the United States and New Zealand, where the state will indemnify the individual wrongdoers. There is a further distinction between the United States, where the individual will be responsible legally, and New Zealand, where the entity will be responsible for the payment of any remedy.

4. Is Fault Relevant?

The relevance of fault has already been alluded to in the earlier discussion of immunities. The standard of liability to be applied to this cause of action has been of importance in each of the three jurisdictions.

Standard of liability concerns the general legal expectation that fault will be the 'determinant' of liability.[206] Generally, the defendant's fault or intent will be a requirement of the cause of action and good faith will be a defence. Strict liability, on the other hand, denotes those cases where fault

202 *Maharastra* (n 191 above) 305; *SAHELI* (n 97 above) 516.

203 Jeffries (n 201 above) 50.

204 *Baigent's Case* (n 5 above) 718; *Hobson* (n 5 above); *Innes v Wong* [1996] 2 HRNZ 618, 624.

205 New Zealand Law Commission, *Crown Liability and Judicial Immunity: A Response to* Baigent's Case *and* Harvey v Derrick (Wellington, NZLC r37, 1997); R Harrison, 'The Remedial Jurisdiction for Breach of the Bill of Rights' in G Huscroft and P Rishworth, (eds), *Rights and Freedoms: The New Zealand Bill of Rights Act 1990 and the Human Rights Act 1993* (Wellington, Brookers, 1996) 401.

206 W Rogers, *Winfield and Jolowicz on Tort*, 14th edn, (London, Sweet & Maxwell, 1994) 27–45.

is not required for liability to be established. The focus is more on the need for equity between victims, than on the defendant's conduct. The basic question is whether fault or intention on the part of the defendant is required as a prerequisite to the cause of action. While the standard of liability is usually portrayed as being either fault-based or strict, in reality it may be that 'fault-based and strict liability exist on a continuum badly defined where they meet at the middle'[207]; fault-based and strict liability are a 'sliding scale'.[208] Thus, it may be possible that other protections from suit may 'soften' a strict liability.

In both India and New Zealand, the cause of action is explicitly strict liability. In India, the Courts have stressed that the purpose of the monetary remedy is compensatory, and not punishment, as the 'objective is to apply balm to the wounds'.[209] As the focus is on the rights-holder and the rights, the wrongdoer's intent or otherwise is largely irrelevant. Clearly, the cause of action in India 'is a claim based on strict liability',[210] and the bona fides of the official or entity will not be relevant at the stage of determining liability. Nevertheless, it should be noted that the early cases, in particular, focussed on the *mala fides* of the defendant as justification for developing the monetary remedy in constitutional law.[211]

In New Zealand, the cause of action was held not to require fault in an early case.[212] Thus, the cause of action does not allow for a defence of good faith or require an examination of intention. The Chief Justice considered that there was no principled basis for circumscribing the cause of action, in the absence of any indication in *Baigent's Case* that limitations should be considered part of the cause of action. Later cases have considered this matter to be conclusively determined.[213]

As New Zealand statutory immunities do not apply to such a public law cause of action, it appears that the cause of action is, *prima facie*, actionable in relation to the actions of the judiciary.[214] There are, however, indications that 'mere judicial error' will not be sufficient to found the cause of action, suggesting that a partial fault element will be relevant in relation to the actions of, at least, the judiciary.[215]

In the United States, by contrast, the intention of the defendant is of the utmost relevance in almost every case as a good faith immunity applies to

207 I Englard, *The Philosophy of Tort Law* (Aldershot, Dartmouth, 1993) 21.

208 P Birks, 'The Concept of a Civil Wrong' in D Owen, (ed), *Philosophical Foundations of Tort Law* (Oxford, Clarendon Press, 1995) 42.

209 *Basu* (n 49 above) 318.

210 *Ibid*, p 314.

211 Eg *Rudul Sah* (n 7 above); *SAHELI* (n 97 above).

212 *Whithair* (n 101 above).

213 *Kerr v Attorney-General* (Unrep, NP 233/95, District Court Timaru Registry, Judge Ryan, 7 August 1996) 9; *Manga* (n 5 above) 70.

214 *Harvey v Derrick* [1995] 1 NZLR 314; *Upton (2)* (n 109 above).

215 *Harvey* (n 214 above) 322.

most officials and public organizations.[216] If the defendant can prove good faith, no liability attaches. As discussed above, the Supreme Court has created a test for good faith which is close to encompassing all actions of governmental officials not made in explicit bad faith: only 'the plainly incompetent or those who knowingly violate the law' will not be able to rely upon an immunity.[217] The test is substantially objective, which allows the immunity to apply when conduct violates established rights of which a reasonable person would have known.[218]

The Supreme Court has stated that the purpose of the good faith immunity is to ensure the proper functioning of the state and 'thereby to protect the public at large, not to benefit its agents'.[219] Thus, the immunity applies only to public officials and not to private individuals, for whom the issue of intention will have less relevance. As has been discussed previously, however, this has little practical effect as the Supreme Court has strictly enforced a requirement of state involvement, so that the only private individuals and entities who will be amenable to suit will be co-conspirators.[220]

Finally, it should be noted that, regardless of whether intention will be required as a component of the cause of action, it may be of relevance in other aspects of the cause of action. Good faith—and, conversely, bad faith—may be relevant in determining the sort and amount of damages awarded.[221]

5. Summary

The comparison of the three jurisdictions' approaches to the issue of against whom the remedy is available shows conceptual and substantive differences. While all three jurisdictions require a public component for the cause of action to exist, the boundaries of what is defined as 'public' varies between the jurisdictions.

More interestingly, it also shows differences in the importance placed on the issue. In the United States, the defendant's identity is a primary question. It is the issue around which much of the jurisprudence has centred; it is an important aspect of all Section 1983 and *Bivens* decisions.

216 Burris (n 177 above) 140–41.
217 *Malley* (n 177 above).
218 *Harlow v Fitzgerald* 457 US 800, 102 S Ct 2727 (1982).
219 *Wyatt v Cole* 504 US 158, 112 S Ct 1827 (1992).
220 *Dennis* (n 143 above).
221 Punitive damages will be available in the United States: *Smith v Wade* 461 US 30, 103 S Ct 1625 (1983). Early Indian cases suggest that the money awarded was in the nature of exemplary damages or costs: *Hongray* (n 7 above); and *Bhim Singh* (n 7 above). In New Zealand, there is a suggestion that lower awards will be made in cases in which good faith could be argued: *Kerr* (n 213 above); and *Manga* (n 5 above) 70.

In comparison, New Zealand and Indian jurisprudence treats this as an issue of importance equivalent to many others.

E. WHAT DOES THE COURT ORDER?

This question is the integral feature of the cause of action. As studying the actual amount of money awarded under the cause of action would be of limited use in a comparative analysis, it will not be discussed here. Rather, issues influencing the final amounts awarded and the nature of what is awarded will be considered. The broad and eclectic issues discussed under this heading may go beyond what would normally be expected in a study of quantum; they are united by their effect on the amount of money awarded by the Courts. Having considered, in the earlier sections of this chapter, the parts of the structure that are more usually separated out from remedy, this section considers those elements of the cause of action that are purely remedial.

1. What Terminology is Used?

A preliminary factor to consider is one of definition. Throughout this book, I have referred to the 'monetary remedy', and not to either 'damages' or 'compensation', in an attempt to encompass both concepts and avoid assumptions. The term is manufactured and not one that is generally used in the judgments.[222] At this point in the discussion, it is timely to consider the difference in terminology.[223]

In general, judges describe what they are doing in these cases as awarding either 'compensation' or 'damages'.[224] Theoretically, the terms are legally distinct, and are often expressly differentiated from one another.[225] Generally, it seems that compensation is the primary aim of damages.[226] Thus, damages will aim to compensate the plaintiff for loss

222 Gault J, in dissent, in *Baigent's Case* (n 5 above) 712 refers to 'an action in the nature of tort for a monetary remedy'. The Court of Appeal's judgments in *Wilding v Attorney-General* [2003] 3 NZLR 787, 791; and in *PF Sugrue Ltd v Attorney-General* [2004] 1 NZLR 207, 236 refer to 'a monetary remedy'.

223 An exegesis on the differences between compensation and damages is beyond the scope of this book.

224 There is an exception in India, where cases have referred to awards of 'exemplary costs' (see *Hongray* (n 7 above); *Bhim Singh* (n 7 above)) and a 'fine' (see *MP v Trivedi* [1995] (3) SCALE 343, cited in *Basu* (n 49 above) 308) in situations where it is difficult to distinguish the award from those described as damages or compensation. The use of the fees jurisdiction in the United States could also fall within the criteria of a monetary remedy.

225 *Halsbury's Laws of England: Damages*, Vol 12(1), 4th edn, Reissue, (London, Butterworths, 1998) para 803.

226 Eg see B Kercher and M Noone, *Remedies*, 2nd edn, (Sydney, Law Book, 1991).

suffered, to place her in the position she would have been had the wrong not occurred.[227] Compensation is 'pecuniary recompense which a person is entitled to receive in respect of damage or loss which he has suffered, other than as a result of an actionable wrong'; damages are recoverable in respect of actionable wrongs.[228]

Both terms are used to some extent in all three jurisdictions and three approaches are evident: the monetary remedy may be referred to as one or the other of the two terms, or by reference to both terms interchangeably. By this I mean that judges will use both terms within the same judgment to refer to the same award, without acknowledging a distinction between the two.

For example, in *Baigent's Case*, two of the majority judges refer to both 'damages' and 'compensation' in their judgments, once in the same paragraph.[229] This is despite Cooke P clearly distinguishing between the two in his leading judgment. In discussing Judicature Act 1908 Section 19A, regarding the definition of pecuniary damages for the purposes of determining whether trial by jury is available, Cooke P stated: 'That section is referring to common law damages, not public law compensation. This is more than a fine point as to the meaning of "damages": the term can no doubt be used loosely and conveniently enough to cover Bill of Rights compensation.'[230]

Although the plaintiffs in question claimed 'damages',[231] both Cooke P and Casey J awarded 'compensation' without further comment as to the distinction.[232] This mirrors the *Maharaj* judgment of the Privy Council, cited extensively by the New Zealand Court, in which Lord Diplock states: 'The claim is not a claim in private law for damages for the tort of false imprisonment, under which the damages recoverable are at large and would include damages for loss of reputation. It is a claim in public law for compensation for deprivation of liberty alone.'[233]

In comparison, Lord Hailsham in dissent refers to the unavailability and undesirability of 'damages'.[234] Perhaps the use of the term 'compensation' masked what this judge saw as an undesirable extension of tort law into public law and so the distinction between the two terms was untenable to him.

Later New Zealand cases have reflected the mixed terminology. For example, in *Grayson*, the Court referred to 'damages or compensation' for

227 D Walker, *The Oxford Companion to Law* (Oxford, Clarendon Press, 1980) 323. Note that this refers to restitution as the primary aim.

228 *Halsbury's* (n 225 above) para 815.

229 *Baigent's Case* (n 5 above) 700; 718.

230 *Ibid*, p 678.

231 The pleadings are annexed to the judgment of Cooke P.

232 Eg *Baigent's Case* (n 5 above) 678; 692.

233 *Maharaj* (n 187 above) 400.

234 *Ibid*, p 409.

breach of the New Zealand Bill of Rights Act[235]; in *Whithair*, the Chief Justice used both terms interchangeably[236]; and in *Sugrue*, the Court of Appeal referred to '*Baigent* damages' as a form of compensation.[237] In *Innes*, Cartwright J quoted Cooke P's distinction in *Baigent's Case* between public law compensation and private law damages; referred to 'public law damages' in the following two sentences; and reverted to 'public law compensation' in the next paragraph.[238] While in *Upton (2)*,[239] *Martin v Tauranga DC*,[240] *M and E*[241] and *Brown v Attorney-General*[242] the remedy was clearly identified as being 'compensation', in *Hobson* the Court referred to 'damages'.[243]

In *Hewitt*, on the other hand, the Court distinguished between the two terms: 'We accept there is a distinction in principle between awards of damages at common law and compensation for breach of the NZBORA'.[244] The same approach was taken in *Dunlea*.[245] In both these cases, the High Court and Court of Appeal were called upon to consider the relationship between monetary relief under *Baigent's Case* and that awarded in tort law. The terminology was important to signify to which of the sorts of monetary relief the Court referred. The Courts also seemed to use it to explain the differences between Bill of Rights cases and the common law.

The distinction was considered in detail in *Wilding*, in which the submission was made that the use of the terminology 'damages' in Section 394 of the Accident Insurance Act 1998 was in contradistinction to 'compensation' used elsewhere in the section and in Cooke P's judgment in *Baigent's Case*.[246] The Court of Appeal held, however, that the term 'damages' in that Act 'must in context include all forms of monetary award intended to compensate for the personal injury suffered' and so *Baigent's Case* compensation or damages were statute-barred.[247] It was noted that the two terms appear indistinguishable in both the Accident Insurance Act and in the *Baigent's Case* judgments,[248] and the 'tentative view' was expressed that *Baigent's Case* 'monetary compensation' could still be awarded, despite the bar, so long as the award was quantified so as

235 *Grayson* (n 27 above) 411.
236 *Whithair* (n 101 above) 56–57.
237 *Sugrue* (n 222 above) 236–37.
238 *Innes* (n 204 above) 634.
239 *Upton (2)* (n 109 above) 20.
240 *Martin* [1995] 1 NZLR 491.
241 *M and E v Attorney-General* [1997] 2 NZLR 746.
242 *Brown* (n 30 above).
243 *Hobson* (n 5 above).
244 *Attorney-General v Hewitt* [2000] 2 NZLR 111, 126.
245 *Dunlea* (n 28 above) 149.
246 *Wilding* (n 222 above) 791.
247 *Ibid.*
248 *Ibid*, p 792.

not to provide compensation for the injury itself; exemplary damages may also be available.[249]

Thus, in New Zealand, it seems that the judiciary may have distinguished between 'damages' and 'compensation' largely to signify distinctly either tort or public law. That distinction has been extremely important in New Zealand for reasons of general legal principle, immunity and procedure.[250] Nevertheless, it seems that judges have assumed that it was unnecessary to distinguish the terminology once such matters had been determined—in other words, once it had been decided that the cause of action was at public law and not at private law.

In India, the distinction between public law compensation and private law damages is also evident, but a different approach is taken. In *Rudul Sah*, the first monetary remedy case, the remedy was categorised as 'compensation' and contrasted with 'private law damages'; the Article 32 compensation was 'interim' to the filing of a final damages claim at private law.[251] Thus, the Court considered it necessary to distinguish between the monetary remedy granted in a constitutional public law case and that which would be granted in a civil law case. This was repeated in *Basu*, in which a monetary remedy was awarded 'not by way of damages as in a civil action but by way of compensation under the public law jurisdiction for the wrong done ... . Public law proceedings serve a different purpose than the private law proceedings.'[252] The judgment clearly identifies the monetary remedy it grants as compensation, and not damages. It seems that most Indian judgments refer only to compensation.[253]

In the United States, in comparison, the language is very clearly one of 'damages' but, unlike in New Zealand and India, there is no major discussion of the difference between compensation and damages to explain why this term was chosen. This may be because the United States legal tradition includes the concept of a constitutional tort—and so damages at public law—which in the Indian and New Zealand common law classically has not been considered possible. Thus, consideration of the distinction between 'compensation' and 'damages' in a public law cause of action in those jurisdictions was inescapable, while in the United States it was unnecessary.

249 *Ibid*, p 793.

250 Generally, damages are not available at public law in New Zealand; the various statutory immunities that apply to tort law causes of action were held not to apply in this cause of action; and, as the remedy was not 'pecuniary damages', jury trial was not inevitable.

251 *Rudul Sah* (n 7 above).

252 *Basu* (n 49 above) 313–14.

253 See Eg *Nilabati* (n 55 above) 2904; (cf the concurring judgment of Anand J, 2912: 'The relief of monetary compensation, as exemplary damages'); *Mehta* (n 7 above); *Charanjit Kaur v Union of India* AIR 1994 SC 1491; *Supreme Court Legal Aid Committee v State of Bihar* (1991) 3 SCC 482; *PUDR v Police Commissioner, Delhi* (1989) 4 SCC 730.

The normality of awarding damages at public law in the United States was evident in *Bivens*, where the Court held that the 'ordinary remedy'—that is, damages—was available for breach of constitutional rights despite the constitutional silence on the matter.[254] Rather than expressly contrasting the cause of action and remedy with private law damages, defendants in the United States are 'sued directly under § 1983 for monetary ... relief' in the constitutional tort.[255] All plaintiffs and judgments refer to damages.[256]

While it is arguable whether the difference in terminology has any actual effect on the approach taken to the remedy awarded, it signifies important rhetorical differences and philosophical bases. Further, it signifies the difference in the nature of the causes of action, with Section 1983 and *Bivens* having more tort law features than the Article 32 and *Baigent's Case* causes of action.

2. Step 1: Should the Monetary Remedy be Ordered?

The remainder of this section is a discussion of a series of steps that courts take in determining quantum. The first step a court must take, once a rights breach has been established, is to determine whether or not the monetary remedy should be ordered. This has involved determining the importance of the concept of a right to a remedy and whether there are any situations in which a remedy will not be awarded, including whether this remedy, rather than any other, is preferable.

Article 32 of the Indian Constitution guarantees a right to move the Supreme Court for enforcement of the other rights so that '[w]henever the fundamental rights are flouted or legislative protection ignored to any citizen's prejudice, the Supreme Court will give appropriate relief'.[257] In early cases under the Constitution the Indian Supreme Court held that Article 32 amounted to a right to a remedy.[258] Further, the existence of alternative remedies is no bar to Article 32.[259] The Indian Supreme Court retains a discretion, however, as to which remedy to award.[260] The value ascribed to remedies in this jurisdiction is reflected in the fact that the

254 *Bivens* (n 15 above) 2004.

255 *Monell* (n 141 above) 2035.

256 Eg *Owen v City of Independence Missouri* 445 US 622, 100 S Ct 1398 (1980), 1415–16; *Farmer v Brennan* 511 US 825, 114 S Ct 1970 (1994); *Schweiker v Chilicky* 487 US 412, 108 S Ct 2460 (1988); *McCarthy v Madigan* 503 US 140, 112 S Ct 1081 (1992); *Davis* (n 16 above); *Carlson v Green* 446 US 14, 100 S Ct 1468 (1980); *Butz* (n 46 above).

257 M Singh, *VN Shukla's Constitution of India*, 8th edn, (Lucknow, Eastern Bd, 1990) 219.

258 *Kochunni* (n 25 above) 729.

259 Eg *Shukla's Constitution* (n 257 above) 226; *Kochunni* (n 25 above) 730.

260 See *Shukla's Constitution* (n 257 above) 219.

Indian Supreme Court has used this freedom to allow a monetary remedy even when one has not been claimed in the original writ.[261]

There are some indications, however, that the Supreme Court's approach to Article 32 cases may not have such a significant effect as first impression suggests. For example, the Court may hold that cases have been inappropriately brought under Article 32, thus dismissing them without a remedy for the individual plaintiff.[262] Obviously, this has much the same effect for the plaintiff as finding that no remedy exists in the particular case. Theoretically, however, the sanctity of the remedy is left unblemished while the width of the guaranteed rights and of Article 32 itself will be narrowed.[263]

Further, the Supreme Court has been keen to delineate the group of cases in which the monetary remedy can be ordered:

> We are deliberately using the words 'in appropriate cases' because we must make it clear that it is not in every case where there is a breach of a fundamental right committed by the violator that compensation would be awarded by the Court in a petition under Article 32. The infringement of the fundamental right must be gross and patent, that is, incontrovertible and ex facie glaring and either such infringement should be on a large scale affecting the fundamental rights of a large number of persons or it should appear unjust or unduly harsh or oppressive on account of their poverty or disability or socially or economically disadvantaged position to require the persons or persons affected by such infringement to initiate and pursue action in the civil Courts.[264]

It seems, therefore, that the monetary remedy will be awarded in India once a right has been breached and the Court is assured that justice requires such compensation because of the nature of the breach and the situation of the plaintiff. Clearly, the majority of cases that are considered to come within this definition are those that have involved the right to life and liberty of economically disadvantaged people,[265] or that are part of

261 Eg *Mehta* (n 7 above) 1089.

262 Eg *Neelu Sarin v India* (1991) Supp 1 SCC 300 and *Kochar v Union of India* AIR 1983 SC 1107. Also see cases sent back to the High Court for consideration under Art 226: *Brahmbhatt v State of Gujarat* AIR 1987 SC 1159; and *Kumar v Municipal Corporation of Delhi* (1987) 4 SCC 609.

263 Judicial comments elsewhere suggest that this is undesirable: La Forest J in *B v Childrens Aid Society* [1995] 1 SCR 315, 389 argued that limitations only should be imposed under the balancing section of the Canadian Charter of Rights, thus leaving the right itself wide. This has not always been followed. Eg in New Zealand, in *Quilter v Attorney-General* [1998] 1 NZLR 523 it was held that the Marriage Act's requirement for marriage to be between a man and a woman was not a breach of the rights of the plaintiff lesbians, thus limiting the scope of the right to marriage; the Court could have held that such a limitation was a breach but was 'reasonable'. Cf J Beatson, 'The Discretionary Nature of Public Law Remedies' [1991] *NZ Rec L Rev* 81 who, in the context of judicial review, believes that factors should be factored into the question of whether a ground for review is made out, rather than being considered at remedy.

264 *Mehta* (n 7 above) 1091.

265 Eg *Rudul Sah* (n 7 above); and *SAHELI* (n 97 above).

shocking behaviour by government officials such as the custodial death cases,[266] death caused by the military,[267] and the systematic blinding of prisoners.[268]

In the United States, once a rights breach has been made out, the Court will consider remedy as a second stage. There is no right to a remedy as a plaintiff must prove that a particular remedy should be ordered in the particular case.[269] Further, as the Court can only award damages sought in the pleadings, the way in which the matter has been pleaded will be extremely important.[270] Having said that, it seems that a monetary remedy will be awarded if the right has been breached, no special factors counsel hesitation, it has been pleaded correctly and no immunities exist.[271] In the United States, the monetary remedy is not reserved for exceptional cases, but is considered a normal response to a rights breach.

In New Zealand cases considering whether the remedy should be awarded, much has been made of the unavailability of any other remedy and the idea that a remedy must follow a rights breach. These two factors combined to justify the development of the monetary remedy in *Baigent's Case*.[272] The decisions in *Grayson* and *Shaheed* made it clear that there will be no presumption of a particular remedy in New Zealand; 'the full range of possible remedies' should be left open to ensure flexibility and appropriateness in each case.[273] All the issues that may have been relevant in limiting the cause of action before it got to this stage, will become relevant in determining the exact remedy to be awarded as the Court will consider which remedy is the most appropriate in all the circumstances of the particular case. In New Zealand, as a result, the remedy is likely to be available if a right has been breached and no other remedy is available that is as effective: 'The Court's role is to ensure than an adequate remedy is available to vindicate the right, and the choice of remedy lies entirely within the discretion of the judge.'[274]

The latest cases considering the remedial approach suggest that in some cases monetary relief would not be awarded. In fact, in *Brown*, the High Court indicated that the monetary remedy would be available only in exceptional cases.[275] Other limitations on the granting of the remedy have

266 Eg *Re Death of Grover* [1995] Supp (4) SCC 450; *Nilabati* (n 55 above); and *Basu* (n 49 above).

267 Eg *Hongray* (n 7 above); and *Kaur* (n 253 above).

268 Eg *Khatri* (n 20 above).

269 Schwartz and Kirklin (n 17 above) 287–88.

270 This jurisdiction differs from the other two jurisdictions in the importance placed on pleadings.

271 *Bivens* (n 15 above); *Davis* (n 16 above).

272 Eg *Baigent's Case* (n 5 above) 676: 'We would fail in our duty if we did not give an effective remedy ... the only effective remedy is compensation'.

273 *Grayson* (n 27 above) 412; *Shaheed* (n 29 above).

274 Smillie (n 199 above) 199.

275 *Brown* (n 30 above) 345.

been considered possible. In particular, it may be that a declaration would be considered to be sufficient if an award of tort law damages was granted.[276] A monetary remedy would only be awarded if necessary to vindicate the rights. Equally, the Accident Insurance legislation may statute-bar the monetary remedy in some cases in which the Bill of Rights has been breached.[277]

3. Step 2: What Amount to Order?

Having decided that the remedy should be awarded, the Court's second step is to decide the actual amount to award. This involves first determining the method for calculating the amount and, second, considering what factors are deemed to be relevant and how they are to be used in the calculation. In other words, it is necessary to consider the methods to be used in these cases in the determination of quantum.[278]

(a) What Method is Used to Calculate Quantum?

The first factor to consider then, is the method used in each jurisdiction for determining quantum. Tort law will be the usual starting point, but not the sole source, for determining quantum. The nature of the cause of action—fundamental rights—has also been of great importance, at least rhetorically. Much has been made of the need for the Courts to uphold the paramountcy and dignity of rights and to prevent state actors from taking advantage of their position to the detriment of individuals.[279] Each jurisdiction has developed its own approach from those two factors.

In New Zealand, a remedial tailoring approach has been developed. In *Baigent's Case*, it was suggested that the remedy would 'depend on the nature of the right and of the particular infringement, and the consequences of the infringement'.[280] This suggestion was followed and developed in *Grayson* which emphasised 'a rights-centred approach' to remedy.[281] The Court of Appeal clearly wished the remedy to be considered flexibly and by taking into account not only the individual's perspective, but also the wider community's interests.[282] The judgment suggested ensuring that a remedy was appropriate to the 'circumstances of

276 *Dunlea* (n 28 above); *Hewitt* (n 244 above).

277 *Wilding* (n 222 above).

278 Shelton (n 1 above) 70: Jurisdictions differ in the methods used both to assess the recoverable elements and in the amounts awarded.

279 Almost all the early cases in all three jurisdictions make these points to some extent eg *Baigent's Case* (n 5 above); *Bivens* (n 15 above); and *Rudul Sah* (n 7 above).

280 *Baigent's Case* (n 5 above) 718.

281 *Grayson* (n 27 above) 411.

282 *Ibid*, p 412.

the breach' which included considering 'the nature and seriousness of the breach'.[283] Courts will take 'a flexible approach to do justice and to meet the circumstances of the particular case'.[284] New Zealand judges have expressly stated that there is no exact mathematical calculation for quantum, which must respond to the particular case.[285] This seems to amount to leaving the consideration of all potential limiting factors until liability has been determined and then considering them as factors to assist in calculating quantum. In other words, the existence of loss, injury, intention and negligence will be considered during the assessment of remedy. Such a discretion is the extreme form of a remedial tailoring approach.[286]

In India, likewise, judges do not often refer to amounts awarded in similar cases as an aid to determining quantum,[287] but seem to begin from the particular case itself and the likely award at civil or criminal law. The use by the Court of the language of 'interim' awards illustrates this sort of comparison with other causes of action leading to a monetary remedy.[288] The Court has clearly stated that quantum will depend on the facts of the individual case and 'no strait jacket formula can be evolved in that behalf'.[289] At least one commentator has suggested that the lack of basis for quantum suggested that 'the judges went by their intuition rather than any rational basis'.[290]

As the causes of action in the United States are constitutional torts, the normal tort law methods of calculation provide a strong basis for the approach to be taken. Generally, tort law principles will provide a 'starting point' for constitutional torts in the United States.[291] Thus, it may be that precedent has more of an impact in this jurisdiction than in either India or New Zealand. Be that as it may, juries determine quantum following legal direction from the trial judge in the United States and, as a result, '[j]ury

283 *Ibid.*

284 *Hewitt* (n 244 above) 127; see also *Shaheed* (n 29 above) 122.

285 *Upton (2)* (n 109 above) 23.

286 Note that remedial tailoring is not globally liked: P Birks, 'Rights, Wrongs and Remedies' (2000) 20 *OJLS* 1, 23.

287 There is an exception: In *Supreme Court Legal Aid Committee* (n 253 above) 483, the sum calculated was that 'ordinarily paid in the case of death', although it is difficult to see exactly how this amount was reached. Eg in *SAHELI* (n 97 above), also a case brought by a mother in which death was caused by the police, the amount awarded was Rs75,000 cf Rs20,000 in the *Legal Aid* case. Admittedly, the *Legal Aid* case involved the death of an adult, whereas *SAHELI* concerned the death of a child.

288 Eg *Rudul Sah* (n 7 above) for an example of a comparison with civil law; *Gautam* (n 165 above) 'interim compensation' for an example of a comparison with criminal law.

289 *Basu* (n 49 above) 318.

290 S Jain, 'Money Compensation for Administrative Wrongs through Article 32' (1983) 25 *JILI* 118, 121.

291 *Carey* (n 49 above) 258.

attitude probably affects damages in civil rights cases more than legal rules do'.[292]

(b) What Factors are Relevant in the Calculation?

Each jurisdiction has, therefore, created its own methodology for this final calculation in the cause of action but at the same time has allowed for certain factors to be considered within the particular approach. The following five factors are the most common and influential.

(i) Injury. The first factor considered must be the actual injury suffered. Clearly, if actual injury can be proven, this would be compensated. In India, the Supreme Court seems to have used the likely monthly income of a dead person as the basis for determining the amount of a monetary remedy.[293] In both the United States and New Zealand, the Court has compensated for actual loss of earnings.[294] These calculations generally mirror tort law calculation of loss.

The question arises as to whether loss or injury to the plaintiff is a necessary precondition to the awarding of a monetary remedy and is the only sort of harm that may be the subject of an award. The other option would be that the cause of action is actionable without proof of harm to anything but the impugned right; and that the monetary award will encompass that abstract harm.

For compensatory or actual damages to be awarded in the United States, actual loss or injury to the applicant will be required; nominal damages will be awarded if no such loss can be shown.[295] The terminology used in the United States is that 'presumed general damages' will not be available for constitutional rights cases, although damages for emotional distress will still be available, if proved.[296] It is clear that the abstract value of rights cannot form the basis for an award of general damages.[297] Proving injury in the United States will, therefore, be very important and will require 'something personal to the plaintiff'.[298]

Indian case law assumes the need for injury, although judgments will often include statements concerning the damage to the right.[299] Individuals

[292] D Dobbs, *Dobbs Law of Remedies*, Vol II, 2nd edn, (Minnesota, West Publishing, 1993) 341.

[293] *Nilabati* (n 55 above) 2909.

[294] *Memphis Community School District v Stachura* 477 US 299, 106 S Ct 2537 (1986); *J v Attorney-General* (1995) 2 HRNZ 311.

[295] *Carey* (n 49 above).

[296] *Ibid.*

[297] See in particular *Stachura* (n 294 above), in which the first instance court had issued jury instructions allowing the jury to award damages based on their valuing of the constitutional right breached; this was reversed by the Supreme Court.

[298] Dobbs (n 292 above) 336.

[299] Eg *Rudul Sah* (n 7 above); *Basu* (n 49 above); *Nilabati* (n 55 above); *Gautam* (n 165 above).

in this jurisdiction have suffered some extravagant losses in which injury has been fairly easy to establish. It has included personal injury as well as economic injury, projected loss as well as actual loss.[300] It may be that the nature of rights breaches in India and of the jurisdiction itself mean that plaintiffs will almost always suffer some personal harm, in addition to the abstract harm to the right when a right is breached.[301] Loss has been used to justify both the existence of the cause of action and the level of quantum awarded.[302] The tort law approach to loss has clearly provided the framework by which quantum will be calculated, especially as quantum is often expressed as being interim to a final award under civil law.

The New Zealand jurisprudence has given a wide scope to the form of injury required. Both intangible and projected losses will be sufficient to found the cause of action.[303] It seems that a mere injury to a right will be necessary for the cause of action to be brought, and the consequent loss to the plaintiff will become relevant when quantum is considered.[304] Nevertheless, while quantum will reflect the importance associated with vindicating rights, it seems that when a plaintiff is unable to show actual damage, the monetary remedy awarded will differ little from nominal damages as the amount awarded will be very small.[305] It is unclear whether the same small amounts would be awarded in cases in which the Accident Insurance Act prevented the quantification of *Baigent's Case* damages by reference to the personal injury, and so the monetary remedy was limited to compensation for the affront to the plaintiff's rights.[306]

Thus, it seems that in all three jurisdictions courts will use any actual injury or loss suffered as the starting point for determining quantum. This is unsurprising, and usually seems to follow closely the tort law rules governing recovery. It is in relation to the more abstract and intangible loss that tort law is of less direct use.

(ii) Defendant's Conduct and Identity The second factor to consider when calculating quantum is the defendant's conduct and identity. Identity seems to be relevant to the extent that the cause of action is only available, generally, as a response to governmental incursions into individual rights,

300 Eg *Rudul Sah* (n 7 above) (calculates the amount of lost earnings as well as general harm); *Nilabati* (n 55 above) (calculation on the basis of monthly income of deceased).

301 By this I mean that the socio-economic reality of India may be such that the impact of a rights-breach is proportionately greater than in a developed country.

302 The early cases were justified on the basis of the very great harm to the plaintiff, and this factor was important as a justification for quantum. Eg *Rudul Sah* (n 7 above); *SAHELI* (n 97 above) and the custodial death cases such as *Basu* (n 49 above); and *Nilabati* (n 55 above).

303 *Baigent's Case* (n 5 above) 678; *J v Attorney-General (1)* [1995] 2 HRNZ 311, 316–18.

304 *Upton (2)* (n 109 above) 20; *Lewis* (n 109 above) 49; *Manga* (n 5 above) 70.

305 In *Kerr* (n 213 above), $NZ20 was awarded.

306 *Wilding* (n 222 above) 793.

and the courts have required high standards of governmental officials.[307] Thus, despite the cause of action being strict liability in New Zealand and India, the issue of *mala fides* and intention come into play at this point. Although it is difficult to quantify, it appears that where the court was disturbed by the lawlessness or disregard of the relevant officials, the amount of money awarded will be higher.

For example, the New Zealand Court was concerned, on the one side, with the police's poor attitude in *Baigent's Case* and, on the other side, with the very real care on the police's part in *Kerr*.[308] It appears that this factor may operate to either increase damages, if bad faith exists, or to reduce damages, if good faith exists.[309] The impression is that a punitive element for a defendant's bad conduct or a reduction in quantum in the case of a mere technical breach will be incorporated into the tailored remedy. There will be no separate amount specified as exemplary, punitive or aggravated damages.[310]

In India, the Supreme Court has made strong pronouncements when *mala fides* was evident. In *Rudul Sah*, the Court was deeply disturbed by officials' behaviour and warned against the dangers to 'civilization' of such incursions into rights by governmental officials.[311] The monetary remedy was clearly seen as a way in which the Court's distaste for such behaviour would be expressed, so producing a deterrent effect.[312] This emphasis on the intention and mindset of the individual official has been enhanced by the Court's suggestions that the state should seek repayment for the monetary remedy from individual breaching officials.[313]

As a result, the punitive element is obvious in India, with 'exemplary costs' being awarded in early cases in which the defendant's *mala fides* was evident.[314] The focus is, to some extent, on the defendant and not the plaintiff when this aspect of the calculation is made. It could be argued that the monetary remedy in India is best understood as 'exemplary compensation', as this factor is so evident in all awards. Examples of technical breaches, on the other hand, are rare.

Even in the United States, where the cause of action requires some sort of fault as a prerequisite to the finding of a breach, the defendant's intention will be relevant in determining quantum insofar as punitive

307 The identity of the defendant and the unequal balance of power between the 'Leviathan' state and simple individual is clear in all three jurisdictions: In particular, see *Rudul Sah* (n 7 above) 1089.

308 *Baigent's Case* (n 5 above); *Kerr* (n 213 above).

309 This is surely double-counting: Good faith is not symmetrical.

310 *Baigent's Case* (n 5 above) makes it clear that quantum will be calculated as a global award.

311 *Rudul Sah* (n 7 above) 1089.

312 'Administrative sclerosis leading to flagrant infringements of fundamental rights cannot be corrected by any other method open to the judiciary to adopt': *Rudul Sah* (n 7 above) 1089.

313 *Maharastra* (n 191 above) 305; *SAHELI* (n 97 above) 516; *Basu* (n 49 above) 317.

314 Eg *Hongray* (n 7 above); *Rudul Sah* (n 7 above); and *SAHELI* (n 97 above).

damages may be awarded.[315] The test for such damages is difficult to express, but amounts to requiring a state of mind element, as well as overt misconduct.[316] Thus, in the United States, the intention of the defendant may be relevant as a threshold issue as well as at quantum.

(iii) Plaintiff's Conduct It has been said of tort law that in general 'bad people get less'.[317] This aspect concerns the unease with which judges may approach less than pure plaintiffs. This is an especially important point in New Zealand, where the majority of cases claiming Bill of Rights protection involve some criminal element, so much so that it has attracted the doubtful accolade of a 'rogues' charter'.[318]

The question of the relevance of the plaintiff's actions has been raised in the post-*Baigent's Case* jurisprudence. *Kerr* involved the unsavoury allegations that the plaintiff was a member of a neo-Nazi gang, and that the breach arose during a contrived confrontation in which the police acted in good faith.[319] Considering himself bound by the decision in *Whithair*[320] to hold that it was not necessary to allege bad faith on the part of the Crown, Judge Ryan found that there had been a breach of freedom of movement. In assessing damages, however, he felt it necessary 'to reflect the general standing of a plaintiff in the community'.[321] This approach is consistent with the view of Cooke P prior to the decision in *Baigent's Case*, when in *Noort* he commented that: 'the conduct of both appellants ... was plainly such that in my view there could be no question of compensation ... . The Bill of Rights Act would fall into disrepute if they were entitled to compensation as well [as the quashing of their convictions].'[322]

Having said that, the impact of this on monetary awards in the absence of *Kerr*-like expressions of concern is obviously difficult to gauge. Similar considerations could be expected to be mirrored in the United States where juries' decisions are likely to reflect their dissatisfaction with giving large awards to culpable plaintiffs. It is possible that nominal damages could be used in such cases.[323]

In India, a large number of the plaintiffs who have brought Article 32 petitions seeking the monetary remedy have been prisoners, but there is no discernible impact upon the remedy awarded as a result. It may be that in India, the breaches are often so outrageous, that this outweighs any

315 *Smith* (n 221 above)
316 Dobbs (n 292 above) 348; *Smith* (n 221 above) confirms that it will include recklessness.
317 T Weir, *A Casebook on Tort*, 9th edn, (London, Sweet & Maxwell, 2000) 258.
318 D Paccioco, 'The Pragmatic Application of Fundamental Principles: Keeping a Rogues' Charter Respectable' in *The New Zealand Bill of Rights Act 1990* (Auckland, Legal Research Foundation, 1992) 1, 2.
319 *Kerr* (n 213 above).
320 *Whithair* (n 101 above).
321 *Kerr* (n 213 above) 11–12.
322 *Noort* (n 26 above) 275.
323 *Carey* (n 49 above).

judicial unease with awarding money to those who have committed offences. There is, however, a suggestion that public interest litigation is little used in relation to the breach of the constitutional rights of individuals such as terrorists and armed militants, who do not enjoy public sympathy. As such cases are not considered by the Courts, there is no jurisprudence on the matter.[324]

(iv) Wider Interests The fourth factor involves the wider interests raised by the case. In particular, the interests of the community and good government will be considered, including issues associated with the public interest. Such interests have been uppermost in the minds of judges in all three jurisdictions, perhaps because of the common emphasis on constitutional rights being for the benefit of the entire community: 'society as well as the individual victim is injured when human rights are violated'.[325] This creates two practical, and possibly conflicting, influences on the determination of quantum. First, the remedy should be high enough to reflect this wider sense of harm. Second, the money paid should not be so high that society suffers to the benefit of the individual victim.

In the United States, the community's interest in having rights vindicated through the causes of action has been recognised in the context of attorney fees. In *Rivera*, the Supreme Court held that plaintiffs 'secure important social benefits' to the community at large and this warranted a large attorney fees award even in the absence of a large damages award.[326] In *Millikin v Bradley (2)*, a United States desegregation case, the Supreme Court held that when designing a remedy, account must be taken of a state's interest in governing its own affairs.[327] The United States approach to remedying constitutional rights breaches will be 'interest balancing'. The Court will ensure that all wider interests will be included in determination of quanta, although the involvement of juries in final decisions will obviously blur legal details somewhat.

In India, the appropriateness of making large damages awards from an extremely limited public fund is an important consideration.[328] The same

324 P Singh, 'Protection of Human Rights through Public Interest Litigation in India' (2000) 42 *JILI* 263, 271 re Jammu and Kashmir, where 'terrorism and armed militancy is more acute' than elsewhere in India.

325 Shelton (n 1 above) 50.

326 *Rivera* (n 59 above).

327 *Millikin v Bradley (2)* 433 US 267, 97 S Ct 2749 (1977) 281–82.

328 Eg 2000 corpses were discovered in the Punjab in the 1990s that had been 'disappeared' by the police. The Supreme Court held that compensation was due to the families of the 585 identified corpses and gave the National Human Rights Commission the task of determining amounts to be paid. The monetary compensation to be paid will obviously be significant and will have a substantial impact upon the state's financial position. The matter was considered in a series of cases: *Paramjit Kaur v Punjab* (1996) 7 SCC 20; (1996) 8 SCALE 6; (1998) 5 SCALE 219. See further Singh (n above) 270; and N Vaid, 'Two Thousand Corpses Paved the Way to Peace' (1997) *The Lawyers Collective* 24. I am grateful to Sara Hossein, Interights, for a discussion concerning the desirability of a monetary remedy in this case.

issue obviously exists in all three jurisdictions, although it is writ large in the least developed country. The Court's solution seems to have been to support the state gaining reimbursement of such money from the actual wrongdoer.[329] Other than that, the community's interest in deterrence and the protection of rights will override other interests. It has been suggested that the 'paramount considerations of national security and law and order' have been taken into account by the Supreme Court when deciding remedies, that the Supreme Court has been loathe to 'make police officers into adversaries' by granting large monetary remedies, and that remedies have been more readily available, and more adequately enforced, in relation to breaches of the rights of lawyers and the judiciary.[330] In fact, it has been suggested that compensatory awards against the police have been arbitrary, inadequately enforced and in some cases, once made not disbursed.[331]

In New Zealand, the wider interests raised by these cases will presumably be considered as part of the general survey into quantum and incorporated into a global award. In *Manga*, the 'public dimension' of Bill of Rights claims was stressed as changing the context of these cases.[332] The community's interest in having rights breaches compensated has overriden even a judicial immunity, although it is probable that this factor will be relevant in determining quantum.[333]

(v) Aims and Purposes of the Remedy Finally, the aim and purpose of the remedy will obviously be expected to have some impact upon the amount of money awarded. An international survey of remedies for breach of constitutional rights, in fact, saw this as a major reason for differences between the monetary remedy in different jurisdictions.[334]

Damages are the method by which both compensation and deterrence, the major aims of the United States causes of action, are ensured; there is a 'public interest in deterrence of unlawful conduct and in compensation of victims'.[335] Thus, 'the basic purpose of a § 1983 damages award should be to compensate persons'.[336]

These two aims are also dominant in New Zealand and India, where the use of the terminology of compensation to describe the remedy may signify rather more of a focus on the need to compensate the victim and vindicate the right, than on deterrence. While both New Zealand and Indian judges refer to deterrence as an important aim of the remedy and seem to

329 *SAHELI* (n 97 above) 516; *Basu* (n 49 above) 317.
330 Ahuja (Vol I) (n 71 above) 95; 152.
331 *Ibid*, p 96.
332 *Manga* (n 5 above) 81.
333 Eg *Upton* (n 109 above).
334 Shelton (n 1 above) 70.
335 *Harlow* (n 218 above) 2739.
336 *Carey* (n 49 above) 1047.

envisage an 'exemplary' element to the monetary remedy awarded,[337] judgments are clear that vindication and compensation are the primary aims.[338]

There seems to be agreement between the three jurisdictions that compensation of the plaintiff will be the primary purpose of the monetary remedy, although this ought not to conflict with the vindication of the rights. Deterrence, and possibly punishment, ought to be secondary purposes. Needless to say, most often the judge's aims are not clearly identified in individual judgments and remedies will attempt to achieve all three aims. The actual remedy awarded may reflect a general sense of the appropriate amount of money, rather than the result of any analytical exploration of the different purposes and the way in which quantum may reflect them.

Further, it is difficult to see any real differences occasioned by this factor in remedies awarded in the three jurisdictions studied. Although the rhetoric may differ, at their base, the jurisprudence of all three jurisdictions ranks the aims in the same order, with differences merely in emphasis. In any case, real differences in quanta seem associated with individual judges' level of distaste for the actions and affinity with the victim: without mathematical formulae to determine quantum, such intuitive responses seem to be the most likely indicator of differences. Intuition may be dignified by being described as all the circumstances of the breach being taken into account, or by the important need to vindicate rights.

4. Step 3: Should other Directions be Ordered?

The third step for a Court determining the monetary remedy concerns the issue of other directions that are ordered in addition to quantum.

In India, such orders are often made. These have directed where the money is to be paid and how it is to be used, continuing the Court's involvement in the case beyond the final decision. In *Supreme Court Legal Aid Committee*, the sum calculated was paid to the legal representatives of a man who died in police custody, and the District Judge was ordered to satisfy himself as to who the relevant heirs were; if the Judge was 'of the

337 Eg *Baigent's Case* (n 5 above) 678; *Hongray* (n 7 above) 548–49; *Bhim Singh* (n 7 above) 499.

338 Eg *Baigent's Case* (n 5 above) repeated in *Innes* (n 204 above) 634: 'The emphasis must be on the compensatory and not the punitive element. The objective is to affirm the right, not punish the transgressor'; 692: 'A remedy which will best vindicate the right infringed'. The New Zealand Court of Appeal expressly distinguished the New Zealand search and seizure jurisprudence from the United States Fourth Amendment jurisprudence: 'The objective of s 21 is vindication of individual rights rather than deterence and disciplining of police misconduct' (*Grayson* (n 27 above) 407). *Basu* (n 49 above) 317–18: 'In the assessment of compensation, the emphasis has to be on the compensatory and not on punitive element. The objective is to apply balm to the wounds and not to punish the transgressor'.

view that the money should be held in a long term fixed deposit in favour of the rightful heir it is open to him to do so'.[339]

In other cases, the Court has provided directions as to how the money should be used once it is paid. For example, in *PUDR* the Court ordered the money to be 'invested in some scheme under the Life Insurance Corporation, so that the destitute family may get some amount monthly and the money may also be kept secured'.[340] In *Nilabati*, the Court ordered the money to be paid as a three-year term deposit in the name of the mother of the deceased, during which period she would be entitled to the interest and at the end of which she would be entitled to the principal.[341]

Courts do not tend to make such orders in the United States and New Zealand, where judicial involvement in cases will typically end with a court ordering the payment of a monetary remedy, unless parties later seek enforcement.

Other directions that a Court may consider after awarding a monetary remedy concern the appropriateness of other causes of action being brought in addition to the constitutional cause of action. In New Zealand, *Baigent's Case* made it clear that the Court considered that other awards must take into account any remedy granted under the Bill of Rights or, alternatively, that the *Baigent's Case* award must expressly be a global award incorporating all others.[342] In *Wilding*, the Court of Appeal expressly refuted the need for a *Baigent's Case* remedy 'where an effective remedy can be granted by other means'.[343] These could include statutory forms of relief, as well as declaratory relief under the Bill of Rights Act.

Likewise, in India, the emphasis on constitutional monetary awards being merely 'interim' shows an awareness of the need to ensure that double benefits do not occur.[344] It seems that civil cases brought on the same grounds as those for which a constitutional monetary remedy has already been made must take into account the earlier award. Practically speaking, it may be unlikely that it would be worth the expenditure of time and money to bring any other action following a successful Article 32 petition.

339 *Supreme Court Legal Aid Committee* (n 253 above) 483. Also note *Sodhi v UP* 1991 (2) SCALE 81 [463] where the Supreme Court stayed disbursal of compensation pending an investigation to determine recipients: Ahuja (Vol I) (n 71 above) 95 and 137–38 indicates that in this particular case, it seems that the money was never disbursed.

340 *PUDR* (n 253 above) 731.

341 *Nilabati* (n 55 above) 2909. As it is reasonable to assume a higher than average education in at least two of the cases in which money was paid directly to the petitioner, it may be that these orders evidence a paternalistic approach by the Supreme Court towards less educated plaintiffs and heirs: *Bhim Singh* (n 7 above) 499 (Member of Parliament); and *Hongray* (n 7 above) (widows of a headmaster and an assistant pastor, both of whom had been army officers).

342 *Baigent's Case* (n 5 above) 678. This was emphasised in *Manga* (n 5 above); *Hewitt* (n 244 above); and *Dunlea* (n 28 above).

343 *Wilding* (n 222 above) 792.

344 Eg *Rudul Sah* (n 7 above); *Gautam* (n 165 above).

Costs or fees are the final 'other direction' possible. In early Indian cases, costs appeared to have had an exemplary nature and were the way in which the monetary remedy was awarded. In *Bhim Singh*, for example, the Court referred to its ability to 'award monetary compensation by way of exemplary costs or otherwise'.[345] Further, the Courts have directed Indian states to pay for any commissions of inquiry instituted by the court in public interest litigation.[346]

In the United States, 'attorney fees' are of the utmost relevance. *Rivera*, by deciding that attorney fees would be available even if only nominal damages were awarded, enhanced the importance of this aspect of the monetary remedy.[347] An award of attorney fees will be a significant component of a monetary remedy. The importance of attorney fees can be seen in the fact that most texts in the area include significant studies of the subject.[348]

In New Zealand, costs are likely to be awarded to the victorious party in accordance with the usual rules although, in many cases, the parties will be encouraged to settle the matter themselves.[349] As costs will very rarely cover the true cost of the case, and will not contain an exemplary element, such awards will not play the same role in New Zealand as in the United States and India.

5. Summary

Determining quantum in constitutional rights cases will not be straightforward and will not necessarily involve precedent or strict rules. Both the interests involved and the loss are usually non-pecuniary and involve abstract ideals. In this context, the different fact situations in New Zealand and the United States, on one hand, and India, on the other, may be determinative.

It appears that determination of quantum will be specific to each jurisdiction, if not each case. At the same time, it involves an assessment of factors common to all three jurisdictions. To some extent, quantum will reflect a judge's (and jury's, in the case of the United States) intuitive response to the case: once breach has been proven and the decision taken to grant the remedy, some cases will attract a large monetary remedy, while others will attract a smaller amount. Discussing the relevance of causation in the award of damages by the Strasbourg Court, the English

345 *Bhim Singh* (n 7 above) 499. See further *Hongray* (n 7 above) 548–49 in which 'exemplary costs' were awarded.

346 Ahuja (Vol II) (n 71 above) 789.

347 *Rivera* (n 59 above).

348 Eg E Chemerinsky, *Federal Jurisdiction*, 2nd edn, (Boston, MA, Little Brown, 1994) 422; Schwartz and Kirklin (n 17 above).

349 *Baigent's Case* (n 5 above) 678.

Law Commission 'guessed' that in some cases 'the Court feels sympathy towards certain applicants based on the particular circumstances and will go out of its way to award damages'.[350]

This survey suggests a similar sympathy is evident in the judgments in the United States, India and New Zealand. The most obvious conclusion to draw from this survey seems to be that in each jurisdiction, quantum is determined by reference to the specific fact situation in each individual case, rather than by the application of rules. Justifications for differing quanta may be the aim of the particular remedy or the interests of the community—either way, judges seek to ensure that their perception of justice is met.

F. CONCLUSIONS

The four questions in this chapter set out the cause of action and so its boundaries in the United States, India and New Zealand. A generic structure is inferred, within which the specificities of each jurisdiction fit. Each jurisdiction has considered the issues existing within these questions, although the interpretations and priorities given often differ greatly. As we have seen, at times the question is not only answered differently, but asked differently. The story is, therefore, one of both similarity and difference. The similarity is not particularly surprising: the cause of action aims to, overall, fill the same hiatus and solve the same problems in each jurisdiction.[351] A commonality of experience is to be expected in that context.

It has been observed that constitutions are based on an underlying agreement about fundamental principles which are not express, yet which make possible and precede the written law.[352] This survey has substantiated this claim concerning individual jurisdictions at an international level: the judgments of the apex courts in these three jurisdictions express an underlying agreement on the structure of this cause of action.

The differences between the causes of action and the way in which they are approached, on the other hand, raise further interesting questions. The jurisdictions studied share similar legal systems and legal history, so that differences cannot be attributable merely to those factors. If the starting

[350] Law Commission and Scottish Law Commission, *Damages Under the Human Rights Act 1998* (Law Com No 266, Scot Law Com No 180, 2000) 45. Given that the role of judges will be crucial to damages claims, it is not surprising that the importance of the method of judicial appointment has been identified as intrinsically important to the protection of constitutional rights in Canada: D Beatty, 'The Canadian Charter of Rights: Lessons and Laments' [1997] 60 *MLR* 481, 498.

[351] M Bogdan, *Comparative Law* (Deventer, Kluwer, 1994) 19: 'The problems in society that require legal regulation are often identical, or at the least very similar'; P Craig and S Deshpande, 'Rights, Autonomy and Process: Public Interest Litigation in India' (1989) 9 *OJLS* 356: 'Legal systems, for all their very real diversity, are often faced with similar endemic problems'.

[352] F Hayek, *The Constitution of Liberty* (London, Routledge, 1960) 181.

point is the individual legal system, and the end point is the establishment of a monetary remedy for breach of constitutional rights, then something else must intervene to create the evident differences.

The following chapter addresses what causes the differences between the causes of action in the three jurisdictions. By doing so, that chapter completes a structured description of the cause of action in the United States, India and New Zealand.

6

Overarching Influences

A. INTRODUCTION

THIS CHAPTER CONSIDERS what creates the differences between the causes of action in each jurisdiction. In doing so, it constructs a list of overarching influences on the nature of the cause of action. The influences are 'overarching' in that they affect the content of the answers given to all the questions making up the structure of the cause of action. Interestingly, the same influences are evident in relation to all three jurisdictions and all four common questions, although they are not of uniform importance and individually only provide part of the explanation. These influences, therefore, explain both the existence of choices in relation to the cause of action and the choices that the jurisdictions have made.

The four overarching influences on the causes of action are its source, its age, its wider context, and its internal context. These influences illuminate the answers given in each jurisdiction to the questions set out in the previous chapter, and so complete the picture of the structure of a generic cause of action. The conglomerate of the ideas set out in these two chapters, therefore, provides an outline of the causes of action in the United States, India and New Zealand.

Superimposed over the four influences discussed here is the existence of an international consensus, or 'international human rights common law' against which each jurisdiction seems to assess itself and which can be seen to impact upon all answers. This is discussed in rather more detail in the second section of this chapter, which concerns the influence of the age of the cause of action.

B. WHAT IS THE SOURCE OF THE CAUSE OF ACTION?

1. Introduction

This influence encapsulates questions concerning two aspects of the source of the cause of action. It involves looking to the very base of the cause of action, to its legal source. A preliminary point should be made: the constitutional documents upon which the causes of action in the three jurisdictions are based are very similar:

> The phenomenon of borrowing and transplantation from the international to national, from the national to international, from national jurisdiction to national jurisdiction is now commonplace. At the level of constitutional human rights protection, Bills of Rights provisions in one country increasingly affect the drafting of equivalent provisions in other countries. Although most post-Second World War constitutions have specifically laid down elements which set them apart, most also have a common core of human rights provisions that are strikingly similar and this is not merely coincidental.[1]

Despite that, differences do exist in relation to the type of constitutional document and the type of provision from which the cause of action developed. It is with those differences that this section is concerned.

2. What is the Foundation Document?

The first aspect concerns the foundations for the causes of action. These differ greatly. In the United States and India, the causes of action are based on rights contained in constitutions, entrenched pieces of fundamental legislation, holding a special place in the legal system. These are 'constitutional causes of action' in the sense that each cause of action is derived from a reading of the constitution and relates to constitutionally guaranteed rights. In this way, despite the fact that Section 1983 is a statutory section, albeit referring to a constitution, it is still a constitutional cause of action; the other two causes of action (India and *Bivens*) are examples of implied constitutional interpretation. In comparison, the New Zealand Bill of Rights Act is neither fundamental nor entrenched, but is a normal statutory instrument. There, the cause of action is not derived from a constitution, but from a piece of legislation.

The difference is obviously fundamental. While constitutions are enacted by legislature they are not concerned with the quotidian aspects of governance, but with abstract statements of the values and focus of society. Because of this, a special place is kept in society and law for them. In New Zealand, much of the debate concerning the Bill of Rights before it was enacted concerned whether or not it should be entrenched law; the legislature decided in the negative.[2]

1 C McCrudden, 'A Common Law of Human Rights? Transnational Judicial Conversations on Constitutional Rights' (2000) 20 *OJLS* 499, 501.

2 P Joseph, *Constitutional and Administrative Law in New Zealand* (Sydney, Law Book, 1993) 847.

It is perhaps surprising to note that this difference has had little, if any, effect on the causes of action. Although the legal position of the New Zealand Bill of Rights Act is much weaker than that of a constitutional document, this has had no real practical impact because of the legal and cultural importance now associated with the statute: it would be a very brave, or very foolish, legislator who tried to alter the Bill of Rights with a simple majority. Not only have judges not argued that the Bill of Rights has a different effect from other international documents guaranteeing rights, but despite its potential weaknesses, the Bill of Rights Act has been given a force beyond that which many critics had considered it to have.[3]

Further, judgments from jurisdictions in which the rights guarantees are contained in fundamental documents have been considered highly persuasive in the establishment and development of a New Zealand indigenous rights jurisprudence. For example, in *Baigent's Case* the New Zealand Court of Appeal quoted generously from Canadian, Indian, Irish and Tobagan cases.[4] In all these jurisdictions the rights are contained in entrenched Bills of Rights or constitutions and the cause of action is correspondingly founded in those documents. The New Zealand Court of Appeal seemed to assume that this distinction was not relevant to the remedying of breaches: '[r]emedies implicitly authorised by an enacted declaration of rights cannot differ *in nature* from remedies authorized by a generally-worded remedies clause'.[5]

Thus, in reality the New Zealand Bill of Rights Act occupies much the same position as the United States and Indian constitutions and this particular difference does not seem to influence the resultant causes of action. References in the United States and Indian jurisprudence to the special nature of the rights and the cause of action are repeated in New Zealand despite the major differences in law between the status of the documents. This feature appears to be of utmost importance in these three jurisdictions and all four 'foundation cases' mention the importance of rights.[6] It is interesting that this seems intrinsic to the rights, and not to the document within which rights are carried.

3. From what Legal Provision did the Cause of Action Develop?

The second aspect concerns the specific source for the cause of action: the legal provision from which the cause of action developed. This aspect may

[3] *Ibid*, p 848.
[4] *Simpson v Attorney-General (Baigent's Case)* [1994] 3 NZLR 667.
[5] *Ibid*, p 676.
[6] Ie *Monroe v Pape* 365 US 167, 81 S Ct 473 (1961); *Bivens v Six Unknown Named Agents of Federal Bureau of Narcotics* 403 US 388, 91 S Ct 1999 (1971); *Rudul Sah v State of Bihar* AIR 1983 SC 1086; and *Baigent's Case* (n 4 above).

partially account for the jurisdictions' differing resolution of the common elements. The three jurisdictions studied illustrate causes of action developed out of three extreme options.

The classic basis of a cause of action would be an express provision—that is, a statutory or constitutional provision stating that a cause of action sounding in a monetary remedy existed for breach of the fundamental rights, wherever those rights are contained. This is almost the case in relation to Section 1983 in the United States, which provides that a person who breaches the constitution 'shall be liable ... in an action at a law, suit in equity, or other proper proceeding for redress'. The existence of a cause of action sounding in the monetary remedy was not doubted in this jurisdiction; it is the details of the cause of action, such as immunities, that have attracted judicial attention.[7] These are not fundamental concerns about the cause of action, but definitions of its scope.

Article 32 of the Indian Constitution is less explicit. It provides the Supreme Court with the power to remedy breach of the constitutional rights, without specifying that the monetary remedy in particular is available. In fact, Article 32 only mentions the prerogative writs as possible remedies. Despite that, the jurisprudence later held that a monetary remedy must be included within the Supreme Court's power to remedy breaches.[8] In India, therefore, there is an implied monetary remedy. Concerns were expressed in the secondary literature at the time about its existence and what its boundaries might be,[9] and the first cases felt it necessary to justify the existence of the remedy by reference to the need to do justice in the face of extravagent breaches.[10] As the remedy has developed, its existence has been accepted and the focus has shifted to define authoritatively the boundaries of its application and less to justify its existence.[11]

In New Zealand, the Bill of Rights contains no mention of remedies should the rights be breached: the cause of action and remedy were entirely implied into the statute. There is no one provision to which one might refer when considering the remedy or cause of action. The *Baigent's Case* cause of action was sourced in the judiciary's wish to ensure that,

[7] Including *Monell v Department of Social Services of the City of New York* 436 US 658, 98 S Ct 2018 (1978), one of the early decisions that opened up the cause of action.

[8] *Rudul Sah* (n 6 above).

[9] Eg S Sathe, 'Constitutional Law—I (Fundamental Rights)' (1983) XIX *ASIL* 178, 215; S Sathe, 'Constitutional Law—I (Fundamental Rights)' (1986) XXII *ASIL* 359, 397; and S Sathe, 'Constitutional Law—I (Fundamental Rights)' (1987) XXIII *ASIL* 76, 100.

[10] Eg *Rudul Sah* (n 6 above) 1089: Necessary to provide such a remedy to ensure 'civilisation does not perish' and to ensure that 'there will be no more poor Rudul Sahs'; *Bhim Singh v State of Jammu and Kashmir* AIR 1986 SC 494, 499: No other way to 'wash away the mischief or malice and the rights invasion'.

[11] Eg *Nilabati Behera v State of Orissa* [1993] Cri LJ 2899; and *Basu v West Bengal* 1996 (9) SCALE 298 which 'tidy-up' the debate concerning sovereign immunity.

prima facie, an effective remedy existed for all rights breaches.[12] All aspects of the cause of action had, therefore, to be determined by jurisprudence. Secondary literature questioned the appropriateness of such an implied cause of action.[13]

The same is true for the *Bivens* action in the United States, which was implied from the general terms of the United States constitution.[14] The major difference is, obviously, that a tandem cause of action exists in the United States. The existence of the Section 1983 cause of action has been extremely important as the two causes of action were held to be equivalent for the purposes of immunities, so that many of the Section 1983 limitations were grafted onto the *Bivens* cause of action.[15]

It is clear, therefore, that there is a great difference between the jurisdictions in relation to the source of the cause of action. This appears to be part of the explanation for the different choices jurisdictions have made in relation to the questions discussed in the previous chapter.

That is, to some extent, entirely expected. Obviously, causes of action based upon express provisions will be governed by the wording of those provisions. The absence of express wording will equally impact on the cause of action: if the cause of action is based upon a general, rather than an express, provision, much of the determination of its scope will centre around what is meant by the existing wording, as well as what is not included. This raises questions concerning statutory interpretation and, in particular, legislative intent.[16]

There will be differences, therefore, between causes of action based in provisions with different wording. Quite simply, certain factors will be rendered either relevant or irrelevant, depending on the wording of the legislative provision and, in particular, the level of ambiguity. These differences will be enhanced in relation to causes of action not based on any provision. In such causes of action, issues may become of increased importance for judicial scrutiny in the absence of a legislative conclusion. Alternatively, issues may be considered irrelevant, in the absence of a legislative direction that they be considered in the awarding of a monetary remedy.

The differences occasioned by the source provisions of the causes of action can be seen in each of the four questions discussed in the previous chapter. The first question discussed involved the rights and breaches—the subject matter of the cause of action. Most obviously, the similarity

12 Eg *Baigent's Case* (n 4 above) 676: 'We would fail in our duty if we did not give an effective remedy to a person whose legislatively affirmed rights have been infringed'.

13 As was noted by the Court in *Brown v Attorney-General* [2003] 3 NZLR 335, 345. See eg J Smillie, 'The Allure of "Rights Talk": *Baigent's Case* in the Court of Appeal' (1994) 8 *Otago L Rev* 188; J Hodder, 'Editorial' (1997) 20 *TCL* 19.

14 *Bivens* (n 6 above).

15 *Butz v Economou* 438 US 478, 98 S Ct 2894 (1978).

16 See R Cross, *Statutory Interpretation*, 3rd edn, (London, Butterworths, 1995).

between the rights to which each of the causes of action relates is due to the similarity between bills of rights; and these guarantee much the same core set of rights. This shows that some of the similarities between the causes of action can be attributed to similarities in provisions.

Other aspects of the subject matter element illustrate differences. For example, the Section 1983 cause of action may be available for the breach of rights other than constitutional rights, due to the express wording of the provision.[17] The other causes of action, without this express wording, seem to limit application to constitutional rights. It is interesting to note that even in relation to the Section 1983 cause of action, the application to other than constitutional rights has been severely curtailed over time.[18] Something seems to have overridden the statutory wording here, to create an approach that is more similar to the other causes of action that were not based on the statute.

It is clear that the wording (or absence thereof) of the foundation provision will greatly influence the determination of the sort of breach that will be necessary to establish the availability of the cause of action. Whereas in the United States, Section 1983 has been held to only apply when rights are breached in certain circumstances,[19] in India and New Zealand this is not so. In India, the fact that Article 32 is a guaranteed right itself has created a right to a remedy, so that once a right has been breached, a remedy will be granted.[20] The New Zealand jurisprudence has focussed on the wider context of the Bill of Rights, perhaps inevitably in the absence of a particular provision upon which to focus. The Courts have emphasised the right to a remedy[21]; and the doctrine that in the absence of legislative intent, there is no basis for courts to proscribe limitations on the cause of action.[22] This feature of the New Zealand cause of action has meant that the sort of breach deemed necessary will be very wide.

The second question was the relevance and identity of the plaintiff. Once again, there are some obvious examples of express statutory wording creating differences between jurisdictions. The United States Constitution has a 'case and controversy' requirement, thus creating a set of constitutional grounds governing standing.[23] Prudential grounds have been

[17] *Maine v Thiboutot* 448 US 1, 100 S Ct 2502 (1980), based on the wording of §1983: 'Rights, privileges, or immunities secured by the Constitution and laws'.

[18] *Pennhurst State School and Hospital v Halderman* 451 US 1, 101 S Ct 1531 (1981); and *Middlesex County Sewerage Authority v National Sea Clammers* 453 US 1, 101 S Ct 2615 (1981): For a federal statute to be actionable, it must confer substantive rights and its remedies must not be exclusive of any others.

[19] That is, not military, employment or social security.

[20] *Kochunni v State of Madras* AIR 1959 SC 725.

[21] *Baigent's Case* (n 4 above).

[22] *Whithair v Attorney-General* [1996] 2 NZLR 45.

[23] Art III(2); see *Singleton v Wulff* 428 US 106, 96 S Ct 2868 (1976) 2873.

developed as a complement.[24] United States law, perhaps as a result, contains strict rules in relation to standing.

In comparison, the Indian and New Zealand documents do not directly refer to standing. The focus in the Indian Constitution is on the rights, rather than the rights-holder[25]; and community, compared with individual, rights have an enhanced importance. Both of these factors seem to have contributed to the extremely wide definitions of standing employed in India, and in particular the expansive, and rabidly anti-procedural, public interest litigation.[26]

The New Zealand Bill of Rights Act rights are mostly available for individuals, and contain few limitations.[27] This, combined with the *Whithair* approach of minimal court-proscribed limitations in the absence of legislative intent,[28] suggests that standing will be wider than for a normal statute, but perhaps not as wide as the Indian approach.

The third question in the previous chapter concerned the defendant, and once again it has been affected by the provisions upon which the causes of action were based. As each foundation provision and Bill of Rights suggests a public law cause of action, with limited private effect, no real difference exists between the jurisdictions.[29] Each jurisdiction has considered the boundaries of what is meant by a public body amenable to suit, and reached remarkably similar conclusions.[30]

Differences exist in relation to the question of immunities. Certain express immunities are included in the United States Constitution, and further immunities have been implied into the United States causes of action.[31] In comparison, in India and New Zealand, where there is no express provision on this point, the Courts have held that immunities should not be implied.[32] In New Zealand, this decision was expressly

24 *Ibid.*

25 Art 32 guarantees a right to move the Court by proceedings 'for the enforcement of the rights' and does not refer to standing.

26 Eg *Gupta v President of India* AIR 1982 SC 149; *Morcha v Union of India* AIR 1984 SC 802.

27 S 29 states that the rights apply for the benefit of all legal and natural persons. S 12 is an example of a limited right—it is available only to citizens.

28 *Whithair* (n 22 above).

29 §1983 requires an action to be made 'under color of law', which has been held to amount to state action; Art 12 of the Indian Constitution defines 'state'; and s 3 of the New Zealand Bill of Rights Act refers to public entities and functions.

30 There is substantial jurisprudence in all three jurisdictions concerning the boundaries of who may be a defendant in the cause of action. In the US, much of the discussion has concerned 'state action'; in India, the ambit of 'public authority' has increased beyond its ordinary meaning; and in New Zealand, the position of state owned enterprises has come under scrutiny.

31 Eg Eleventh Amendment, extended by *Will v Michigan Department of State Police* 491 US 58, 109 S Ct 2304 (1989); in addition, various absolute and qualified immunities have been held to exist.

32 *Basu* (n 11 above) and *Nilabati* (n 11 above) state that the cause of action is strict liability and that sovereign immunity will not apply. *Whithair* (n 22 above) states that good faith will not be a defence.

attributed to the lack of statutory authorization for such a limitation on the scope of the cause of action.[33] Whether or not the courts are explicit about this, it seems that the more legislative constraints exist in relation to a cause of action, the more inclined judges will be to imply further constraints.

Because the United States Constitution creates different causes of action for different defendants, the question of pleadings has been one of great relevance and a body of rules has developed.[34] In New Zealand and India, the matter of pleadings is not subject to such rules and, in both jurisdictions, the way in which a matter is pleaded will not defeat the cause of action. Nevertheless, the extremely unfettered Indian approach is not repeated in New Zealand, where it appears that the Court will alter pleadings which have named an incorrect defendant to refer to the correct defendant.[35] The difference in source clearly does not wholly account for the difference in approach; another factor must intervene to explain fully the difference between the jurisdictions in this regard.

In relation to the standard of liability, the New Zealand concern not to delimit the Bill of Rights in the absence of clear legislative intent has meant that the cause of action has been held to be absolute liability.[36] Likewise, the cause of action is absolute in India, due to the Court's adherence to the contextual clues that the rights are of utmost importance.[37] In comparison, the more formalistic approach and more precise provision in the United States has lead to a wide good faith immunity.[38]

The wording of the provision has less direct influence on the final question. Obviously, terminology has been affected—in the United States, the provision has wording that cannot be ignored and creates a certain sort of cause of action,[39] while in New Zealand and India, the lack of description of the cause of action has allowed judges to consider which terminology best fits the cause of action and remedy as they have developed.[40]

33 *Whithair* (n 22 above).

34 Immunities mean that bringing a suit against individual officers in their personal capacity is the only way in which a plaintiff can succeed. This is, however, a matter of form and not substance: J Jeffries, 'In Praise of the Eleventh Amendment and Section 1983' (1998) 84 *Virg L Rev* 47, 62.

35 *Hobson v Harding* [1995] 1 HRNZ 342.

36 *Whithair* (n 22 above).

37 *Basu* (n 11 above) and *Nilabati* (n 11 above).

38 Almost all officials will enjoy some immunity (A Burris, 'Qualifying Immunity in Section 1983 and *Bivens* Actions' (1992) 71 *Texas L Rev* 123, 140) and qualified immunity will immunize all but the plainly incompetent or those who knowingly violate the law (*Malley v Briggs* 475 US 335, 106 S Ct 1092 (1986) 1096).

39 §1983 creates a constitutional tort, and so 'damages' is the obvious, and appropriate, terminology.

40 In both jurisdictions, the courts distinguished the new cause of action from tort by using the terminology of 'compensation' rather than 'damages'.

Contextual influences have affected the calculation of quantum. In New Zealand, in the absence of a statutory provision, courts consider the right to a remedy and the need to vindicate rights as primary concerns. As the New Zealand court is unconstrained by statutory direction, it has been free to create a largely unfettered remedial discretion that is not possible in jurisdictions with legislative limitations and authorisations. Nonetheless, there is no right to a remedy in the Bill of Rights which has perhaps been reflected in the suggestion that the remedy will be tailored to the particular circumstances in New Zealand—which will sometimes mean that no remedy, or nominal damages only, will be awarded.[41]

The limitation of the remedy to 'appropriate cases' in the Indian jurisprudence is related to the wording of Article 32 which provides a right to move the court 'by appropriate proceedings'.[42] As Article 32 is a guaranteed right itself, the court will grant a monetary remedy once a breach is made out.[43] In the United States, the wording of the provision answers many of the questions. The remedy in the United States is granted by juries due to express constitutional provision.[44] This imports an unpredictable element to quantum that is difficult to assess, but is consistent with a constitutional tort, as is created in the constitution.

4. Summary

Despite this list of clear differences between the jurisdictions, it seems that the simple fact of a difference in source has had surprisingly little influence on the scope of the cause of action. The differences between the provisions are so pronounced that a much greater influence upon the causes of action could have been expected. In the United States, for example, the *Bivens* cause of action has been deemed to almost replicate the Section 1983 cause of action—the most highly defined by provision of all those studied. If the differences between jurisdictions based on explicit provisions, and those based on constitutional interpretation were really influential, some real differences would be expected between these two causes of action as no

41 A Beck, 'Bill of Rights Litigation' [1997] *NZLJ* 427, 428; E Thomas, 'Criminal Procedure and the Bill of Rights: A View from the Bench' in *The New Zealand Bill of Rights Act 1990* (Auckland, Legal Research Foundation, 1992); D Paccioco, 'The Pragmatic Application of Fundamental Principles: Keeping a Rogues' Charter Respectable' in *The New Zealand Bill of Rights Act 1990* (Auckland, Legal Research Foundation, 1992) 1. See *PF Sugrue v Attorney-General* [2004] 1 NZLR 207; *Wilding v Attorney-General* [2003] 3 NZLR 787; and *Brown* (n 13 above).

42 Eg *Mehta v Union of India* AIR 1987 SC 1086.

43 *Kochunni* (n 20 above); *Khatri v State of Bihar* (1981) 1 SCC 627.

44 The Seventh Amendment provides right to jury trial for §1983 cases in which damages in excess of $20 are sought.

real contextual differences exist. In fact, there are only relatively unimportant differences.

In New Zealand, the *Baigent's Case* cause of action has been based on the jurisprudence of jurisdictions with provisions, despite being the least defined cause of action.[45] As has developed in the United States, the New Zealand Court of Appeal clearly did not see the difference in provisions as determinative of the cause of action. While the differences are interesting, they are not of great importance.

Overall there appears to be a correlation between the degree of statutory definition of the cause of action and the degree of limitations placed by judges on the cause of action. It seems that more express provisions are mirrored by a more formalistic and perhaps restrictive approach. This is not, however, necessarily a strict causal link: other factors will exist that both explain the exceptions to this correlation and, perhaps, amount to other correlations or links themselves.

It seems that judges will play down the impact of the source of the cause of action in recognition of the importance of constitutional rights. The mere source of the cause of action seems to be unimportant in the development of a common international human rights jurisprudence. Likewise, the nature of the document upon which the cause of action is based is an irrelevant distinction in terms of its impact on the cause of action.

Rather than determining the shape of the cause of action, therefore, it seems that the differences in the document and provision upon which a cause of action is based will influence the way in which the cause of action develops, the rhetoric used by judges, and the legal issues discussed in the case law. Judges do not ignore the wording of provisions where they exist, but usually choose to emphasise the importance of rights as an overwhelming consideration. This has resulted in the evolution of an international consensus.

C. WHAT IS THE AGE OF THE CAUSE OF ACTION?

1. Introduction

The four causes of action discussed in this book developed at different times. This section addresses the impact this factor has on the cause of action. Overall, it seems that differences exist between jurisdictions in which the cause of action is a recent creation, and those in which the cause of action was developed longer ago. In fact, the way in which jurisdictions deal with the development of the cause of action seems to be correlated with its age. Indeed, unlike the source of the cause of action discussed in

45 *Baigent's Case* (n 4 above) 677.

the previous section, there may be a causal connection between the age of the cause of action and its nature.

2. The Relative Ages of the Causes of Action

The starting point must be the actual relative ages of the causes of action. Section 1983 was enacted in 1871 but remained largely unused until 1961, when the Court decided *Monroe,* indicating its true significance.[46] Its potential ambit had, perhaps, become evident in a series of cases starting in the 1920s.[47] *Bivens* was decided in 1971, although the line of argument had been suggested in 1946.[48] The monetary remedy in India was first awarded in 1983, having been discussed but not granted in a series of cases during the previous two years.[49] The New Zealand cause of action was developed in 1994, having been foreshadowed two years earlier.[50] It seems two patterns are evident here: first, that in each jurisdiction the cause of action was foreshadowed before it was finally determined either to exist, or to be used to its full potential. Second, it seems that in the later causes of action, the development from that foreshadowing to the full use of the cause of action was quicker than in the earlier causes of action.

Further, in each case, the fundamental rights which the cause of action aims to protect had been enacted earlier. The United States Constitution came into practical effect in 1789; the Bill of Rights took effect from 1791. The Indian Constitution was enacted in 1949 and the New Zealand Bill of Rights Act in 1990. It seems that another two patterns are evident: first, that there is a gap between the enactment of the rights and the development of the remedy; and, second, that the length of the gap has decreased over time.

These patterns influence the gestation and actual birth of the cause of action. It seems that there will be a gap between the time at which the cause of action could first be expected to develop and its actual development, as well as between the time at which the cause of action is first suggested, and the time at which it actually develops. It also seems that modern causes of action are likely to develop rather more quickly, so that all the possible gaps will be shorter.

46 *Monroe* (n 6 above).

47 E Chemerinsky, *Federal Jurisdiction*, 2nd edn, (Boston, MA, Little Brown, 1994) 422: A series of voting registration cases.

48 *Bivens* (n 6 above); foreshadowed by *Bell v Hood* 327 US 678, 66 S Ct 773 (1946).

49 The monetary remedy was discussed but not granted in *Khatri* (n 43 above); *Kochar v Union of India* AIR 1983 SC 1107; and *Chaturvedi v MP* 1983 (2) Cri LJ 1928 (SC) and granted for the first time in *Rudul Sah* (n 6 above).

50 *Baigent's Case* (n 4 above) and *Auckland Unemployed Workers' Rights Centre Inc v Attorney-General* [1994] 3 NZLR 720 were decided on the same day. They had been foreshadowed by *Noort v Ministry of Transport* [1992] 3 NZLR 260, two years earlier.

3. Tidal Fluctuations

So far, so abstract; do these patterns influence the details of the cause of action, beyond the initial birth? It seems so. Differences are particularly clear when one considers the court-proscribed limitations to the causes of action. Starting from the most general level, it is clear that currently the causes of action in the United States—the older causes of action—are narrower than those in India or New Zealand; there are many more limitations on the United States causes of action. This has meant that plaintiffs in the United States will face a more complex cause of action, and will be required to prove many preliminary factors before liability is established and remedy considered.[51]

In India, on the other hand, almost anyone may bring the cause of action in relation to almost anything. The Indian Supreme Court has considered many of the elements that the United States courts have used to create limitations, but has almost exclusively reached generous interpretations.[52] In New Zealand, the youngest cause of action, many of these questions have not come up for consideration.[53]

This snapshot of the causes of action suggests that the older the cause of action, the more developed the limitations. Although this is by no means conclusive as the difference could, of course, be attributed to influences other than the age of the cause of action,[54] two points support it. First, it should be noted that the differences do correlate with the time development—for example, New Zealand is more similar to the United States socially and economically than to India, and yet is more similar to the Indian cause of action in terms of limitations on the causes of action. Second, the observation is confirmed by abandoning the snapshot approach and taking a deeper, historical approach to the causes of action. This indicates that it may be that the difference relates to an evolution in each cause of action over time.

It seems that the evolution over time in these causes of action resembles a pattern of tidal fluctuations, with an ebbing and flowing of the limitations to the causes of action. In general, the cause of action starts out as an unknown; limitations then retreat, to create a very much wider

[51] Eg cases will be unsuccessful if close attention is not paid to the questions surrounding immunities and the pleadings: Jeffries (n 34 above); Burris (n 38 above).

[52] Ie wide standing and relaxed procedural rules through public interest litigation: *Gupta* (n 26 above), *Morcha* (n 26 above); and strict standard of liability without the protection of sovereign immunity: *Basu* (n 11 above) and *Nilabati* (n 11 above).

[53] Most of the early cases involved questions of application of *Baigent's Case* (n 4 above) to other circumstances. In *Whithair* (n 22 above) a limitation (good faith defence) could have been imposed, but was not. In *R v Grayson and Taylor* [1997] 1 NZLR 399, the Court chose not to limit the cause of action to officials, but included co-conspirators.

[54] Eg the difference could be attributed to the different social context of the causes of action: See following section.

application. Following this retreat, the limitations of the cause of action expand, to reduce the application of the cause of action. Obviously, this is no more than a general pattern: occasional cases will not accord with it, but the overall impression given is of such a progression. In relation to the three jurisdictions discussed, the Section 1983 cause of action illustrates the entire pattern, while the Indian cause of action is perhaps just entering the third phase, and the New Zealand cause of action may be at the beginning of the second phase, having somewhat bypassed the first.

It can, therefore, be seen most explicitly in relation to the United States. The narrowness of the United States causes of action has clearly not been historically constant. At first, the Section 1983 cause of action was not used to any great extent due largely to the severe limitations that existed.[55] Following that period, its scope was greatly increased by a series of cases which reduced the ambit of the often implied limitations.[56] It was at this point that the *Bivens* cause of action was developed. As early cases decided that it was equivalent to the Section 1983 cause of action, all the limitations were deemed to apply and so, to some extent, *Bivens* bypassed much of the first and second evolutionary stages. The narrowing of the cause of action indicates a third stage in the chronology.[57]

Despite the current width of the Indian cause of action, the earliest cases showed somewhat more caution and fewer cases were successful at this time.[58] A period of rapid expansion was obvious in the 1980s and 1990s.[59] While there may be some indications that the current approach is somewhat narrowing in the more recent cases, this is by no means dramatic.[60] According to the United States pattern, a decrease in ambit may soon become apparent in India.

[55] Political and social influences may have prevented the cause of action being used, as did narrow judicial interpretations of 'under color of law' and which rights would be covered: Chemerinsky (n 47 above) 427; L Levy, *et al*, *Encyclopedia of the American Constitution*, Vol IV (New York, MacMillan, 1986) 1640.

[56] From the 1960s, more cases were heard by the courts because of the increased social and political influence of the civil rights movement and the opening up of public interest litigation: M Schwartz and J Kirklin, *Section 1983 Litigation: Claims, Defences and Fees* (New York, Wiley Law Publications, 1986) 4–5. *Monroe* (n 6 above) was a watershed, increasing the ambit of 'under color of law' and overriding to some extent the emphasis on state autonomy. *Lynch v Household Finance Corporation* 405 US 538, 92 S Ct 1113 (1972) held that property as well as personal rights would be covered.

[57] Eg *Will* (n 31 above); *Harlow v Fitzgerald* 457 US 800, 102 S Ct 2727 (1982); *Kentucky v Graham* 473 US 800, 105 S Ct 3099 (1985); *Correctional Services Corporation v Malesko* 534 US 61, 122 S Ct 515 (2001).

[58] It took two years for the remedy to develop from the first suggestion that it was possible, and the Court awarded the monetary remedy as an exception in early, outrageous cases eg *Bhim Singh* (n 10 above); and *Hongray v Union of India* [1984] 3 SCR 544.

[59] Continual increase in width codified in *Nilabati* (n 11 above); and *Basu* (n 11 above) in the 1990s.

[60] *Narmada Bachao Andolan v Union of India* AIR 2000 SC 3751 illustrates a retreat in the public interest litigation sphere; this suggests that there will be fewer cases seeking the monetary remedy under Art 32 as the two aspects are so closely linked.

Finally, in New Zealand, the cause of action was wide from the beginning,[61] and while subsequent cases generally extended the scope still further,[62] the very latest cases indicate some narrowing of its scope.[63] It may be that the New Zealand cause of action is rather like the *Bivens* cause of action in the United States, so that having taken advantage of all the developments in the older causes of action, it has curtailed the effect of the tidal pattern. Alternatively, it may simply not have had the requisite number of years to allow for a full judicial backlash to its width.

If this pattern of fluctuations is evident in relation to the overall picture of the cause of action, it is equally evident in relation to the specifics of the elements that make up the cause of action. At that specific level, fluctuations are especially obvious in relation to the issue of public interest litigation. In the United States, public interest litigation was very important in the 1960s, causing what was considered possible in constitutional law to expand to the point that the two causes of action discussed here developed.[64] More recently, the use of public interest litigation in the United States has become more limited, at the same time as the boundaries of the causes of action have contracted.[65]

In India, the issue gained in importance in the 1980s–1990s and, as in the United States, both assisted in the creation of the cause of action and has been strongly influenced by those cases.[66] Public interest litigation in India has maintained an expansive interpretation, although later cases suggest an unease at its ambit.[67] Nevertheless, even though some decrease is probable, it seems unlikely that public interest litigation would become as little important in India as it has in the United States in more recent years.

In New Zealand, the issue has not been raised at all. As the *Baigent's Case* cause of action was created with great width, it may not stimulate the development of public interest litigation—and public interest litigation, if

61 *Baigent's Case* (n 4 above) held that the cause of action was at public law and so the general state immunity was not available.

62 *Whithair* (n 22 above) held that good faith would not be a defence. *Hobson* (n 35 above) held that the Attorney-General would be substituted as defendant in Bill of Rights cases brought wrongly against other entities, rather than deciding that such cases would fail for having been pleaded wrongly.

63 *Brown* (n 13 above) stressed that *Baigent's Case* monetary remedy was available only in exceptional cases; *Wilding* (n 41 above) held that the Accident Insurance Act applies so that the *Baigent's Case* monetary remedy cannot compensate for personal injury; and *Sugrue* (n 41 above) stressed that the remedy was discretionary and therefore undue delay may prevent it being awarded in a particular case.

64 Schwartz and Kirklin (n 56 above) 5.

65 See A Chayes, 'The Role of Judges in Public Law Litigation' (1976) 89 *Harv L Rev* 1281; A Chayes, 'The Supreme Court 1981 Term Forward: Public Law Litigation and the Burger Court' (1982) 96 *Harv L Rev* 4.

66 Many monetary remedy cases have been brought as public interest litigation, including *Rudul Sah* (n 6 above).

67 *Narmada* (n 60 above).

developed, may not add to the cause of action's development—in the way it has in the United States and India. It may be that the issue has not been raised in New Zealand yet because of the newness of the cause of action, or it may be that the cause of action has bypassed this issue, for whatever reason.

While some sort of tidal instinct may be inherent in the continuing development of causes of action, it is unclear to what extent. For example, it is unclear whether all the features that became limitations in the United States will become relevant in India and New Zealand over time. It may be that the experience of the older causes of action means that the pattern may be bypassed in relation to certain issues in later causes of action.

In fact, as has been alluded to above, it seems that this has happened to some extent in New Zealand. There, it seems that the initial 'unknown' quality phase has been bypassed; the cause of action began wide and subsequent cases have largely provided detail. Thus, it is possible that the pattern will not be replicated in New Zealand for a reason which is intrinsic in the pattern: jurisdictions will learn from each other.

Clearly, when the cause of action was developed in New Zealand, the previously developed jurisprudence from other jurisdictions was taken into account. In fact, the President of the Court of Appeal was keen to ensure New Zealand jurisprudence did not 'lag behind' other jurisdictions with a monetary remedy for constitutional rights breaches.[68] The resulting cause of action was, therefore, created at a more optimal level, evolutionary speaking, than the older causes of action, which learnt rather more by trial and error. Additionally, of course, other reasons may intervene to upset the pattern such as the contextual matters discussed in the next section, or simply other matters similarly associated with the age of the cause of action; these will be considered in what follows.

4. Number of Cases

Until this point, I have referred to the age of the cause of action. It is, however, probably more exact to consider that it is the number of cases that have come before the Courts that contribute to this factor. This will, of course, usually amount to the same thing. Bentham's description of the common law as 'dog law' is perhaps apposite here: 'Do you know how [judges] made [law]? just as a man makes law for his dog. When your dog does anything you want to break him of, you wait till he does it, and then beat him for it. This is the way you make laws for your dog: and this is the way the judges make laws for you and me.'[69]

[68] *Baigent's Case* (n 4 above) 676.

[69] Quoted in G Postema, *Bentham and the Common Law Tradition* (Oxford, Clarendon Press, 1986) 277.

The previous description of the fluctuations in the causes of action over time illustrates the importance of judicial decision-making in relation to the development of the causes of action, as the cause of action develops through the introduction and reduction of limitations on the cause of action as decided, primarily, by judges. Obviously, therefore, the cause of action will only develop along the lines allowed by the cases brought to the courts; judicial decision-making is dependant to this extent on both the social reality of the community and lawyers' choices in the cases brought and arguments made. The cause of action will develop further, and perhaps more quickly, in jurisdictions in which a higher proportion of constitutional rights breaches coincides with an active legal community, thus resulting in more cases being taken to the courts.[70] While there may be some debate about the extent to which constitutional rights law is (and ought to be) reactive, rather than constitutive of societal standards, at least insofar as the cause of action is developed by judicial consideration of cases it will inevitably evolve in reaction to the wrongdoer's wrongdoings.

Using Bentham's analogy, in New Zealand there has been less time for judges to beat the law into shape because of the few cases that judges have had to consider. In the absence of many (if any) express statutory boundaries for the cause of action, this has left a cause of action with few existent limitations. Against that background, *Whithair*, in which a limitation was held not to exist, has had a disproportionate effect.[71] In comparison, the large number of cases in the United States has allowed judges there to develop a plethora of rules relating to the causes of action. There is also a large number of cases in India. This is partly due to the age of the causes of action in the United States and India, partly to the number of breaches in each jurisdiction, and partly to the size of the populations compared with that of New Zealand. The result is that many factors have been considered by the courts more than once, so that authoritative decisions have been taken in relation to many aspects of the cause of action.

In the United States, it is obvious that the large number of cases allowed the Supreme Court to alter its approach on some matters over time, for example, the issues of the liability of municipalities, immunities and punitive damages.[72] In India, the Court has almost exclusively used the

70 See next section in which the issue of the legal context is discussed in more detail. F Cross, 'International Determinants of Human Rights and Welfare: Law, Wealth or Culture' [1997] *Indiana Intl & Comp L Rev* 265 attempts to provide statistical analysis to support such a contention.

71 *Whithair* (n 22 above). The risk of a single case having a disproportionate effect in New Zealand's small democracy was noted in *Manga v Attorney-General* [2000] 2 NZLR 65, 82.

72 This aspect evolved through the decisions in *Monroe* (n 6 above) (municipalities are immune); *Monell* (n 7 above) (municipalities are not immune); *Mt Healthy City School District Board of Education v Doyle* 429 US 274, 97 S Ct 568 (1977) (boundaries of municipalities); and *City of Newport v Facts Concerts* 453 US 247, 101 S Ct 2748 (1981) (no punitive damages against municipalities).

number of cases to widen the boundaries although, as discussed above, it may be that the United States pattern is followed in India in the future.[73] The large number of cases in relation to the blinding of prisoners and custodial deaths in India has allowed the courts to develop special responses to those particular fact situations.[74]

Interestingly, the number of cases coming before the Indian Supreme Court has been the subject of judicial comment. It has, therefore, directly influenced the cause of action in India, in addition to the indirect influence discussed above. The Court began to refer cases back to the High Courts for decision, as the explosion in cases filed had almost paralysed the Supreme Court.[75] This can be seen as a limitation on the cause of action.

Although the age of the cause of action and number of cases are usually related, that will not necessarily be so. For example, in New Zealand many *Baigent's Case* type cases are not taken to Court but are settled, in an attempt by the Crown to avoid unfavourable decisions.[76] This, therefore, gives fewer cases than might be expected in a cause of action of the particular age and correspondingly fewer chances for judges to develop the cause of action. As most cases that are settled include a confidentiality clause, it is not possible to calculate the real numbers, the effect on other decisions, or the amount settled upon.

Further, because the *Baigent's Case* cause of action began later, after equivalent causes of action internationally had built up significant jurisprudence, it is likely that when taking the decisions to settle cases on the basis of the likelihood of losing, the Crown will take into account international decisions of a similar nature. It is likely that newer causes of action, in general, may benefit from the experiences of the older causes of action in this way and so avoid decisions, particularly those negative to the Crown, even being taken: 'man learns by experience. Such experience need not be confined to the bounds of one's own national territory'.[77]

While it is by no means inevitable that the New Zealand and Indian causes of action will follow the United States' fluctuation pattern, the age

[73] *Basu* (n 11 above) confirmed *Nilabati* (n 11 above) that sovereign immunity would not apply to this strict liability cause of action. *Morcha* (n 26 above) stated that a letter purporting to commence a public interest litigation petition should be addressed to the court as a whole and not individual judges; *Mehta* (n 42 above) stated that it would be wrong to reject a letter merely because it was addressed simply to one judge rather than the whole court; *Narmada* (n 60 above) suggests a general narrowing of public interest litigation in India.

[74] Eg *Khatri* series of cases (n 43 above) re: Blinding of prisoners; *Nilabati* (n 11 above) and *Basu* (n 11 above) re: Custodial death.

[75] *Kumar v Municipal Corporation of Delhi* (1987) 4 SCC 609; *Brahmbhatt v State of Gujarat* AIR 1987 SC 1159.

[76] The stance of the Crown is more conciliatory than in many other areas of law: Eg *Rawlinson v Rice* (1997) 3 HRNZ 480, 493 where it is reported that the Crown accepted liability for Bill of Rights Act damages and was willing to negotiate as to an appropriate sum. In *Brown,* both the paucity of cases brought to court, and the fact that others had settled, was noted: *Brown* (n 13 above) 345.

[77] D Basu, *Comparative Constitutional Law* (New Delhi, Prentice-Hall, 1984) 4.

of the cause of action or number of cases before the Courts will, nonetheless, influence them in this less direct way.

5. International Human Rights Common Law

There is yet another aspect to this feature that seems to interplay with the fluctuations: it may not be only the age of the cause of action (or numbers of cases) that is relevant but also when, historically, the cause of action began.[78] This builds upon the observation that the tidal fluctuation pattern has allowed newer causes of action to learn from the pattern of older causes of action, suggesting that they will avoid the excessive fluctuations.

It is quite possible that the cause of action can be viewed internationally, as part of something akin to an 'international human rights common law'. Seen thus, it may have its own independent age. The concept of an international human rights common law has already been seen to be an important factor intervening in the previous section: despite the wide variations in the source of each of the causes of action, they are all remarkably similar. In relation to the age of the cause of action, it seems that the cause of action in each national jurisdiction is affected by when in the timeline of the international human rights common law it developed.

For example, as seen at the beginning of this section, the length of the gap between the enactment of each set of rights, and the development of the cause of action in each jurisdiction has shortened over time. This time gap has decreased from 100 years for the United States causes of action, to 30 years for the Indian, and four years for the New Zealand cause of action. It may be that the existence of the cause of action begins to seem more inevitable following its development in other jurisdictions so that in jurisdictions in which written rights guarantees are recent creations, there is less resistance to the development of a new cause of action. It was certainly seen as inevitable in New Zealand that a cause of action sounding in a monetary remedy would develop.[79] Further, the international consensus seems to have affected the development of the details of the cause of action in New Zealand: it was said to be 'utterly surprising' if issues confronted in other jurisdictions did not become relevant in New Zealand.[80]

[78] In the context of state liability, a similar influence has been noted: 'It is the historical phase for human rights at a particular time in each country that actually determines the level and scope of state liability': T Fuke, 'Historical Phases of State Liability as Law of Remedies—Some Introductory Remarks' in Y Zhang, (ed), *Comparative Studies on Governmental Liability in East and Southeast Asia* (The Hague, Kluwer, 1999) 1, 4.

[79] *Baigent's Case* (n 4 above) 676.

[80] *Manga* (n 71 above) 82.

This suggests that jurisdictions 'learn' from international human rights common law, thus avoiding both problems that earlier jurisdictions have solved and slow trial and error development. This could be expressed in another way: the development of the cause of action in many jurisdictions has created a new contemporary historical period, when the development of such causes of action seems reasonable and desirable. Internationally, rights-talk is active and important. Further, when viewed like this it seems that the ebb and flow pattern itself has evolved over time, in response to the changing legal context brought about by the increased number of domestic causes of action for breach of fundamental rights. New Zealand can thus be seen as an example of the more evolved pattern.

Noting the ebb and flow pattern and the 'learning' aspect associated with it allows a final observation: there is a suggestion that in all jurisdictions, the causes of action tend towards similar conclusions, over time. This can be seen even in relation to factors where wildly different conclusions have been reached. For example, statutory rights in the United States may be the subject of Section 1983 cases, in direct contrast with India and New Zealand[81]; nevertheless, later cases softened this difference so that although the United States somewhat differs from the 'norm' at international common law on this point in theory, in practice the cause of action remains much the same.[82]

Obviously, this entire book is premised on the idea that differences do exist between jurisdictions, but the evolutionary aspect suggests that causes of action move towards, at the least, similar questions. Local conditions may lead to different answers. It seems that these causes of action may be intrinsically and subtly attracted to similarity.[83] This suggests a movement towards, once again, a common international human rights norm, affecting not only all the elements discussed, but also the general mood of the cause of action as a whole.

This raises the interesting question of why this occurs. Intuitively, it seems that there are only so many answers available for the same questions. Thus, this sort of meandering towards a common law, through a common path, is to be expected. Although illuminating the differences between the causes of action, the age of the cause of action also, therefore, explains the similarities between jurisdictions. Contributing to this is the increasing 'globalization' of the law and the resulting tension between indigenous and international jurisprudence. Both of these factors are addressed in rather more detail in the following sections.

81 *Thiboutot* (n 17 above).

82 Two exceptions were later implemented: *Halderman* (n 18 above); and *National Sea Clammers* (n 18 above) so that this has not been a significant aspect of the cause of action.

83 This is, in fact, an idea borrowed from the behaviour of physical systems. For example, two isolated systems with different temperatures will, when they come into contact, tend towards a common and stable temperature different from either of their original temperatures.

6. Summary

Overall, then, it seems that certain of the differences evident in the way in which the jurisdictions have decided the questions discussed in the previous chapter may be attributed to the age of the cause of action. Various different influences are covered by the concept of the age of the cause of action.

First, it is possible that the number of years a cause of action has been existent may affect the way it looks; a pattern resembling tidal fluctuations in the width of the cause of action may be the result. Second, this may be better attributed to the number of cases brought under the cause of action, rather than the number of years a cause of action has existed, although the two are usually related. Third, the time at which the cause of action developed may be equally relevant, meaning that historical or international legal context affects the existence of a cause of action. Finally, an international human rights common law appears to exist, either towards which causes of action tend over time or by which causes of action are affected.

D. WHAT IS THE WIDER CONTEXT OF THE CAUSE OF ACTION?

1. Introduction

This influence probably best accounts for the differences between the causes of action. This is unsurprising, of course, because each cause of action must be a product of the context within which it exists and develops.

Kahn-Freund argued that the proper use of comparative law 'requires a knowledge not only of the foreign law, but also of its social, and above all its political, context'.[84] Even comparative lawyers who consider that the similarities between legal systems far outweigh the differences note that 'it is essential for us to understand the social, political and cultural background of the foreign law and comprehend the organic nature of its rules'.[85] Law 'is a reflection of the country's experience'.[86] As a result, empirical studies have attempted to determine the correlations between human rights, and law, wealth and culture.[87]

[84] O Kahn-Fruend, 'On Uses and Misuses of Comparative Law' (1974) 37 *MLR* 1, 27.

[85] A Watson, *The Making of Civil Law* (Cambridge, MA, Harvard University Press, 1981) 44–45.

[86] M Glendon, *et al*, *Comparative Legal Traditions* (St Paul, MN, West Publishing, 1982) 10.

[87] Cross (n 70 above). J Strouse and R Claude, 'Empirical Comparative Rights Research: Some Preliminary Tests of Development Hypobook' in R Claude, (ed), *Comparative Human Rights* (Baltimore, MD, John Hopkins University Press, 1976) 51. While the value of such empirical studies may be questionable, they support the intuitive impression that these factors are influential in some way.

It has been argued that, despite the existence of 'historically unique and various circumstances surrounding the development of legal guarantees of rights from country to country ... the worldwide concern for human rights transcends the differences among political and economic systems'.[88] This book has likewise found that some sort of international common belief seems to exist that transcends cultural differences.[89] This section does not err from that path, but considers the impact of contextual differences on constitutional rights remedies.

A further point to note is that the awarding of a remedy tends to be discretionary.[90] This means that it involves a calculation in which decisions may well involve a judge's personal views of what is right and wrong which, in turn, cannot be separated from the cultural context within which they exist. It is possible, therefore, that contextual differences between the jurisdictions are especially influential at the remedial level. Thus: 'remedial rules on the national level are intertwined with legal procedure and the social, historical, economic, and technological environment of the legal system.'[91]

This section is an attempt to assess the cultural and legal context of the causes of action. The factors I consider are exogenous to the causes of action. As 'culture' is a rather amorphous term and a precise definition is unnecessary for the purposes of this book, I will assume that socio-economic, political and religious factors as ordinarily understood make up the concept. This part will assess the wider context of the cause of action and the term 'culture' will be used to include all non-legal aspects of the contexts within which the causes of action exist.

The second part will assess the wider legal context of the cause of action. Issues internal to the causes of action will be considered in the following section which will look at the tension between indigenous and comparative jurisprudence.

2. What is the Cultural Context?

This book does not address the reasons for cultural distinctions, assess their value, or the reasons for any differences between jurisdictions on account of these cultural distinctions; it is enough to note that differences exist and that they cannot be ignored when considering the causes of action.

[88] R Claude, 'Preface' in R Claude, (ed), *Comparative Human Rights* (Baltimore, MD, John Hopkins University Press, 1976) ix.
[89] See especially last section.
[90] Eg J Cassels, *Remedies: The Law of Damages* (Toronto, Irwin Law, 2000) 1: 'The law of remedies provides perhaps the richest entry point into the study of the nature of Judge-made law'.
[91] D Shelton, *Remedies in International Human Rights Law* (Oxford, OUP, 1999) 57.

The primary difference is development. Whichever method is used to determine socio-economic development, the United States is the most developed country, New Zealand the second, and India the third. In addition, the gap between the United States and New Zealand is significantly smaller than that between New Zealand and India. India is, quite simply, in another category of development. The classic measure for development is gross domestic product per head of population:[92]

United States	$37,562
New Zealand	$22,582
India	$2892

The United Nations Development Programme's Human Development Index combines life expectancy, literacy, educational enrolment and GDP, to provide a measure that encompasses more than mere economic wealth. The Index measures development in a scale from 0 to 1. Countries which score over 0.8 have high human development; scores from 0.5–0.79 indicate medium human development; and those under 0.5 have low human development:

United States	0.944
New Zealand	0.933
India	0.602

On the Human Development Index, the United States is ranked 10th, New Zealand is 19th, and India is 127th.[93] The United States is paradigmatic of a western country and, despite its geographical position in the South Pacific, New Zealand is also 'western'. India, on the other hand, is not a western country. In both New Zealand and the United States, the major religions are Judeo–Christian; while in India the majority of people are Hindu or Muslim,[94] there is a great diversity of religion.[95] In New Zealand and the United States, most citizens share the same language; in India, there are 15 official languages, with little or no mutual understanding.[96] Politically, the three jurisdictions differ greatly from one another: India and the United States are both federal; New Zealand and the United States are both primarily two-party systems[97]; India and New Zealand have more

[92] United Nations Development Programme, *Human Development Report 2005* (www.undp.org) 219–22.

[93] *Ibid*, p 149.

[94] *CIA World Factbook 2005* (www.cia.gov/cia/publications/factbook).

[95] J Johari, *Indian Political System* (New Delhi, Anmol, 1996) 3.

[96] *CIA World Factbook 2005* (n 94 above). In addition, English is an associate language.

[97] *Ibid*; Johari (n 95 above) 240.

regulated economies than the United States.[98] Corruption is most prevalent in India, while it is almost non-existent in New Zealand[99]; New Zealand and the United States have higher political stability,[100] government effectiveness[101] and accountability than India.[102]

There are, therefore, significant cultural differences between these jurisdictions primarily occasioned by socio-economic development. In terms of constitutional rights, this developmental difference is key:

> the function of human rights (and discourse on them) in Asia is quite different from that in the West … . The role of human rights [in the West] is to fine-tune the administrative and judicial system and fortify rights and freedoms that are largely uncontroversial. In Asia, on the other hand, human rights have a transformative potential … . Human rights are therefore a terrain for struggle for power and the conceptions of good society.[103]

The difference can be seen particularly clearly in the fact situations that are brought to the courts. In India, the earlier cases out of which the cause of action developed concerned life and liberty issues: a 14-year illegal detention,[104] death at the hands of the military,[105] blinding of prisoners,[106] death and assault by the police.[107] Understandably, there is a sense of urgency in relation to such institutionalised and grave constitutional rights breaches. Indian commentators refer to the 'lawlessness' of the Indian state as the impetus for the activist approach of the Supreme Court.[108]

Similar fact situations do not generally exist in the United States and New Zealand. There, the cases tend to concern negligence rather than intention, and procedural rather than life and liberty rights. So, for example, the cause of action in the United States was developed primarily

98 Johari (n 95 above) 10–11; *CIA World Factbook 2005* (n 94 above).

99 Control of corruption, 2004 percentile rank: India 55.8, New Zealand 97.1 and United States 93.8: D Kaufmann, A Kraay and M Mastruzzi, *Governance Matters IV: Governance Indicators for 1996–2004* (World Bank Research Papers, 2005, http://econ.worldbank.org/).

100 Political stability, 2004 percentile rank: India 24.3, New Zealand 97.1 and United States 60.7: Kaufmann, *et al* (n 99 above).

101 Governmental effectiveness, 2004 percentile rank: India 55.8, New Zealand 97.1 and United States 93.8: Kaufmann, *et al* (n 99 above).

102 Voice and accountability, 2004 percentile rank: India 53.9, New Zealand 97.1 and United States 89.3: Kaufmann, *et al* (n 99 above).

103 Y Ghai, 'Human Rights and Governance: The Asia Debate' (1994) 15 *Australian Year Book of International Law* 1, reprinted in P Alston, (ed), *Human Rights Law* (Aldershot, Dartmouth, 1996) 219, 239–40.

104 *Rudul Sah* (n 6 above).

105 *Hongray* (n 58 above).

106 *Khatri* (n 43 above).

107 *SAHELI, a Women's Resources Centre v Commissioner of Police, Delhi* AIR 1990 SC 513.

108 Eg U Baxi, 'Preface' in M Mridul, *Public Interest Litigation—A Profile* (Jaipur, Bharat Law House, 1986) iii; and P Singh, 'PIL' (1993) XXIX *ASIL* 245, 253 re development of public interest litigation; M Jain, *Indian Constitutional Law*, 4th edn, (Bombay, Tripathi Private, 1987) 600 re development of monetary remedy in *Rudul Sah* (n 6 above).

through cases concerned with illegal search and seizure.[109] In New Zealand, *Baigent's Case* also concerned an unlawful search and seizure, where that was the sole illegality.[110]

The differences between jurisdictions are stark when the role of children in these cases is compared. In India, there are cases involving child labour and children killed by police.[111] In the United States, the court was called to consider the state's responsibility in not preventing parents from abusing children[112] and due process rights in the suspension of secondary school students.[113] In New Zealand, the Court of Appeal has considered the state's responsibility in relation to children whose parents refused, for religious reasons, to allow necessary blood transfusions.[114]

Simply described, in these examples the Indian state and its employees are often guilty of heinous breaches, whereas in the United States and New Zealand, the state's guilt (if it is held to exist) is in omitting to prevent parental actions. Even when the United States and New Zealand cases do involve the acts, rather than omissions, of state actors the level of intention, the impetus and, perhaps most importantly for the victim, the effect of the breach are often different: there are, for example, few intentional illegal deaths in the United States and New Zealand.[115] As Craig and Deshpande describe it, in India 'the nature of the substantive problems to be solved will often be more acute than those normally faced within the West'.[116]

It is interesting to consider the possible impact of these factors on the general development of the cause of action. As India is a less developed country, with consequent limited resources, the existence of a monetary remedy must be balanced against the need to use limited money for other

109 Including *Monroe* (n 6 above) and *Bell* (n 48 above).

110 *Baigent's Case* (n 4 above).

111 *Mehta v Tamil Nadu* AIR 1991 SC 417 (children employed in match factories); *SAHELI* (n 107 above) (child killed by police).

112 *DeShaney v Winnebago County Department of Social Services* 489 US 189, 109 S Ct 998 (1989).

113 *Carey v Piphus* 435 US 247, 98 S Ct 1042 (1978).

114 *Re J (An Infant)* [1996] 2 NZLR 134.

115 Eg the cases concerning the United States military involved experiments with LSD that severely reduced quality of life (*US v Stanley* 483 US 669, 107 S Ct 3054 (1987)), while in India the military were guilty of causing death and refusing to participate in the legal process (*Hongray* (n 58 above)); in relation to prisoners, the United States Supreme Court has considered procedural rights (*Cleavinger v Saxner* 474 US 193, 106 S Ct 496 (1985) and *McCarthy v Madigan* 503 US 1401, 112 S Ct 1081 (1992)), and in New Zealand the Court has compensated a prisoner for a 252 day wrongful imprisonment on the basis of a mistaken interpretation of the law (*Manga* (n 71 above)), whereas in India, the Supreme Court has been required to consider the systematic blinding of prisoners by authorities (*Khatri* (n 43 above)) and 14-year illegal detentions (*Rudul Sah* (n 6 above)); in New Zealand, the police has failed to give the proper advice to suspects (*J v Attorney-General* (1995) 2 HRNZ 311), while in India, the police have caused death (*SAHELI* (n 107 above)) and forced people to work for them (*PUDR v Police Commissioner, Delhi* (1989) 4 SCC 730).

116 P Craig and S Deshpande, 'Rights, Autonomy and Process: Public Interest Litigation in India' (1989) 9 *OJLS* 356.

governmental functions. In that context, a breach of procedural rights without an extreme effect on an individual or group of individuals may not have been sufficient impetus for the development of the cause of action in India. Money is, of course, a limited resource in New Zealand and the United States as well, and it may be that Indian courts would have developed the monetary remedy for procedural cases. Nevertheless, the less developed nature of India means, simply, that extreme cases exist which directly led to the development of the monetary remedy. In a country in which 25 per cent of the population lives below the poverty line,[117] more basic concerns for food, water and shelter will take precedence over technical breaches of constitutional rights. For whatever reason, constitutional rights breaches are rife.

Up until this point, this subsection has considered the effect that the cultural context has on the fact situations that come before the courts. It is timely to now consider the impact that the sort of fact situations has on the decision-making process in these cases. It seems that the nature of cases and of society also influences the approach of the courts.

This is particularly obvious in India, where there is the impression that the cause of action should be used to try to improve society. In fact, this is perhaps partly reflective of the Constitution: it has been wryly commented that although the Constitution does not guarantee a right to happiness, it does set out 'similar high-sounding aims'.[118] The Indian Supreme Court has evolved a sense of responsibility for itself, which extends to a 'sacred duty' to condemn unconstitutional acts by the state.[119] Faced with such extreme fact situations, judges seem to perceive themselves as the saviours of the 'have-nots' before the courts and in the Article 32 writ jurisdiction employ vivid rhetoric about the nature of the breaches.[120]

It is here that the discretionary nature of decisions becomes especially obvious in relation to the monetary remedy. As one commentator described the cases establishing the Indian monetary remedy: 'the administrative wrong was of such magnitude that it shocked the conscience of the judges to such an extent that even without caring for the technicalities of the law they awarded compensation to the victims'.[121] In fact, in relation to the cases which developed the monetary remedy '[p]erhaps the judges went by their intuition rather than any rational basis'.[122] This emotional element to the monetary remedy is evident in the way it has been awarded

117 *CIA World Factbook 2005* (n 94 above): 2002 estimate.

118 J Derrett, 'Human Rights and Fundamental Freedoms in India' in Recueils de la Société Jean Bodin Pour L'Histoire Comparative des Institutions *XLVII: L'Individu Face au Pouvoir Deuxième Partie: Afrique, Asie, Amérique* (Paris, Dessain et Tolra, 1988) 159, 201.

119 *Basu* (n 11 above) 302.

120 *Morcha* (n 26 above) 811; *Nilabati* (n 11 above) 2909.

121 S Jain, 'Money Compensation for Administrative Wrongs Through Article 32' (1983) 25 *JILI* 118.

122 *Ibid*, p 121.

since then: 'The most striking feature of compensation awards is their arbitrary nature. The courts have responded to cases with charity, and have avoided the need to decide upon a case by awarding interim compensation. No formal scheme for the compensation of those wronged has been framed.'[123]

Judicial style in the United States and New Zealand, without those fact situations, is less overtly emotional, and the concept of an overriding judicial responsibility for society is less obvious. While in India judgments often focus on the facts as a justification for judicial decisions, in the United States and New Zealand the focus is often on determining the appropriate legal relationship between public bodies and private individuals.[124] The causes of action in the United States and New Zealand are part of the courts' general decisions regarding the liability of the state for its actions. In India, the cause of action is part of the court's 'poverty jurisprudence' and is concerned primarily to vindicate constitutional rights.[125]

In addition to the development of the cause of action and the associated judicial style, the cultural differential is also evident in relation to matters of substance in the cause of action. Principally, many of the niceties of the cause of action in the United States and New Zealand are ignored in India, presumably for the reasons of style and focus discussed above. When India is compared to the other two jurisdictions, major differences in substance seem to be directly attributable to the difference in developmental level.

The context of the cause of action has affected the very fundamentals of the cause of action: the rights themselves. In India it has been suggested that the Indian vision of rights has 'its own base in ancient Indian culture and civilisation' and not in western conceptualisations of rights.[126] This may have meant more of a focus on groups in the Constitution than is evident in other cultures.[127] Rights in the United States and New Zealand tend to be more individually oriented, consistent with the general socio-political climate.

The most obvious substantive difference caused by the contextual differences exists in relation to the nature of the plaintiff in the cause of action. Perhaps the most identifiable feature of the Indian cause of action is the existence of public interest litigation; not only has it greatly

123 S Ahuja, *People, Law and Justice: Casebook on PIL*, Vol II (London, Sangam, 1997) 790.

124 Eg *Rudul Sah* (n 6 above); cf *Bivens* (n 6 above) and *Baigent's Case* (n 4 above).

125 See S Sathe, 'Preface' in S Ahuja, *People, Law and Justice: Casebook on Public Interest Law*, Vol I (London, Sangam, 1997) xxxv.

126 A Palai, *National Human Rights Commission of India: Formation, Functioning and Future Prospects* (New Delhi, Khama, 1998) 26.

127 Derrett (n 118 above) 167.

influenced the cause of action, but it has been a factor which has received international attention.[128]

Public interest litigation in India, of course, only exists because a large proportion of the community is unable for reasons of social or economic disadvantage to use the legal system itself.[129] This relates to educational attainment, as much as to income and language, and for these reasons there is a significant difference between India and western countries.[130] In that context, the development of public interest litigation whereby responsibility for rights rests in the community as a whole, rather than simply with the individual rights-holder, is perhaps unsurprising.

Obviously, public interest litigation first developed in the United States despite the great disparity between India and the United States in terms of socio-economic development. The reason for this can perhaps also be attributed to context: at the time that public interest litigation developed in the United States, the socio-economic situation was very different from the contemporary picture. In any event, it is clear that in relative terms there is a much greater continued need for public interest litigation in India now than in the United States.

The decision as to the nature of the remedy and calculation of quantum is perhaps the most discretionary part of the cause of action. As expected, this is an area in which cultural context plays an important part in judicial decisions.

The perception that Indian judges decide to grant the remedy on the basis of 'intuition' and with a sense of 'charity' in mind has been discussed above.[131] This may create a sort of paternalism in the way in which judges determine remedy in India. Specifically, the monetary awards are often directed to be paid in a certain way.[132] Further, the monetary remedy is usually 'interim' which reflects both the urgency associated with these cases, and the judicial concern to provide money to the victims.[133] In the United States and New Zealand, in comparison, perhaps because recipients of awards are likely to be more used to money than those in India, such

128 Eg J Chambers, *et al*, (eds), *Public Interest Litigation Around the World—Report of a Symposium held at Columbia University in May 1991 with Descriptions of Participating Legal Organizations from Twenty Countries* (New York, Columbia Human Rights Law Review, 1992) 7; see also C Baar, 'Social Action Litigation in India: The Opportunities and Limits of the World's Most Active Judiciary' (1992), reproduced in V Jackson and M Tushnet, *Comparative Constitutional Law* (New York, Foundation Press, 1999) 643; J Cassels, 'Judicial Activism and Public Interest Litigation in India' (1989) 37 *Am J Comp L* 495.

129 Eg *Gupta* (n 26 above); *Morcha* (n 26 above).

130 H Dembowski, *Taking the State to Court: Public Interest Litigation and the Public Sphere in Metropolitan India* (New Delhi, OUP, 2001) 49 points to poverty, lack of education and social exclusion as factors that reduce access to the legal system.

131 See Jain (n 121 above) 121; and Ahuja (n 123 above) 790.

132 Eg *PUDR* (n 115 above) 731; *Nilabati* (n 11 above) 2909.

133 Eg *Rudul Sah* (n 6 above); *Gautam v Chakraborty* (1996) 1 SCC 490.

paternalism is not evident in the way in which the monetary remedy is awarded.

Procedural rules especially illustrate the difference that social context has on the cause of action. In the United States, a complex interplay of rules has developed which severely limits the cause of action.[134] In New Zealand, certain procedural aspects of the cause of action have been addressed by the courts. In particular, Cooke P in *Baigent's Case* annexed a statement of claim to his judgment, indicating to future plaintiffs how the cause of action should be pleaded[135]; and it has been held that the Attorney-General should be named as the defendant in these cases.[136] In the United States and New Zealand, there is no social imperative to make it easier to use the cause of action. In India, in comparison, procedural rules have been downplayed. The breadth of the 'epistolary jurisdiction'[137] of the Indian Supreme Court would appear unusual in a country in which the human development index was as high as in New Zealand or the United States. In India the relaxed procedure is the only way in which many people whose rights have been breached are able to have the breach brought to the courts. Procedural rules similar to those in the United States would have a disproportionate effect here, because of the lower levels of literacy and higher levels of poverty in the Indian populace.

Finally, it should be noted that while the majority of the differences referred to in this section compare India with the United States and New Zealand, this is because these are the most striking and not because differences do not exist between the United States and New Zealand. In fact, the different political context, in particular, but also the pure numbers of people and geographical size of the countries cause real differences between the United States and New Zealand causes of action; there are 'particular dilemmas' associated with a 'small scale, intimate society'.[138] In particular, those distinctions may well be reflected in the sort of decisions judges reach in relation to immunity. The small size of the New Zealand population, as well as the high degree of state involvement in the community, may well affect the nature of expectations that people have of government with the consequence that the sort of limitations imposed in the United States are not evident in New Zealand.

134 As immunities apply to almost all officials and entities, the way in which a case is pleaded will determine whether or not it succeeds. This is often a matter of form and not substance: J Jeffries, 'In Praise of the Eleventh Amendment and Section 1983' (1998) 84 *Virg L Rev* 47, 62.

135 *Baigent's Case* (n 4 above) 678–83.

136 *Hobson* (n 35 above).

137 *Mehta* (n 42 above) 1089.

138 *Manga* (n 71 above) 82.

3. What is the Legal Context?

Constitutional rights causes of action cannot be considered in isolation from the rest of the legal system that exists in each jurisdiction.[139] Various aspects of the legal system and, in particular, the judiciary, will influence the decisions that evolve the cause of action:

> No statute, however radical or important its objectives, can be interpreted in isolation from the legal system of which it forms a part. Its meaning will inevitably be dependant, to some degree, on the expectations and preconceptions of those subject to its requirements; and those expectations will rightly be reflected in the process of judicial interpretation.[140]

Perhaps the most important distinction is in relation to the constitutional arrangements of the three jurisdictions. First, both the United States and India have written constitutions, while New Zealand does not. This issue has been discussed in the first section to this chapter and so will not be addressed further. Second, the United States and India are republics, while New Zealand is a constitutional monarchy. Perhaps because of the shared colonial heritage, it is difficult to identify any real effect of the factor on the three jurisdictions.

Third, the apex courts for the United States and India are their Supreme Courts while, at the time that *Baigent's Case* was decided, the apex court for New Zealand was the Privy Council in London.[141] This seems to have had little, if any, impact. The Attorney-General decided, on the Solicitor-General's recommendation, not to appeal *Baigent's Case* from the New Zealand Court of Appeal to the Privy Council. As it is difficult to imagine a judgment that is more far-reaching and clearly contrary to the government's interest than this one, this suggests that for the purposes of Bill of Rights matters, the New Zealand Court of Appeal was in effect the apex court in New Zealand even before the judicial arrangements were changed in 2004. Once again, it seems that the fundamental nature of constitutional rights brings New Zealand into line with the other jurisdictions.

The previous part of this section considered judges as members of the cultural context within which they exist; in this part, judges are considered as members of the legal context within which they take their decisions. Judges will inevitably be influenced in their decisions by the legal system surrounding the decisions. Ultimately, all three jurisdictions have very

139 Factors internal to the cause of action itself will be addressed in the following section.

140 T Allan, *Law, Liberty, and Justice: The Legal Foundations of British Constitutionalism* (Oxford, Clarendon Press, 1993) 79.

141 The right to appeal from New Zealand-based courts to the Judicial Committee of the Privy Council was abolished as from 1 January 2004 with the establishment of the Supreme Court: Supreme Court Act 2003.

similar legal systems as they share the English common law base. While the differences in legal systems are, therefore, fairly minor from an international comparative perspective, differences do exist that may affect legal reasoning.

In New Zealand, it is still possible to 'reason in the traditional way—ie by a conceptual analysis of judgments—while in North America, this is not possible because the sheer volume of reports makes it impossible'.[142] This is the same in India.[143] Inevitably, the large number of cases influences decisions in the ways discussed in the previous section concerning the age of the cause of action. The other side of the coin is that the small number of cases in New Zealand means that individual decisions of principle may have had a disproportionate importance as they are so few and far between.[144]

Any resultant difference in reasoning is not easy to see in the judgments. Nevertheless, it would be surprising if there was not some difference considering that, at a practical level, while it is possible to gather almost all New Zealand cases on a particular topic, it will generally only be possible to gather the more important Indian and United States cases. Inevitably, this will result in different sorts of reasoning.

Another difference relates to the position of the law within society. Both the United States and India have litigious populations and the legal profession is influential in society. In India, the role of lawyers is immense; to an outsider, it appears to be a profession deeply involved in social change. Interestingly, public interest litigation in India had its origins not in a popular, or even professional movement, but in the actions of the judiciary of the Supreme Court and the legal profession.[145] Public interest litigation in India has, primarily, involved cases brought by lawyers on behalf of the rights-holders and not by non-governmental organizations. In fact, in many of the cases, lawyers not only act as representatives or advocates, but are the named parties: 'the strength of Indian public interest law has drawn from the fact that prominent and well-known lawyers have chosen to espouse public interest causes and fight the cases emanating from such causes with tenacity.'[146]

This has meant that public interest litigation has continued to be used aggressively which, in turn, has led to the development of the monetary

142 G Hammona, 'Rethinking Remedies: The Changing Concept of the Relationship Between Legal and Equitable Remedies' in J Berryman, (ed), *Remedies: Issues and Perspectives* (Ontario, Carswell, 1991) 87, 89. Note further the many differences in 'United States' law as a result of federalism: P de Cruz, *Comparative Law in a Changing World* (London, Cavendish, 1995) 109.

143 Baar (n 128 above).

144 In *Manga*, the Court commented on the risk of a disproportionate effect of individual cases in a small democracy like New Zealand: *Manga* (n 71 above) 82.

145 Baar (n 128 above).

146 R Dhavan, 'Promises, Promises ...: Human Rights in India' (1997) 39 *JILI* 149. Cf Baar (n 128 above): No financial support by law firms for public interest litigation in the United States.

remedy through cases which would otherwise not make it to the courts. A cycle has developed, encouraging the usage and development of the cause of action and remedy. This is accentuated by what appears to be a high level of legal awareness in the general population: 'The public are litigious, and knowledge of the complicated processes of law is widespread. Although law is very far from being the whole of life, it is a safe indication of an aspect of life … . India works its law.'[147]

Law in India is seen as a process of social transformation. This may be because the wider socio-political context has meant that 'the court has been compelled to take up issues which ought to have been taken up by other co-ordinate organs of government but had not been done by them'.[148] The judiciary has by no means shied away from this task: it is activist and takes its responsibility in these cases seriously. It seems that, in India, the Supreme Court will intervene by way of the Article 32 petition even when other parts of the law could intervene, but may take longer.[149] Legally, this distinction is important: while in the United States, the Supreme Court enforces the concepts of ripeness and exhaustion of remedies to ensure lower court actions are complete, the Indian Supreme Court will operate on an interim basis, regardless of the status of the case, if it considers that to be appropriate in the circumstances.[150]

A final point concerns the level of corruption in the system. Whereas in New Zealand and the United States there is very little state corruption, in India it appears to be rather more commonplace.[151] In fact, corruption is almost endemic throughout the governmental system which causes a 'strong ambivalence' to the judiciary in the minds of the Indian public.[152] While the public perceive the judiciary as serving the interests of justice, it also widely regards the judiciary as both corrupt and inefficient.[153] In fact, while judges are held in high esteem in India, this may be only in relation to the view held of other societal institutions: this high level of respect is in 'relative and not abstract terms'.[154] The same rumbles of discontent are less audible in New Zealand and the United States.

4. Summary

Clearly, the cultural and legal context of the Section 1983, *Bivens*, Article

147 Derrett (n 118 above) 159.

148 S Sathe, 'Constitutional Law—I (Fundamental Rights)' (1983) XIX *ASIL* 178.

149 This is evident in the way in which the monetary remedy evolved as 'interim' awards of compensation: *Rudul Sah* (n 6 above); *Gautam* (n 133 above).

150 Baar (n 128 above).

151 Kaufmann, *et al* (n 102 above).

152 Dembowski (n 130 above) 47.

153 *Ibid*.

154 *Ibid*, p 56.

32, and *Baigent's Case* causes of action have been influential. This factor seems to account for many of the more obvious differences between the cause of action in India, and those in the United States and New Zealand. Development is the major contextual difference between India and the other two jurisdictions, and seems to have had a significant impact upon the evolution of the cause of action. This section has perhaps shown how the law both is shaped by its context, and is a response to that context.

E. WHAT IS THE INTERNAL CONTEXT OF THE CAUSE OF ACTION?

1. Introduction

There are some decisions that the courts are required to take in each jurisdiction which influence the entire cause of action. The final overarching influence discussed in this chapter concerns the essential nature of the cause of action. The factors considered here are internal to the cause of action and as such they create internal contextual influences on the questions established in the previous chapter.

2. What are the Aims and Rationale?

It is rare that a court will decide, after hearing argument, an authoritative version of the aims and purposes of the cause of action. Rather, it will be developed incrementally and impliedly. In any case, principles are often difficult to identify: 'It is rare [internationally] to find a reasoned decision articulating the principles on which a remedy is afforded. One former Judge of the European Court of Human Rights privately states: "We have no principles". Another judge responds, "We have principles, we just do not apply them".'[155]

Much of this has been discussed in earlier sections, in which the paramouncy of rights was emphasised. The importance of the rights has meant that all three jurisdictions have evolved a cause of action in which to some degree the focus is not on the money, but on the rights.

Nevertheless, the intended aim will be important to determine the ends that the remedy is attempting to meet. Generally, the monetary remedy 'assesses the harm that the misconduct has caused and imposes the cost upon wrongdoer'.[156] Usually, the remedy will attempt to compensate the victim. Occasionally, the remedy will be calculated so as to punish the

155 Shelton (n 91 above) 1.
156 *Ibid*, p 55.

wrongdoer or consciously provide a deterrent. Although this sounds relatively simple, it will not necessarily be so nor will it be value-free. There has been much written from a theoretical perspective about the difference in aims and rationales.[157]

The question of aim principally involves deciding the relative importance of compensation, retribution, deterrence and punishment. In all three jurisdictions, much of the jurisprudence and literature emphasises the vindication of rights, with compensation and deterrence expressed as secondary purposes of the cause of action.[158] In other words, the focus is on the rights. If the aim of the remedy was pure compensation or deterrence, the focus might be expected to fall on either the breach, or the identity of either the person who breaches or the person whose rights are breached.

Judges attempting to calculate a monetary figure to attach to the breach are required to undertake a substantially abstract assessment of each case. The remedial outline may, therefore, become somewhat blurred as judges avoid an exact identification of rationale. This is hardly surprising considering the difficult nature of the task. As the aim of the legal process in fundamental rights breaches will be multi-faceted, the remedy awarded will attempt to encompass all the aims. In fact, it seems that all jurisdictions will utilize a flexible, diverse, set of remedial rationales so that 'Courts can move between the rationales, focusing on the one that supports the most palatable result'.[159]

As the three jurisdictions studied appear to share similar aims and rationales for the remedy, this factor causes few differences between the causes of action. Nevertheless, individual cases may vary in terms of aim, so that the focus shifts to emphasise one or other of the aims. Thus, there are cases which seem to be concerned to punish,[160] deter[161] or compensate.[162] It is possible that the vindication of rights is referred to as the appropriate

157 Eg K Roach, 'Section 24(1) of the Charter: Strategy and Structure' (1986–87) 29 *Crim LQ* 222; D Paccioco, 'The Pragmatic Application of Fundamental Principles: Keeping a Rogues' Charter Respectable' in *The New Zealand Bill of Rights Act 1990* (Auckland, Legal Research Foundation, 1992) 1.

158 Re New Zealand: *Baigent's Case* (n 4 above) 692. Re India: *Khatri* (n 43 above) 630 (first case to discuss monetary remedy which refers to vindication of rights as the purpose); and *Basu* (n 11 above) 317–18, although note the Indian Supreme Court's tendency to award exemplary damages and to attempt to 'civilise' society. Re the United States: *Owen v City of Independence Missouri* 445 US 622, 100 S Ct 1398 (1980); *Robertson v Wegmann* 436 US 584, 98 S Ct 1991 (1978); *Carey* (n 113 above); *Bell* (n 48 above). See Shelton (n 91 above) 55: International discussion of the purposes of remedy and argues for restitution as a primary aim; and S Sturm, 'A Normative Theory of Public Law Remedies' (1991) 79 *Geo LJ* 1355, 1378: 'The widely accepted principle that rights should find vindication in an effective remedy'.

159 Paciocco (n 157 above) 42.

160 Eg *Carey* (n 113 above); *Memphis Community School District v Stachura* 477 US 299, 106 S Ct 2537 (1986); *Hongray* (n 58 above); cf *Kerr v Attorney-General* (Unrep, NP 233/95, DC Timaru Registry, Judge Ryan, 7 August 1996), which was keen not to punish.

161 Eg *Rudul Sah* (n 6 above).

162 Eg *Nilabati* (n 11 above).

aim in other cases in which the court attempts to provide a remedy which encompasses all these aims.[163] A decision that one of the aims should be paramount in all cases, could cause great differences not only in the way in which the remedy is awarded, but also in relation to the decisions taken under the cause of action.[164]

3. How are Principle and Pragmatism Balanced?

The relative importance of principle and pragmatism at the remedial stage is a theoretical distinction with practical effect. This is part of a debate concerning the nature of remedy in general, and its relationship with liability. Every remedial decision will involve both the application of principle and pragmatism. In fact, the search for principle will usually include pragmatic considerations.[165] The question here is the extent to which pragmatic considerations are relevant to the remedy.

Generally speaking, a non-discretionary approach to the remedy means that every time liability is established, the remedy will be awarded. Such an approach reduces the discretionary nature of the remedy by reducing the importance of pragmatic considerations. On the other hand, it may be decided that in the particular case the interests of justice are best served by other factors being considered in the remedial response: this is a more discretionary and more pragmatic approach to remedy.

In relation to the New Zealand Bill of Rights Act, it has been argued that there is a public interest objective in preserving the integrity of the administration of justice which may mean that sometimes no remedy is awarded when the exclusion of evidence is sought.[166] In some cases, therefore, despite liability being established, no remedy will be granted. Pragmatism may be juxtaposed with theory and has a long tradition at English law.[167]

The distinction encompasses the divergence between the idea that rights and remedies should be separated, and the idea that they should be considered to be of equal importance.[168] Often, remedies are seen as being

163 Eg *Baigent's Case* (n 4 above) which is a composite of all the aims.

164 Paciocco (n 157 above) 41.

165 K Cooper-Stephenson, 'Principle and Pragmatism in the Law of Remedies' in J Berryman, (ed), *Remedies: Issues and Perspectives* (Ontario, Carswell, 1991) 3.

166 Paciocco (n 157 above) 41.

167 P Atiyah, *Pragmatism and Theory in English Law* (London, Stevens, 1987) defines pragmatism as 'practice'.

168 Eg D Levinson, 'Rights Essentialism and Remedial Equilibrium' (1999) 99 *Col L Rev* 857; P Birks, 'Rights, Wrongs and Remedies' (2000) 20 *OJLS* 1; and J Beatson, 'The Discretionary Nature of Public Law Remedies' [1991] *NZ Rec L Rev* 81; cf O Fiss, 'The Supreme Court 1978 Term Foreword: The Forms of Justice' (1979) 93 *Harv L Rev* 43; and R Dworkin, *Law's Empire* (London, Fontana, 1986); and S Sturm, 'A Normative Theory of Public Law Remedies' (1991) 79 *Geo LJ* 1355.

secondary to rights.[169] This suggests that while rights are somehow pure, remedies are a more pragmatic means to achieve the ends. Thus, remedial decisions must manage 'the tension between the ideal and the real'.[170]

The effect of this issue extends beyond the remedial stage to substantive decisions under the cause of action: 'this dual aspiration affects both the interpretation of rights and the implementation of remedies when rights are violated'.[171] For example, it seems that both rights and remedies will 'be affected by public attitudes and resistance' so that such resistance becomes relevant to the remedial decision.[172] Thus, a remedy may be considered either from the victim's viewpoint alone, or by taking into account other societal interests.[173]

Jeffries has argued that in the United States context, the 'right-remedy gap' is most obvious in relation to the monetary remedy for constitutional breaches on account of the qualified immunity that means fault is required by officials before they will be held liable.[174] As a result, a remedy will not always be available for breaches of rights. Interestingly, he has argued that limiting the monetary remedy has been positive overall for American constitutional law, because it forces the focus to fall on other, future-based, remedies rather than damages. Despite that, it seems that judges will not always be candid about their decisions in this value-laden area because taking pragmatic decisions is usually seen as less justifiable.[175]

It seems that pragmatism and remedial discretion will mean different things in different legal cultures. In New Zealand and the United States, pragmatism usually means that the remedy will not necessarily be awarded, even where all aspects of the cause of action have been made out. In New Zealand in particular, the theoretical debate has concerned the desirability of limiting the remedy, so that the rights will not be distorted.[176] New Zealand judges appear to be developing a highly discretionary remedial approach. Thus, once it has been established that a right has been breached, the monetary remedy is considered as one of a number of remedial options, from which the most appropriate and effective should not only be chosen, but should be tailored to the particular circumstances of the individual case.

This approach was suggested in *Baigent's Case*[177] and followed in

169 Eg Dworkin (n 168 above).

170 P Gewirtz, 'Remedies and Resistance' (1983) 92 *Yale LJ* 585, 587.

171 *Ibid*. Note Gewirtz focuses on resistance in the context of injunctions in relation to race.

172 *Ibid*, p 589.

173 *Ibid*, p 591.

174 Jeffries (n 34 above) 89.

175 See Gewirtz (n 170 above) 589 who argues that public resistance to court injunctions to prevent racial segregation is a valid consideration for judges, despite their reticence.

176 *Brown* (n 13 above) 349; Paciocco (n 157 above); Thomas (n 41 above); C Walker, 'Wilkes and Liberty: A Critique of the Prima Facie Exclusionary Rule' (1996) 17 *NZULR* 69.

177 This idea comes from the concept of an effective and appropriate remedy: *Baigent's Case* (n 4 above) 692; 718.

Grayson and *Shaheed* concerning the classic exclusionary rule. In *Grayson*, the Court explicitly stated that an appropriate remedy would be one that is 'appropriate to the circumstances of the breach rather than a remedy inflexibly applied in respect of all breaches'.[178] This approach involves the Court taking substantive considerations into account at the remedial stage of a case. In *Shaheed*, the Court held that 'the proper approach is to conduct a balancing exercise'.[179] As a result, those considerations that were not factored into the analysis at the earlier stages, such as delay in bringing the case[180] or the defendant and plaintiff's fault and intention, will be considered at the remedial stage.

It is possible, therefore, that in some cases either a very limited amount of money will be awarded, or no money, if the judge considers a declaration to be the best solution in all the circumstances.[181] Theoretically, this approach allows the rights and the cause of action to remain unfettered, while leaving pragmatic decisions for the remedial stage.[182]

In the United States, this debate has principally focussed around the best way in which the 'ideal-real' element of the cause of action and remedy may be managed. The United States courts have considered how a remedy can best achieve its intention, even if that means that the remedy will not be awarded as expected.[183] Thus, the public interest, as well as the public's opinions, will be relevant for the remedy. The United States remedial approach differs from the New Zealand approach in that there are many threshold issues which will often prevent cases from reaching the remedial stage. Unsurprisingly, such substantive issues are not then considered relevant at remedy. A more restricted approach to what amounts to a breach of a right may mean that some decisions are taken earlier in the United States than in New Zealand and India where they will be taken at the remedial stage of the cause of action.

In India, the debate about principle and pragmatism seems to have focussed around a different issue. The use of interim awards has meant that the monetary remedy has been awarded in India even where, on a pure legal analysis, it should not be.[184] Judges have clearly been concerned

178 *Grayson* (n 53 above) 412. See also *Upton v Green and Attorney-General (2)* (Unrep, HC Chch Registry, Tompkins J, 10 October 1996) 20–23, in which this approach was utilized to some extent.

179 *R v Shaheed* [2002] 2 NZLR 377, 122.

180 *Ibid.*

181 *Dunlea* [2000] 3 NZLR 136, 149–51.

182 See Thomas (n 41 above) and Paciocco (n 157 above), both of whom suggest that remedy is the appropriate place to incorporate pragmatism in order to protect a principled response to the BORA and to the wider public interest. In particular, Paciocco argues that it is neither 'new nor offensive' for the Court to refuse to grant a remedy for breach of the Bill of Rights Act because the breach is trifling, the complainant contributed to the breach or it is against the public interest.

183 Gewirtz (n 170 above); Fiss (n 168 above).

184 Eg *Gautam* (n 133 above). See S Jain, 'Money Compensation for Administrative Wrongs through Article 32' (1983) 25 *JILI* 118, 121; Ahuja (Vol II) (n 123 above) 790.

to ensure justice is met in this way. In India, pragmatism and discretion in relation to the remedy have been used to justify widening the scope of remedies, rather than reduce it as is done in the United States and New Zealand. Further, money is awarded in a discretionary manner so that payments are often made in a particular way that the court thinks best in the circumstances of the particular case.[185] The monetary remedy in India has developed as a flexible approach to be used to ensure justice is reached.

In summary, it seems that this very theoretical issue has practical impact. Not only will the sort of remedy, and quantum, be affected but so will the entire nature of the cause of action. It seems that the theoretical debate, in whichever phraseology it is described and however it is finally decided, raises the essential decision as to the width of the cause of action. Most causes of action are likely to be fettered in some way: either through the threshold issues, such as in the United States, or through a wide remedial discretion, such as in New Zealand. The importance of practical considerations in determining remedy is one that will differ between jurisdictions, but also between judges within jurisdictions and between cases.

4. Is it a Public or Private Cause of Action?

The judicial approach to liability has influenced the cause of action in each jurisdiction. This section considers the impact of the fact that the cause of action exists at the intersection of public and private law. While constitutional rights are usually pure public law, a monetary remedy, on the other hand, is usually private:

> I regard public law as being the system which enforces the proper performance by public bodies of the duties which they owe to the public. I regard private law as being the system which protects the private rights of private individuals or the private rights of public bodies. The critical distinction arises out of the fact that it is the public as a whole ... who are the beneficiaries of what is protected by public law and it is the individuals or bodies entitled to the rights who are the beneficiaries of the protection provided by private law.[186]

Although the cause of action sounds in a monetary remedy, and so is markedly different from traditional public law causes of action in common law jurisdictions, it is equally different from traditional tort law causes of action on account of its constitutional nature. The cause of action is public to the extent that it is, generally speaking, only actionable against public entities and in relation to the breach of constitutional or similar guarantees

185 Eg *PUDR* (n 115 above) 731; *Nilabati* (n 11 above) 2909.
186 Lord Woolf, 'Public Law—Private Law: Why the Divide?' [1986] *PL* 220, 221.

of fundamental rights. It is private to the extent that it concerns liability for breach and the remedy of money. The cause of action is a hybrid of the two systems, a matter which is relevant to the questions structuring the cause of action.

In the United States, the causes of action are classified as 'constitutional torts' and are considered to be a subset of the general state and federal tort liability.[187] The causes of action are not in any way exceptional, but are a normal part of the legal arrangements in the jurisdiction. Although the constitutional element is clearly essential to a full understanding of the causes of action, they fit within the general law of liability in the United States. As such, their boundaries are moulded from, and influenced by, the general tort liability. The scope of the causes of action is consistent with general tort liability in the United States. This is particularly obvious in relation to the question of immunities. By positioning the United States causes of action within tort law, the general liability rules are clearly relevant to the question of which immunities should apply to public officials sued under Section 1983 or *Bivens*.

In comparison, the New Zealand and Indian causes of action are separate from questions of tort liability and no such middle category of constitutional tort exists. These causes of action are constitutional causes of action, existing at public law and not tort law. In both jurisdictions, there are explicit statements to this effect, and the cause of action is seen as something of a novelty.[188] This means that the elements of the cause of action are moulded in a unique way, without the need to be consistent with other causes of action in either jurisdiction.

The distinction is equally clear when immunities are considered. In India, where the cause of action is somewhat separated from tort law, the courts decided that the usual immunities would not apply to this sort of case.[189] In New Zealand, where the separation from tort law is conceptually complete, the first cases developing the cause of action explicitly held that tort law immunities would not apply.[190] This was an essential distinction in New Zealand as, if the cause of action had been at civil law, then the usual statutory immunities would have applied and no liability would have existed. Thus, in New Zealand, the cause of action's existence relied upon it being categorized as a public, rather than private, law cause of action.

Interestingly, even in New Zealand and India, tort law has some effect. It seems generally accepted that tort law is the starting point for decisions

187 R Clayton, *et al*, *The Law of Human Rights* (Oxford, OUP, 2000) 1417.
188 *Baigent's Case* (n 4 above); *Nilabati* (n 11 above); and *Basu* (n 11 above).
189 *Nilabati* (n 11 above); and *Basu* (n 11 above).
190 *Baigent's Case* (n 4 above); and *AUWRC* (n 50 above). *Whithair* (n 22 above) held that a good faith liability would not apply.

under the cause of action.[191] In both New Zealand and India, tort law guidelines are used to calculate quantum and in New Zealand it has been suggested that monetary relief will not differ from common law tort awards.[192] Likewise, in the United States, public law elements are relevant in relation to the way in which rights are approached: this is clearly a composite cause of action.

Nonetheless, it is clear that the question of immunities has, to all intents and purposes, determined the width of the cause of action and so the practical availability of the remedy. As civil law causes of action, the United States causes of action are exceptional liability granted by the state and federal governments and so are constrained. As aspects of constitutional human rights law, the Indian and New Zealand causes of action are part of a 'higher order' of causes of action, are wide, and are practised in a rarefied context.

A final point returns to the idea of an international human rights common law. It is possible that a jurisdiction's emphasis on public law, rather than private law, might be attributable partially to the time at which the cause of action developed. For example, at the time the cause of action developed in the United States, such a remedy was, at least, unusual. It may not be surprising, in that context, that the cause of action was classed within an existing part of the legal pantheon.

By the time that the cause of action developed in India and in New Zealand, a cause of action sounding in a monetary remedy for breach of domestic constitutional rights was fairly usual, as was the existence of domestic constitutional rights. The emergence of many causes of action as novel causes of action at public law became the expected approach. It is interesting that both New Zealand and Indian cases make much use of comparative material in relation to the positioning of the causes of action at public law, thus avoiding the limitations of tort law.[193] In discussing the likely approach to be taken to this aspect of the monetary remedy under the United Kingdom Human Rights Act, it has been suggested that 'the "public law" analysis is more consistent with the case law relating to other jurisdictions'.[194] It seems that what may have been unknown at the time the United States causes of action developed, unusual when the Indian cause of action developed, and usual when the New Zealand cause of action developed, has now become expected as the English cause of action

191 In *J* (n 115 above), the New Zealand High Court chose not to rule upon the Crown's submission that the common law elements of a tort cause of action should be used as a starting point in defining the *Baigent's Case* cause of action. Shelton (n 91 above) 57 notes that internationally most causes of action are built around a framework of tort.

192 *Manga* (n 71 above) 84; *Attorney-General v Hewitt* [2000] 2 NZLR 111, 127.

193 See especially the use by *Baigent's Case* (n 4 above) of *Maharaj v Attorney-General of Trinidad and Tobago* [1979] AC 385.

194 Clayton (n 187 above) 1419.

develops. Once again, the international human rights common law is an influential intervening factor.

5. How is Comparative Jurisprudence Integrated?

The final aspect cuts to the heart of this book which is, after all, comparative. Having decided that the international human rights common law will have a significant effect on the cause of action, the tension between comparative law and indigenous jurisprudence within each jurisdiction is especially important.[195] In India, this tension is especially clear in the judgments:

> This Court has held that the provisions of the American Constitution cannot always be applied to Indian conditions or to the provisions of our Constitution. While some of the principles adumbrated by the American decisions may provide a useful guide yet this Court did not favour a close adherence to those principles while applying the same to the provisions of our Constitution, because the social conditions in this country are different.[196]

Clearly, each jurisdiction is unique. This must be beyond argument following the discussion in this chapter of the impact of context on the causes of action. It is equally clear, however, that much of modern constitutional rights law is highly comparative.

Despite comments such as that above, even in relation to the Article 32 writ jurisdiction in India, much of the discussion is comparative.[197] This is especially so in the latest cases of principle. In *Basu*, in fact, the circle is complete: the Indian Supreme Court quoted a passage of the New Zealand Court of Appeal in *Baigent's Case* that cited the Indian case law.[198] The Supreme Court judges felt it important at this point in the development of the cause of action, to support their decisions by reference to decisions of other apex domestic courts internationally. It seems that the use of comparative law has increased over time in India.[199]

The New Zealand cause of action is particularly comparative. Judgments from around the world were generously cited in the *Baigent's Case* decision.[200] The Court of Appeal seems to have had no concerns

[195] This is part of the general international debate concerning the 'globalisation of law': eg Claude (n 88 above) x.

[196] *Air India v Nergesh Meerza* AIR 1981 SC 1829, 1852. See also *Mehta* (n 42 above) 1097: The limits of United States' imports and the need to 'Indianise' international material.

[197] P Tripathi, 'Foreign Precedents and Constitutional Law' (1957) 57 *Col L Rev* 319.

[198] *Basu* (n 11 above) 316–17.

[199] Much of the jurisprudence expressing concern with comparative material occurred earlier than those judgments using such material.

[200] *Baigent's Case* (n 4 above) 699–702 referring to international law, *Maharaj* (n 193 above), Indian, Irish, United States, and Canadian decisions.

about the relevance of citing such judgments, despite such comparative material being based on entirely different constitutional arrangements. Comparative law in this jurisdiction was used to justify the development of the cause of action as well as, to a lesser extent, in the more important decisions of principle since then.[201] In fact, the suggestion in *Baigent's Case* is that comparative material will be especially relevant in such 'big picture' decisions, and less so in determining the details of the cause of action which may be rather more context-specific.[202]

Comparative law has been of rather less use in the United States than in New Zealand and India:

> despite the increasing 'internationalisation' of human rights law over recent decades, the American courts have paid almost no regard to international human rights instruments or case law from other jurisdictions. They have instead developed a strong indigenous tradition over 200 years which has become insulated from developments elsewhere.[203]

This may be attributable to the fact that the causes of action in the United States are considerably older than other common law causes of action.[204] As such, there was not much comparative material to draw upon in the early years of its development in the United States. As was seen above, it seems that comparative material is used most often in relation to the development of the cause of action and in relation to decisions of principle.

Since then, of course, a large body of comparative domestic law has developed in relation to the cause of action. Nevertheless, the United States has not developed a culture of comparative law, perhaps because the issues of principle have been decided already. Further, as the Supreme Court is an arbiter of differences between the state courts, importing further comparative material to such decisions would not necessarily be of assistance. This has not been the case in India, in which the Supreme Court has not been concerned with issues of state autonomy in relation to such causes of action.

Clearly, the use of comparative material in domestic jurisprudence will affect the causes of action. At its most basic, the use of comparative juris-

201 Eg *Grayson* (n 53 above); *Dunlea* (n 181 above) 150–51.

202 *Baigent's Case* (n 4 above) 677: Remedies implied from the Bill of Rights Act do not differ *in nature* from remedies explicitly authorised by statute. In relation to the new Hong Kong Bill of Rights, it has been suggested that as areas of the law are 'explored', there is 'less need' for comparative analysis: Y Ghai, 'Sentinels of Liberty or Sheep in Woolf's Clothing? Judicial Politics and the Hong Kong Bill of Rights' (1997) 60 *MLR* 459, 479.

203 Clayton (n 187 above) 9. E Mearns, 'Emerging Trends in International Constitutionalism: A Comparative Approach' (1996) 28 *Case Western J Intl L* 1 states that there is an attitude in the United States that it has 'little to learn from countries whose constitutions have not reached the two-century mark'.

204 McCrudden (n 1 above) 524 suggests that the longer a country is from independence, the less resort is made to comparative material.

prudence will determine the level to which causes of action will resemble one another. For example, the United States jurisprudence is not only less likely to use comparative material, but is more likely to find that its own jurisprudence is of limited use internationally.[205] It is, as a result, rather different from many other jurisdictions. Further, it seems that the level to which judges will consider comparative material will affect their ability to take decisions that may appear eccentric within their own jurisdiction.[206]

This is particularly clear in relation to the question of immunities. The courts in New Zealand and India took exceptionally unfettered approaches, possibly due to the development of similar stances in other jurisdictions.[207] Likewise, the use of comparative material enabled New Zealand judges to position the cause of action at public law, rather than at civil law.[208] Without the use of the comparative jurisprudence, this may have seemed a cynical ploy by the *Baigent's Case* judges to avoid the statutory Crown immunity in New Zealand that would have applied to a private law cause of action.

It is likely that the use of comparative jurisprudence has an international effect. By this I mean that the move towards a more similar cause of action, internationally, will be increased as jurisdictions increasingly draw upon comparative materials. This emphasises the 'natural' element of constitutional rights, even when they are protected by domestic law and not by international treaty. In turn, this will make the use of comparative material more likely. Once again, the way in which United States decisions are somewhat separate from other common law jurisdictions is a clear example of this in practice.

Obviously, these causes of action are part of domestic law and ought not to be clones of an international standard cause of action. On the other hand, these causes of action are often developed in response to the jurisdiction's need to develop such a cause of action to fulfil its obligations at international law and, to do so, must conform to international standards to some extent.[209] The balance between international and domestic considerations, comparative and indigenous jurisprudence, is likely to be one that continues to evolve as the number of domestic causes of action grows.

Three things are clear. First, comparative material is of great use in the development of constitutional rights law domestically.[210] Judges seem to

205 Clayton (n 187 above) 10.

206 A Gubbay, 'Foreword' [1996] 1 *CHRLD* I: Comparative material will avoid parochial experience or foibles of individual judges.

207 Both jurisdictions made comparative analysis on this point: Eg *Nilabati* (n 11 above) and *Basu* (n 11 above).

208 *Baigent's Case* (n 4 above).

209 *Ibid*, p 700: International treaties mean that New Zealand courts are obligated to provide a monetary remedy at domestic law for breach of human rights.

210 McCrudden (n 1 above) 501.

accept that case law from other jurisdictions will assist in developing the cause of action and remedy in their own jurisdiction:

> It is beyond argument that judicial decisions emanating from Commonwealth courts, whose reputation for the advancement of human rights is high, provide invaluable information and guidance. They point to progressive changes and innovations in international human rights law with which a municipal judge should strive, where possible, to bring domestic law into harmony. A judicial decision has greater legitimacy and will command more respect if it accords with international norms that have been accepted by many jurisdictions, than if it is based upon the parochial experience or foibles of a particular judge or court.[211]

Nevertheless, comparative material may only be used if it is considered in light of indigenous factors. As judges in India described the process, it is necessary to 'Indianise' and 'harmoniously blend' the comparative material with Indian constitutional jurisprudence.[212] This means that judges will choose from which jurisdiction they wish to borrow. Such choices will be made on many grounds.[213] Judges will also choose which judgments to use; there is a suggestion that only those decisions that support the result preferred by the court will be invoked and otherwise foreign decisions will be dismissed as irrelevant.[214] This inclination accentuates the argument that an international consensus exists.

Second, the more that a comparative jurisprudence is developed internationally, the more difficult it is for jurisdictions to avoid using it for domestic determination of this cause of action and remedy. In other words, a sort of impetus develops which is hard to avoid; judges will appear to be taking decisions based not upon the internationally accepted human rights norms, but upon 'parochial experience or foibles', as was suggested in the quotation above by the Chief Justice of Zimbabwe.

Finally, causes of action that develop without reference to comparative material are likely to develop in a significantly different way from the bulk of other such causes of action. Thus, comparative material is less likely to be of use in the future and so the jurisdiction will continue to develop in what may appear to be a more eccentric manner. As a result, the case law in that jurisdiction will not be greatly utilised by other jurisdictions, thus perpetuating the exclusion from the international comparative law. The United States case law exemplifies this point.

211 Gubbay (n 206 above).
212 *Mehta* (n 42 above) 1097 re the definition of 'state'.
213 McCrudden (n 1 above).
214 Ghai (n 202 above) 197.

6. Summary

Certain 'big picture' legal decisions taken by the judiciary in relation to the cause of action will affect the elements of the cause of action and remedy. Aim and rationale may be of great importance theoretically but, interestingly, may have little, if any, practical impact. The relative weighting of principle and pragmatism at the point when the decision as to remedy is taken will be essential. This aspect will greatly impact upon individual decisions which are often impossible to categorise according to strict rational criteria. The positioning of the cause of action at public or private law will have a great impact in terms of both theory and practice: big issues like immunities will largely be determined by this matter. Finally, the use of comparative material is probably unavoidable in modern causes of action, but courts will need to identify how such material will fit into the individual legal system.

F. CONCLUSION

This chapter has provided a discussion of four overarching influences on the way in which jurisdictions answer the questions posed in the previous chapter. These influences operate through a complex interplay, so that some features are more important than others both for specific issues and for certain jurisdictions. The net effect of this chapter has been to show that causes of action can only develop by means of an interplay between the questions that provide a generic structure, and the specificities of the particular jurisdiction.

An interesting side-product of this discussion has been the evaluation of what has been termed an international comparative human rights common law. Such an international consensus may explain the similarities between jurisdictions, despite the significant differences that exist. Conversely, the substance of domestic remedies seem to be influenced by when in the development of the international common law the particular remedy developed; this provides part of the explanation of the differences between causes of action.

There is, of course, nothing exceptionally surprising about the idea of an international human rights common law. In a recent article, McCrudden has assessed the 'meaning and significance' of judges using comparative material in domestic constitutional rights decisions as this has become a commonplace feature.[215] This book has commented on its existence and its great impact on the nature of the domestic monetary remedy for breach of constitutional rights.

215 McCrudden (n 1 above) 499.

The analysis has illustrated the way in which to some extent a common understanding of constitutional rights law has evolved internationally. Simply put, it seems that nations share a general sense of how breaches of constitutional rights should be remedied. In relation to constitutional judicial review, for example, it has been suggested that the Canadian Supreme Court 'has read the Charter in the same way Bills of Rights have been interpreted all over the world'; the judges have developed 'the same set of principles and analytical framework' as are used by other domestic judges throughout the world.[216] The shared approach to the monetary remedy seen in this book appears to have evolved over time and to have responded to developments in jurisdictions and internationally.

216 D Beatty, 'The Canadian Charter of Rights: Lessons and Laments' [1997] 60 *MLR* 481.

PART III

TURNING THE ANALYSIS AROUND

7

The United Kingdom Human Rights Act 1998

A. INTRODUCTION

UP UNTIL THIS point, the book has established a framework of four common questions that structure the cause of action at a general level, and another four overarching influences that will affect the answers given to the four common questions. Together, this taxonomy described the causes of action in the United States, India and New Zealand. At this point, the analysis is turned around to apply this generalized framework to causes of action other than those from which it was inferred. The intention of this chapter is to consider whether the taxonomy may be used to explain jurisdictions beyond the three from which it was developed.

To this end, the new cause of action for breach of human rights sounding in the monetary remedy in England, contained in Section 8 of the Human Rights Act 1998, is considered. The Human Rights Act 1998 incorporates most of the rights set out in the European Convention on Human Rights ('the ECHR') into United Kingdom domestic law and explicitly provides for a monetary remedy should rights be breached. It received royal assent on 8 November 1998, came into force in its entirety on 2 October 2000; and the first House of Lords case providing pointers on the availability of the monetary remedy was decided in 2005.[1]

To recap, the generic structure developed in the preceding analysis involves four questions concerning what the cause of action protects, who it protects, who it is directed against, and what the court orders. These four questions all have sub-questions, the relative weight of which—not to mention the answers given to each—will vary between jurisdictions dependent on over-arching influences. While the meat of the structure will only be determined by the cases as they develop, pointers can be identified by the over-arching influences. The framework will operate as a generic tool by identifying the influences in a particular jurisdiction and then 'applying' them to the structure.

1 *R v Secretary of State for the Home Department, ex parte Greenfield* [2005] UKHL 14.

There are strong suggestions that the framework, drawn as it has been from Commonwealth jurisdictions, will be of use in England in relation to the categorisation of the cause of action as it continues to develop. As the Law Commission stated in its attempt to provide information to assist in the eventual use of the damages remedy in the United Kingdom, '[t]he apparently simple exercise required by Section 8 is, on analysis, an unfamiliar one to English and Scottish courts'.[2] Lord McClusky, in the House of Lords debates on the Human Rights Act, emphasised the likely comparative element of litigation under the Act: 'In future no lawyer will be able to advise a client on any matter which might involve a public authority without studying not just the European jurisprudence ... but also American case law, Canadian case law, and even Indian case law and Australian and New Zealand case law.'[3]

The generic structure developed in the preceding chapters is an easily accessible synthesis of the case law of three of those jurisdictions. In addition to providing a framework for the early cases and debates, it suggests paths along which the cause of action may develop in the future in England.

As 'the primary duty of setting the parameters of the damages remedy falls upon the Courts' under the Human Rights Act,[4] it would be futile to pretend to predict the outcome of the interplay of the overarching influences with the generic structure. The framework produces an outline of the questions with which lawyers and judges are likely to be faced in the early years of the Human Rights Act and so focuses the inevitable debates that will occur. Rather than second guessing the 'avalanche' of writing already commenting on the strengths, weaknesses and likely outcomes of the Human Rights Act and the monetary remedy,[5] this survey provides a unified scheme against which both earlier commentaries and cases and future ones can be assessed.[6]

The chapter will, therefore, identify some of the overarching influences that could be expected to be raised, and consider what effect they may have on each of the questions that structure the cause of action. In other words, in application it is necessary to turn the analysis around, and tackle the overarching influences first, as they are the conduit through which the structure must be considered.

[2] Law Commission and Scottish Law Commission, *Damages Under the Human Rights Act 1998* (Law Com No 266, Scot Law Com No 180, 2000).

[3] HL Debs, Vol 582, col 1268 (3 November 1997) quoted in C McCrudden, 'A Common Law of Human Rights? Transnational Judicial Conversations on Constitutional Rights' (2000) 20 *OJLS* 499, 505.

[4] D Fairgrieve, 'The Human Rights Act 1998, Damages and Tort Law' [2001] *PL* 695, 696.

[5] D Scorey and T Eicke, *Human Rights Damages* (London, Sweet & Maxwell, 2002) v.

[6] See especially Law Commission (n 2 above); Fairgrieve (n 4 above); M Amos, 'Damages for Breach of the Human Rights Act 1998' [1999] *EHRLR* 178; and Scorey and Eicke (n 5 above).

B. COMPLETING THE FRAMEWORK: THE OVERARCHING INFLUENCES

1. Introduction

This section will highlight what appear to be the most important aspects of the four overarching influences in England. It will then be possible to picture in more detail the likely answers to the common questions describing the cause of action and remedy.

2. The Nature of the Foundation Document

This influence encompasses the issues surrounding the document out of which the cause of action developed and upon which the rights are based. The nature of the document has been relevant in relation to the sort of cause of action that has developed and its specific details in the three jurisdictions studied.

England has no written Constitution and, until recently, had no modern Bill of Rights. The cause of action and remedy will be founded in the Human Rights Act which is based on the ECHR. The nature of these two documents will affect all aspects of the cause of action.

The Human Rights Act is neither entrenched nor fundamental law, yet it arguably should 'be characterised as a constitutional instrument'.[7] Its purpose was to incorporate the ECHR into domestic law and as such it principally repeats the provisions of the Convention. Of special significance to a study of remedy is one of the ways in which it differs: Article 13 which provides a right to an effective remedy has been excluded from the Human Rights Act.

This means that relief under the Human Rights Act is discretionary.[8] Nevertheless, the government has argued that the remedial sections of the Act provide sufficiently for an effective remedy.[9] It has been suggested that the remedial provisions of the Human Rights Act may be interpreted so as to meet the requirements of Article 13 of the Convention.[10]

There are two remedial powers in the Act. The first is in relation to legislation, and involves the power to recommend that such legislation that is incompatible with the rights and freedoms guaranteed should be

[7] R Clayton, *et al*, *The Law of Human Rights* (Oxford, OUP, 2000) 67; see also Lord Cooke, 'The British Embracement of Human Rights' (1999) 3 *EHRLR* 243, 244 who describes the Human Rights Act as part of a 'constitutional revolution' in the United Kingdom.

[8] Clayton (n 7 above) 147.

[9] *Ibid.*

[10] D Feldman, 'Remedies for Violations of Convention Rights Under the Human Rights Act' [1998] *EHRLR* 691, 692.

overruled. The second is in relation to actions of 'public authorities'. This is the area within which the monetary remedy exists.

The remedial provision itself is Section 8:

> (1) In relation to any act (or proposed act) of a public authority which the court finds is (or would be) unlawful, it may grant such relief or remedy, or make such order, within its powers as it considers just and appropriate.
>
> (2) But damages may be awarded only by a court which has power to award damages, or to order the payment of compensation, in civil proceedings.
>
> (3) No award of damages is to be made unless, taking account of all the circumstances of the case, including—
>
> (a) any other relief or remedy granted, or order made, in relation to the act in question (by that or any other court), and
>
> (b) the consequences of any decision (of that or any other court) in respect of that act, the court is satisfied that the award is necessary to afford just satisfaction to the person in whose favour it is made.
>
> (4) In determining—
>
> (a) whether to award damages, or
>
> (b) the amount of an award, the court must take into account the principles applied by the European Court of Human Rights in relation to the award of compensation under Article 41 of the Convention.

Prima facie, the statute makes it unlawful for a public authority to act in a way which is incompatible with a Convention right.[11] While the monetary remedy is not available in relation to acts of the legislature, a public authority is defined to include Courts and 'any person certain of whose functions are functions of a public nature'.[12] The statute makes it clear that a person will not be considered a public authority, even if their functions are of a public nature, if the nature of the act in question is 'private'.[13]

The Human Rights Act will apply, therefore, to the Courts, but an immunity is provided for judicial actions taken in good faith. The only exception to the definition of public authority is the two Houses of Parliament. It seems that liability will be vicarious, so that an individual will not be liable unless she or he is also a public authority—it is the public

11 S 6(1).
12 Ss 6(3) and 6(6).
13 S 6(5).

authority that will be liable.[14] A debate has arisen as to the extent that the Act will apply 'horizontally', to private actions.[15]

The public authority will not be liable for a breach of a Convention right if it was unable to act differently in accordance with primary legislation.[16] An act will include, other than in relation to the introduction of legislation, the failure to act.[17] The wide definition of 'act' that has been adopted is likely to include decision-making and policy.[18] The statute allows the victim to bring proceedings directly under the Human Rights Act, or to choose to rely upon the Convention in other legal proceedings.[19] Thus, the European Court's jurisprudence will be of indirect influence also.

To be a 'victim', one must be a victim pursuant to Article 34 of the Convention as brought before the European Court of Human Rights.[20] The 'victim' requirement may restrict the cause of action, as public interest litigation may not be possible, beyond assistance for particular individuals and by the use of amicus briefs.[21] The European Court will not hear abstract challenges or hypothetical breaches: 'The test applied by the Court is that the applicant must show that he or she has been personally or directly affected by the alleged Convention violation'.[22]

The statute makes it clear that the money awarded should be considered damages, which may include within it the concept of compensation. Mirroring the Strasbourg jurisprudence, the Act requires the Court to consider the totality of the remedial picture when making a damages award.[23] Damages awards will be 'residual', in that they will be available only if necessary to afford just satisfaction.[24] The Human Rights Act requires the domestic courts to consider the Strasbourg jurisprudence as they develop the remedy, and only courts which currently have the power to award damages will be able to award the remedy.

14 C Baker, (ed), *Human Rights Act 1998: A Practitioner's Guide* (London, Sweet & Maxwell, 1998) 23.

15 B Markesinis, 'Privacy, Freedom of Expression, and the Horizontal Effect of the Human Rights Bill: Lessons from Germany' (1999) 115 *LQR* 47; R Buxton, 'Horizons of Horizontality' (2000) 116 *LQR* 217; M Hunt, 'The "Horizontal Effect" of the Human Rights Act' [1998] *PL* 423; G Phillipson, 'The Human Rights Act, "Horizontal Effect" and the Common Law: A Bang or a Whimper?' (1999) 62 *MLR* 824; and D Oliver, 'The Human Rights Act and Public Law/Private Law Divides' [2000] *EHRLR* 343 re the United Kingdom.

16 S 6(2).

17 S 6(6).

18 Baker (n 14 above) 23.

19 S 7.

20 *Ibid.*

21 Baker (n 14 above) 25; Feldman (n 10 above) 696. Although cf P Leach, *Taking a Case to the European Court of Human Rights* (London, Blackstone, 2001) 62: '[T]he European Court rules relating to capacity and standing are not restrictive'. Art 34 allows for applications by individuals, non-governmental organizations and groups of individuals.

22 Leach (n 21 above) 68–69.

23 Baker (n 14 above) 26.

24 I Leigh and L Lustgarten, 'Making Rights Real: The Courts, Remedies, and the Human Rights Act' (1999) 58 *CLJ* 509, 527; Fairgrieve (n 4 above) 697.

In summary, Section 8 of the Human Rights Act means that the remedy in the United Kingdom 'must be just, appropriate, necessary to afford just satisfaction and perhaps even effective'.[25] Although the boundaries of the remedy are set out in statute, it is by no means clear how it will develop and speculation has been rife.[26]

In terms of impact upon the remedy in England, the first point to note in relation to this overarching influence is that much of the scope of the cause of action has been statutorily defined. In common with the Section 1983 cause of action in the United States, many elements were decided at its inception and, in this aspect, the English remedy will differ from those in India or New Zealand. Not only does the Human Rights Act set out answers to specific questions about the cause of action, but it also provides direction as to how the courts ought to approach matters.

Nevertheless, the amount of discussion now in the United Kingdom on the details of even those points that have been set out in the Human Rights Act show that it is not that simple[27]; statutory interpretation allows for almost as many points of view as defining an implied cause of action. As was stated in a discussion of the use of foreign precedent in constitutional law, '[e]ven the most exhaustive attempts at codification leave scope for authoritative interpretation'.[28] Further, the cause of action set out in Section 8 leaves many issues to be resolved. In fact: 'The brevity of the statutory language means that the primary duty of setting the parameters of the damages remedy falls upon the courts.'[29]

The uncertainty of the parameters may be especially marked in the case of fundamental rights decisions. As one English judge noted prior to the Human Rights Act coming into force, in the United States interpretative questions extend beyond settling details to determining 'whether on the constitution's true interpretation the right claimed exists at all'.[30] Whether or not the United Kingdom courts choose to take such a wide view of their role in constitutional interpretation, some aspects of the ambit of the rights, the cause of action and the remedial jurisdiction will be developed through the case law.[31]

This means that it may not be easy to predict with certainty individual elements in the cause of action. The English cause of action will, regardless

25 Amos (n 6 above) 194.

26 Eg Law Commission (n 2 above); Amos (n 6 above); Feldman (n 10 above); Leigh and Lustgarten (n 24 above); R Carnwarth, 'ECHR Remedies from a Common Law Perspective' (2000) 49 *ICLQ* 517.

27 Eg the Human Rights Act sets out the identity of the plaintiff and defendant, and provides guidelines for the calculation of quantum. Despite that, there has been much discussion about what amounts to a 'just and appropriate' remedy, and whether the Act will apply horizontally or vertically.

28 D Tripathi, 'Foreign Precedents and Constitutional Law' (1957) 57 *Col L Rev* 319.

29 Fairgrieve (n 4 above) 696.

30 *R v Lord Chancellor, ex p Witham* [1997] 2 All ER 779, 783.

31 Eg definition of public authority.

of the niceties of parliamentary sovereignty, be largely judicially created and judicial interpretations cannot be conclusively predicted. If the first impression was that statutory context matters in the scope of the cause of action, then this conclusion 'blurs' the edges somewhat.

The comparative analysis of the United States, India and New Zealand raised another point that in some ways is an outright contradiction of the judicial freedom in interpreting provisions, as well as of the importance of statutory context: ultimately, similar conclusions were reached about the causes of action in these three jurisdictions. This was most obvious in relation to the two United States causes of action which are almost identical despite the different statutory basis. In relation to the question of who can be sued, for example, the four causes of action have roughly reached the same conclusion whether or not there is a statutory basis, explicit or otherwise, for that.

In England, this pull to commonality may be exacerbated by the fact that the Human Rights Act was drafted with reference to the experience of other jurisdictions, notably Canada and New Zealand. In fact, it has been suggested that Section 8 of the Human Rights Act makes 'explicit that which the New Zealand court found to be implicit' in *Baigent's Case*; '[i]t is certainly more articulate'.[32] Thus, the actual statutory wording is closer to the commonly accepted end product.

A further point is that English courts have a statutory direction in the Human Rights Act to utilize comparative materials under the ECHR. While it is inevitable that it will be greatly influenced by its common law context, the different focus and starting point of examinations under this statute may well result in conclusions that differ from the common law. The English approach to the cause of action may be different from the other jurisdictions studied, therefore, as none of them have drawn upon the European civil law tradition which is an important part of the European jurisprudence. Having said that, cases decided before the enactment of the Human Rights Act suggest that in many instances, there will be little difference between decisions under the common law and those under the Convention.[33] The overall point remains, however, that the cause of action in the United Kingdom is likely to be very comparative, particularly in relation to the Strasbourg Court's jurisprudence, on account of the statutory direction. As the House of Lords stated in *Greenfield*, '[i]t is, therefore, to Strasbourg that British courts must look for guidance on the award of damages'.[34]

In relation to the specificities, the reference to the well-defined jurispru-

32 Lord Cooke (n 7 above) 257.

33 *Derbyshire CC v Times Newspapers* [1993] AC 534 (HL).

34 *Greenfield* (n 1 above) para 6; cf *Anufrijeva v London Borough of Southwark* [2003] EWCA Civ 1406, para 52 which states that due regard should be given to the Strasbourg jurisprudence, but that it will provide only 'limited' assistance.

dence under the ECHR will obviously have an effect on the English cause of action. It is likely that the *Z v United Kingdom* decision, for example, will not only speed up the development of the cause of action, but will ensure it has a wide scope.[35] Further, specific doctrines developed under the European jurisprudence, such as just satisfaction and proportionality, will be utilized by the domestic United Kingdom courts. Most obviously, damages awards under Section 8, once it has been determined that an award is required, will be calculated by reference to the Strasbourg jurisprudence.[36]

In summary, this influence will be of great impact on the cause of action and remedy in England. The statutory direction to use comparative material and the statutory reference to the European Convention, in particular, are likely to be of great importance. Nevertheless, as became evident in the discussion of the three jurisdictions compared in the previous parts of this book, the fact that the monetary remedy for breach of fundamental rights in England is contained in a statute, rather than a Constitution, will not have a determinative impact upon the cause of action.

3. The Age of the Cause of Action

The analysis of the cause of action in the United States, India and New Zealand suggests that the first cases under the United Kingdom remedy will appear very wide, possibly even extravagant, as the courts evolve the cause of action. Broad statements about the importance of rights and the role of remedies in vindicating those rights, in addition to rhetoric concerning the courts' role, could be expected. Eventually, however, it may be that the cause of action may end up rather narrower.

In England, however, such a pattern has not occurred. The first cases decided concerning Section 8 have been concerned to limit the availability of the remedy and quantum and the rhetoric about the importance of rights has not been marked.[37] This is perhaps because the reference to the ECHR jurisprudence means that the cause of action began half-formed. In some ways, reading the early cases gives a sense of having entered a conversation that has been going on for some time. The early cases have decided the way in which the European jurisprudence will be incorporated into the cause of action.

This is similar to the *Bivens* cause of action in the United States, which in a less express manner began partially formed because of its relationship

[35] *Z v United Kingdom* (2002) 34 EHRR 3. See text accompanying n 70 below.
[36] *Greenfield* (n 1 above) para 19.
[37] *Anufrijeva* (n 34 above); *Greenfield* (n 1 above).

with the Section 1983 cause of action. Many factors were directly imported into the *Bivens* cause of action, without the more usual piecemeal development of the law. This meant that there was more certainty than might have been expected in a new cause of action. Conversely, many of the uncertainties of the Section 1983 cause of action have not been avoided in *Bivens* cases, but have been repeated. In New Zealand, the *Baigent's Case* cause of action likewise seems to have avoided much of the initial phase, perhaps due to the highly developed international human rights common law that greatly influenced the cause of action.

The difference in forum for the ECHR and the Human Rights Act allows the English courts to assess whether and how aspects of European law could be imported into the Human Rights Act cause of action. In this way, the English courts can take advantage of European law to create certainties, but also prefer indigenous solutions in relation to certain other difficult areas. As Lord Cooke of Thorndon has said: 'Judges and practitioners in the United Kingdom have the opportunity to learn from other people's mistakes as well as their more successful efforts.'[38]

In relation to the idea of an international human rights common law, this cause of action will obviously be developed at a time that an international consensus exists about the importance of remedies for breach of fundamental rights. It will probably, as a result, be a wider cause of action than those that exist in the United States. On the other hand, the benefits of hindsight means that the cause of action is not likely to be as wide as that in India or as the New Zealand cause of action began. It is also likely that United Kingdom decisions on certain points mirror, or at least refer to, the bulk of international jurisprudence on the subject. By necessity, the English cause of action will develop according to the European jurisprudence.

In fact, the Human Rights Act illustrates a final step in the development of an international consensus in relation to a human rights monetary remedy. The inclusion of a provision that makes it beyond doubt that the remedy exists recognises that it would be impossible to avoid the judicial development of the remedy at domestic law should it not be statutorily defined. This is especially relevant as Section 8 purports to limit the potential remedy—it assumes that without such limiting terms, the cause of action would be broad in application. The parliamentary wish for an exceptional remedy has been reflected in the early judicial decisions taken under the statute.[39]

This reiterates the point noted in the previous section: comparative

[38] Cooke (n 7 above) 259.

[39] *Anufrijeva* (n 34 above) and *Greenfield* (n 1 above) which, on the whole, treat the new cause of action as analogous to similar cases brought under the Convention to the Strasbourg Court.

jurisprudence is likely. The sort of analysis and decision-making judges undertake in these matters is likely to be positioned within the international consensus, both in terms of substance and of style. Clearly, internationally, domestic human rights causes of action and cases resemble one another. It is to be expected that the English cause of action will be part of the international picture. The time at which the cause of action has developed will affect it insofar as it is likely to learn from other causes of action that have developed earlier.

4. The Wider Context

Many of the differences between the cause of action in the three jurisdictions studied could be traced to their cultural, political and economic context. The biggest contextual difference was between the United States and New Zealand on the one hand, and India on the other. The English socio-economic context is that of a politically stable and developed country.[40] It falls within the group of countries to which United States and New Zealand belong, rather than those more similar to India. This suggests that many of the unique features of the Indian system associated with its context will not be relevant to the English remedy.

Another difference is likely to be in relation to judicial style. As judges in England are unlikely to be faced with fact situations similar to those in India, they are unlikely to use emotive rhetoric such as that evident in India. It may, however, go further. Lord Hoffman has suggested that judicial intervention in highly political issues is expected in the United States but in the United Kingdom decisions on political issues are reserved for parliament.[41] In other words, the role of judges in England may differ from both India and the United States. The role United Kingdom judges take in relation to the Human Rights Act will determine much of the way the cause of action develops. It will also have an influence beyond the Human Rights Act: 'How the judges will define their role [under the Human Rights Act] will be the question which is likely to dominate English jurisprudence in the 21st century.'[42]

40 The United Kingdom is ranked 15th on the UNDP Human Development Index; its GDP is $27,147; and the Human Development Index value for the United Kingdom is 0.939: United Nations Development Programme, *Human Development Report 2005* (www.undp.org).

41 Lord Hoffman, 'Human Rights and the House of Lords' (1999) 62 *MLR* 159, 161. This is perhaps reinforced by Lord Woolf, who may have been thinking of the United States jurisprudence when he stated that the Human Rights Act should not promote 'a public law damages culture': Lord Woolf, 'The Human Rights Act 1998 and Remedies' in M Andenas and D Fairgrieve, *Judicial Review in International Perspective*, Vol II (The Hague, Kluwer, 2000) 429, 433.

42 N Roberts, 'The Law Lords and Human Rights: The Experience of the Privy Council in Interpreting Bills of Rights' [2000] 2 *EHRLR* 147.

The relationship the legal profession and the population as a whole will have with the Human Rights Act will directly influence the cases brought to court and the remedy sought. It will also indirectly affect decisions of principle and substance: in relation to the United States, it has been argued that judges are likely to take public opinion into account in determining the value of the remedy.[43] To some extent this may already be visible in relation to the United Kingdom Human Rights Act, as the Court of Appeal in *Anufrijeva*, stating that modest awards of money would be appropriate, noted that '[i]f the impression is created that asylum seekers whether genuine or not are profiting from their status, this could bring the Human Rights Act into disrepute'.[44] Public opinion will, therefore, impact upon the cause of action in England and this is likely to extend to the elements of the cause of action as well as the availability and amount of quantum.

Common law protections will provide the legal context within which the Human Rights Act remedial jurisdiction will be implemented. Until the enactment of the Human Rights Act, fundamental rights in England were protected by the legislature and courts through the common law. While those guarantees may have been more vulnerable to statutory encroachment and were usually only residual rights,[45] most rights were protected to some extent and the Human Rights Act largely codifies and formalises the common law.

While piecemeal legislative protection of rights exists in the United Kingdom,[46] the criminal and civil law is of interest in relation to the monetary remedy.[47] The intersection of tort law and public law, existing as it does almost wholly at common law, is of particular interest. This is the only way in which a citizen may bring an action against the state for such breaches, as public law does not, in theory, allow damages as a remedy.[48]

Simply put, damages actions for the illegal acts of public officials are 'discouraged' in the United Kingdom.[49] While it was previously difficult to establish a duty of care in cases involving the discretionary exercise of a statutory duty, it was even harder to do so in cases involving either a statutory power or allegations of non-feasance of such powers or duties.[50] The case of *Barrett*[51] seems to have signified an increased scope to tort law

43 J Jeffries, 'In Praise of the Eleventh Amendment and Section 1983' (1998) 84 *Virg L Rev* 47.

44 *Anufrijeva* (n 34 above) para 75.

45 T Allan, *Law, Liberty, and Justice: The Legal Foundations of British Constitutionalism* (Oxford, Clarendon Press, 1993) 135.

46 Eg discrimination and equal pay legislation.

47 A government publication before the enactment of the Human Rights Act argues that these features of United Kingdom law protect various of the rights and freedoms in the UN Declaration of Human Rights: Publishing Services, Central Office of Information, *Aspects of Britain—Human Rights* (London, HMSO, 1995) 13–102.

48 P Craig, 'Compensation in Public Law' (1980) 96 *LQR* 413.

49 Leigh and Lustgarten (n 24 above) 527.

50 *X v Bedfordshire County Council* [1995] 2 AC 633; *Stovin v Wise* [1996] AC 923.

51 *Barrett v Enfield LBC* [1999] 3 All ER 193.

which is at least in part attributable to the influence of European law.[52] Nonetheless, negligence actions against public officials are the exception and not the rule. Further, the law of negligence develops incrementally, on a case-by-case basis, so that it is not always easy to determine whether a particular set of facts will be held to make out the cause of action.

Certain aspects of English public law are of relevance. First, it should be noted that there is a suggestion of a broadening of the definition of what constitutes a 'sufficient interest' in relation to standing, by considering it within all the circumstances of the case.[53]

Second, the ECHR impacted upon judicial review in the United Kingdom even before the Convention was incorporated into English law. For example, *Wednesbury* irrationality was 'adapted to the human rights context' by the Divisional Court in *Smith*,[54] and the issue of human rights was confirmed to be justiciable in the Court of Appeal.[55] In *Brind*, a decision as to the relevance of proportionality was left for the future in recognition of the continuing development of English human rights law and judicial review.[56] This process has been described as a 'semi-incorporation' of the Convention into English law.[57]

Third, the rules of interpretation and construction were likewise broadened in public law cases concerning human rights. Higher standards were considered to apply in contexts concerning 'fundamental constitutional rights' so that express provision was required before Courts would consider that Parliament had intended to abrogate those rights.[58]

Fourth, exemplary damages, generally unavailable at European law, exist at common law. Interestingly, in a recent House of Lords decision on the issue of exemplary damages the Lords limited the availability of exemplary damages.[59] Three of their Lordships referred to the Human Rights Act in their speeches, suggesting that it had changed the law in England in relation to exemplary damages.

A further aspect of the legal context of the cause of action is European law. Since 1966, the United Kingdom has allowed its citizens to petition the European Court in respect of alleged breaches of the ECHR. The United Kingdom Human Rights Act not only incorporates certain rights from this document into domestic law, but also requires domestic courts to

52 P Craig and D Fairgrieve, '*Barrett*, Negligence and Discretionary Powers' [1999] *PL* 626.

53 In *R v Attorney General, ex parte ICI* [1987] 1 CRMLR 72, 106–8, a taxpayer was able to seek judicial review of a decision concerning the affairs of another taxpayer because of the 'exceptional circumstances of the case'. Cf *Inland Revenue Commissioners v National Federation of Self-employed and Small Businesses* [1982] AC 617.

54 *R v Ministry of Defence, ex p Smith* [1996] QB 517, 540 (DC). Note that the applications in question in that case were dismissed.

55 *Ibid*, p 556 (CA).

56 *R v Secretary of State for the Home Department, ex p Brind* [1991] 1 AC 696, 750.

57 McCrudden (n3 above) 505.

58 *Witham* (n 30 above) 788.

59 *Kuddus v Chief Constable of Leicestershire Constabulary* [2001] 3 All ER 193.

consider the Court's jurisprudence when deciding whether or not to award a monetary remedy under the Act. Thus, this jurisprudence will be of direct relevance in the development of the monetary remedy in England and will form an intrinsic part of the legal context as the case law develops.

Of particular importance, it should be noted that Article 13 of the Convention provides a right to an effective remedy before a national authority for anyone who claims a breach of Convention rights.[60] Article 41 relates to the Court's power to award a remedy and refers to the Court's power to 'afford just satisfaction to the injured party'.

The European Court has regularly imposed damages and costs against the United Kingdom as well as other Member States. For example, damages were awarded to employees of British Rail who had been dismissed for refusing to join a union[61]; for breach of property rights[62]; to two people dismissed from the armed services on account of their sexual orientation[63]; and to residents who suffered from night-time noise from Heathrow Airport.[64] In other cases, friendly settlements had been brokered by the Court or Commission in which compensation for non-pecuniary loss and loss of earnings were offered.

Decisions under the ECHR include, therefore, the possibility of a monetary remedy. While damages for pecuniary loss and costs are generally calculated according to expected rules, the awards given for non-pecuniary loss are often awarded on the basis of what seems to be 'equitable'.[65] Of particular importance in relation to the remedy is the doctrine of just satisfaction, which has often been interpreted to limit the availability of a monetary remedy for non-pecuniary harm as the Court considers that the judgment alone gives just satisfaction to the claimant.[66] The Court has applied 'general principles' in assessing just satisfaction, rather than developing any specific means of calculation.[67] Much of the early case law has involved considering the Strasbourg Court's abstract jurisprudence. Much comment on the Strasbourg Court's jurisprudence in

60 As previously mentioned, this section is not part of the United Kingdom law.

61 *Young, James and Webster v United Kingdom* (1983) 5 EHRR 201: The Court ordered £146,000 to be paid, of which £65,000 was for legal costs and the rest for compensation, in different amounts, to each of the applicants.

62 *Gillow v United Kingdom* (1991) 13 EHRR 593: £10,735.

63 *Smith and Grady v United Kingdom* (2001) 31 EHRR 24.

64 *Hatton v United Kingdom* (2002) 34 EHRR 1.

65 Leigh and Lustgarten (n 24 above); Carnwarth (n 26 above).

66 Leach (n 21 above) 196 suggests that there is 'a prevailing view that the primary remedy in Strasbourg is the finding of a violation of the Convention itself'. Clayton (n 7 above) 1422 states that between 1982–91, in 51 cases in which non-pecuniary damages were sought, the Court decided that the judgment alone gave just satisfaction. See esp *Hood v United Kingdom* (2000) 29 EHRR 365; and *Jordan v United Kingdom* (2001) 31 EHRR 6.

67 Leach (n 21 above) 196.

this area has noted difficulties in identifying any 'principles' used in determining quantum.[68] No 'tariff' exists in these cases.[69]

One recent European case of special importance to the remedy under the Human Rights Act is *Z v United Kingdom*.[70] At the domestic level, this case had restated the common law in relation to negligence claims against public authorities.[71] The case was then heard by the European Court of Human Rights, which decided that the claimants' rights under Articles 3 and 13 had been breached by the United Kingdom government.

The Court held that Article 13 guarantees the availability at the national level of a remedy to enforce the substance of Convention rights and freedoms.[72] While States are given discretion as to the manner by which this guarantee is fulfilled, the remedy must be effective and is likely to include compensation. The Court noted that the United Kingdom government 'conceded that the range of remedies at the disposal of the applicants was insufficiently effective ... [but] pointed out that in the future under the Human Rights Act 1998 victims of human rights breaches will be able to bring proceedings in courts empowered to award damages'.[73]

The 'inherently uncertain character of the damage flowing from the violation' made it difficult to calculate reparation, which will 'be determined by the Court, at its discretion, having regard to what is equitable'.[74] Thus, awards made in similar domestic judgments would be of relevance, but would not be decisive. In this case, the European Court awarded pecuniary damages for psychological help, loss of earning potential and non-pecuniary damages for pain and suffering. Costs were also awarded.

The decision suggests that the Court would consider an effective monetary remedy under the Human Rights Act to be the means by which the United Kingdom government fulfils its obligations under Article 13 of the ECHR. Should such a remedy not be developed by the United Kingdom courts, or should the remedy be constrained, it may be that the European Court will hold that the United Kingdom is in breach of its European obligations. It is likely, in this context, that the monetary remedy under the Human Rights Act will be developed by domestic courts in the near future. Further, it is possible that judges will be more astute to avoid

[68] A Mowbray, 'The European Court of Human Rights Approach to Just Satisfaction' [1997] *PL* 647; Clayton (n 7 above); Leigh and Lustgarten (n 24 above); Law Commission (n 2 above); D Shelton, *Remedies in International Human Rights Law* (Oxford, OUP, 1999) 1; Scorey and Eicke (n 5 above); J Hartsthorne, 'The Human Rights Act 1998 and Damages for Non-pecuniary Loss' [2004] *EHRLR* 660, 661–63.

[69] Clayton (n 7 above) 1428.

[70] *Z* (n 35 above).

[71] *X v Bedfordshire County Council* (n 50 above).

[72] *Z* (n 35 above) para 108.

[73] *Ibid*, paras 110–11.

[74] *Ibid*, para 120.

restrictions on the cause of action than might otherwise have been expected.

The European Court of Justice's jurisprudence in relation to rights and remedies is a further part of the context for the new cause of action, especially as its decisions regarding European law are a part of domestic United Kingdom law.[75] The ECJ seems to use the European Convention 'as an aid to the construction of the Community Treaties and the legislative and administrative acts of the Community institutions'.[76] The Court has implied a concept of fundamental rights, linked to the rights in the ECHR,[77] as one of the governing principles of Community law. While such rights were not expressly incorporated into the Community treaties, the increased judicial reference to them has resulted in a general acceptance.[78] This has extended from application to the Community institutions, to application to the actions of member states.[79] The usual remedy is injunctive or declaratory. Nonetheless, the ECJ jurisprudence illustrates that fundamental rights are an intrinsic part of European law.

In *Francovich*,[80] the ECJ 'added a new dimension to its case law by requiring the provision in every Member State of one important form of remedy: a claim for compensation against the State for breach of Community law'.[81] Thus, the Member States were held to be monetarily liable for their failure to implement European directives at domestic law.

Brasserie du Pecheur[82] extended this. The monetary remedy was to be available for directly effective European rights, as well as for non-directly effective European directives. There is a 'right to reparation' where three conditions are met: 'the rule of law infringed must be intended to confer rights on individuals; the breach must be sufficiently serious; and there must be a direct causal link between the breach of the obligation resting on the State and the damage sustained by the injured parties'.[83] The remedy is available when the unlawful act of a Member State gives rise to injury. This has not, as yet, been held to apply to human rights breaches.

Two aspects of the English legal context in particular differ from the other jurisdictions studied. First, the apex domestic court for England is the House of Lords, which includes within it many Privy Council Judges who have been faced with decisions about fundamental rights, if not about

75 P Birkinshaw, *Grievances, Remedies and the State*, 2nd edn, (London, Sweet & Maxwell, 1994) 249.

76 N Grief, 'The Domestic Impact of the European Convention on Human Rights as Mediated Through Community Law' [1991] *PL* 555.

77 *Ibid*, p 566.

78 P Craig and G de Burca, *EU Law*, 2nd edn, (Oxford, OUP, 1998) 296.

79 *Ibid*, p 298.

80 *Francovich and Bonifaci v Italy* [1991] ECR I–5357, [1993] 2 CMLR 66.

81 Craig and de Burca (n 78 above) 236.

82 Cases C–46/93 and C–48/93 *Brasserie du Pecheur SA v Germany, R v Secretary of State for Transport, ex p Factortame* [1996] QB 404.

83 *Brasserie du Pecheur* (n 82 above) 499, para 51.

the monetary remedy directly, in that role. It will be interesting to see whether that experience has any impact upon their decision-making in United Kingdom cases under the Human Rights Act.

While there is some dispute about the value, from a human rights perspective, of many of the Privy Council decisions,[84] it seems that much of the jurisprudence there allows a wider view of governmental liability than the House of Lords has allowed in domestic cases such as *X v Bedfordshire* and *Stovin*.[85] This factor may combine with the previous factors discussed to suggest a widening of this concept in this new area of United Kingdom law.

Second, the Strasbourg Court will operate, in effect, as a second apex court albeit an international one. In addition to the great experience of human rights matters, this may also import considerably more civil law aspects into English human rights law than exists in the United States, India or New Zealand. Clearly, European human rights law contains much from civil law and the influence of certain European human rights law concepts are attributable to that.[86] The effect of this on the English damages remedy is likely to be indirect but undeniable. In any event, the Strasbourg Court's jurisprudence will be a significant part of the domestic cause of action under the Human Rights Act.

5. The Internal Context

Decisions about the internal context of the cause of action determine its legal shape. As such, they will continue to evolve with the first decisions. It is clear, nevertheless, that decisions about the relative weighting of principle and pragmatism, the categorisation of the cause of action as public or private, and the use of comparative and indigenous jurisprudence will be similar to decisions taken in the European context.

The Human Rights Act provides for a remedy that is highly discretionary and which may, in some cases, not be awarded should the Courts consider the judgment to afford just satisfaction. The remedy shall be exceptional; it is to be expected that it will not be awarded as a matter of course. As the Court of Appeal stated in *Anufrijeva*, damages will not be recoverable as of right in a Human Rights Act claim brought for breach of the Convention, unlike tort cases.[87] The Courts are directed to consider relevant factors when taking the decision as to quantum. This aspect has been emphasised in the first cases decided under the Human Rights Act,

84 Eg Roberts (n 12 above) 179.
85 *X* (n 50 above); and *Stovin* (n 50 above).
86 Fairgrieve (n 4 above) 716.
87 *Aunfrijeva* (n 34 above) para 50.

strongly suggesting that a remedy will be available only in exceptional cases and not as a matter of course.[88]

These points suggest that issues of pragmatism will be considered to be part of a principled approach to remedy under Section 8 so that decisions as to remedy under the Human Rights Act cause of action are likely to involve a pragmatic element.

In common with most other jurisdictions, the House of Lords in *Greenfield* made it clear that the cause of action in England will be considered to be a subset of public, rather than tort, law.[89] The Human Rights Act is likely to develop as a separate human rights sphere of the law within which the remedy will be considered. The Human Rights Act will override the general reluctance, at English common law, to grant a monetary remedy against public authorities,[90] and quantum itself will be calculated by reference to European case law.[91] In *Kuddus*, the House of Lords utilised the ECHR to develop the common law[92]; it is likely that the courts will continue to use this 'semi-incorporation' approach following the enactment of the Human Rights Act.[93] Thus, general English law may be greatly affected by the Section 8 cause of action.

As noted earlier, the direction in the Human Rights Act that courts shall use European case law as a guide to decision-making made it certain that the judiciary would utilize international jurisprudence. The early decisions under the Human Rights Act indicate that the delicate balance between comparative and indigenous materials is being undertaken without much difficulty.

Decisions have referred extensively to the decisions of the Strasbourg Court, and the manner in which these decisions should be approached has itself been the subject of judicial scrutiny. In *Anufrijeva*, the Court of Appeal had felt that the 'assistance to be derived' from European jurisprudence was limited.[94] In *Greenfield*, the House of Lords clearly stated that in relation to determining awards, courts in England 'should look to Strasbourg and not to domestic precedents', indicating that the comparative jurisprudence is an intrinsic part of Human Rights Act decisions.[95]

88 See especially *Anufrijeva* (n 34 above); and *Greenfield* (n 1 above).

89 *Greenfield* (n 1 above) para 19. See also Clayton (n 7 above) 1416–19.

90 Eg *R v Home Secretary ex p Dew* [1987] 1 WLR 881, 894: 'there is no general right in an individual to damages for an infringement of a public right'. See also Lord Hoffman (n 41 above) 163: 'The theme that runs through these causes of action is that the fact that public services are provided at the public expense to confer benefits or protection on members of the public does not mean that a person who fails to receive those benefits or protection will be entitled to sue for compensation on the ground that the authority acted negligently in failing to provide them.'

91 *Greenfield* (n 1 above) paras 8–17.

92 *Kuddus* (n 59 above).

93 McCrudden (n 3 above) 505. Such an approach accords with the indirect application to the common law suggested by Hunt (n 15 above).

94 *Anufrijeva* (n 34 above) 52.

95 *Greenfield* (n 1 above) para 19.

Further, it is likely that United Kingdom judges will utilise the more familiar common law: 'The English lawyer will often find the approach of common law judges more familiar and congenial than the Delphic style of the European Court of Human Rights'.[96] This approach will affect all elements of the cause of action, by ensuring that it will take advantage of lessons learnt in similar causes of action throughout the world.[97]

In summary, therefore, although the details of this overarching influence will continue to evolve as the cause of action itself develops, the approaches that will be taken seem clear: the cause of action will be pragmatic, will exist at public law, and will be highly comparative, particularly in relation to the jurisprudence of the Strasbourg Court.

6. Summary

This brief survey of the overarching influences illustrates that the European context and the clear statutory basis to the cause of action will be the most important influences on the common elements forming the cause of action and remedy. The wider socio-economic and cultural context of the cause of action affects it primarily by omission: the first world nature of England means that many of the approaches and decisions taken by the Indian Supreme Court are unlikely to be considered relevant in England.

C. ANSWERING THE COMMON QUESTIONS: TOWARDS AN APPLICATION TO THE HUMAN RIGHTS ACT

1. Introduction

Putting all the previous information together provides some suggestion of the potential of the monetary remedy under the Human Rights Act. This involves looking at the likely impact of the overarching influences on the questions setting out the common structure of the cause of action. As is obvious from all that precedes in this chapter, the principal influences on the cause of action are first, the nature of the statute as the means by which the ECHR is incorporated into United Kingdom law, the content of the statute, and the consequent references to European jurisprudence in the remedial section and, second, the international human rights common law. Other influences are less important when compared with these.

[96] Clayton (n 7 above) 7–8.

[97] *Anufrijeva* (n 34 above) para 54, referring to the Indian Supreme Court's decision in *Nilabati Behera v State of Orissa* [1993] Cri LJ 2899.

2. What does the Cause of Action Protect?

This aspect of the cause of action is set out in the statute: the remedy will be available in relation to actions which are incompatible with the Convention rights covered by the Human Rights Act.[98] These are all the expected rights and freedoms, with one noticeable exclusion: Article 13 of the Convention, which provides a right to an effective remedy at domestic law. As Article 13 is not included, it will not be possible for plaintiffs to receive a monetary remedy under the Human Rights Act for the failure of the English courts to provide a remedy. As was discussed earlier, however, this may have little impact as plaintiffs will still be able to plead Article 13 before the European Court, and *Z v United Kingdom* suggests that the establishment of a monetary remedy under Section 8 of the Human Rights Act will be necessary to prevent the United Kingdom being liable for breach of Article 13.[99]

The case law of the European Court suggests that any 'sufficiently serious' breach of the rights will be sufficient to found a claim under Section 8 and neither negligence nor bad faith will be required.[100] The sort of breach is likely to become relevant when the court considers whether any remedy other than a declaration is required in the particular case and, if so, the level of the appropriate monetary award.[101] In particular, it seems that courts will be unlikely to award damages 'to reflect the mere fact of a violation'.[102]

Interestingly, early cases suggest that the availability of a monetary remedy will be affected by which article of the Convention has been breached. Thus, care should be taken not to read Strasbourg decisions given in relation to one article of the Convention across as applicable to another.[103]

In practice, the subject matter in cases under the Human Rights Act will be equivalent to cases under the Convention decided by the Strasbourg Court. The indication that the remedy may be available only in a limited number of cases means that the nature of the breach will be of importance, as will which right was breached.

The taxonomy developed by the generic structure is, therefore, partially answered. It is clear that the breach of a Convention right is required for the cause of action to be available, and that the interpretation of these will

98 Human Rights Act s 6(1).

99 Z (n 35 above).

100 Fairgrieve (n 4 above) 697–700.

101 Eg *Anufrijeva* (n 34 above) para 68: 'In addition to the violation committed being particularly serious, the manner or way in which the violation took place has in some cases been considered sufficiently serious to lead the EctHR to award damages'.

102 Law Commission (n 2 above) 34.

103 *Greenfield* (n 1 above) para 7, distinguishing Art 6 cases from other cases under the Convention.

be according to European law. There are indications that the issue of the relevance of which right was breached in a particular case is being addressed by the courts in the early cases, as part of the decisions as to the availability of the remedy. Clearly, not every breach of a Convention right will be sufficient to found the cause of action, as the early case law has stressed the exceptional nature of the remedy. It may be that the United States approach, that the remedy is not available in particular contexts may be considered in the future.[104] In any event, the sub-questions under this heading have received the attention of the English courts at this early stage of the cause of action's development, and seem to be categorised as of relevance to the decision as to whether the particular case amounts to one in which a monetary remedy should be ordered.

3. Who does the Cause of Action Protect?

The Human Rights Act explicitly limits the cause of action to those who fall within the ECHR definition of a 'victim'.[105] That definition will include 'pre-emptive strikes' by individuals whose rights may be breached in the future,[106] but will preclude representative actions.[107] As a result, it will be left to group actions which include a named 'victim' and the financial support from non-governmental organizations to ensure that all individuals whose rights have been breached are able to use the cause of action. In any event, the socio-economic context suggests that in England a wide public interest litigation, such as exists in India, would not be a priority of the courts.

In accordance with the ECHR jurisprudence, it is likely that injury will not be a necessary precondition to bringing a claim.[108] This will mean that individuals will merely need to prove that their rights have been breached to found a claim. To receive damages, however, it is likely that individuals will need to prove something more than injury to the right.[109] Some level of causation will be required, considered on a case-by-case basis.[110] This is consistent with international jurisprudence.

This set of questions has, therefore, been largely determined by the statutory definitions referring to the European jurisprudence, which

104 See ch 5(B)(4) above.

105 Human Rights Act s 7(1), s 7(3). See Law Commission (n 2 above) 10–13.

106 Feldman (n 10 above) 696.

107 J Marriott and D Nicol, 'The Human Rights Act, Representative Standing and the Victim Culture' [1998] 6 *EHRLR* 730, 735; *ibid.*

108 Fairgrieve (n 4 above) 707–8.

109 Law Commission (n 2 above). In this way, the actual loss or harm to the plaintiff will become relevant at the remedial stage of the process.

110 *Greenfield* (n 1 above).

provides answers to the questions of the availability of public interest litigation and the requirement for injury.

4. Who is the Cause of Action Directed Against?

Once again, this aspect of the cause of action is set out in the Human Rights Act: the remedy will be available in relation to the actions of 'public authorities'.[111] It will include courts, tribunals and people exercising public functions, but will not include legislative acts or people carrying out private functions. Beyond that, the exact meaning of this phrase is not clear: 'The expression 'public authority' is not defined in the Act, nor is it a recognised term of art in English law, that is, an expression with a specific recognised meaning.'[112]

The case law concerning its meaning 'is opaque and very disappointing', particularly in relation to hybrid authorities.[113] It is difficult to predict a court's decision in any one case. This is an area which will continue to evolve. The comparative analysis highlights varying tests to determine whether particular entities will be amenable to a human rights action; decisions will be jurisdiction-specific on this point.

There has been much discussion of whether or not the statute will have application to the actions of private individuals.[114] Pleadings which name private parties will not be possible as, pursuant to Section 6, only individuals and entities with a public flavour can be defendants under the Human Rights Act. Nevertheless, the Human Rights Act will influence indirectly the construction and interpretation of all law, including that between purely private parties. Consider, for example, defamation being raised in a case with a public defendant, and later in a case with two private parties. Since it would be clearly illogical for one common law to exist for cases involving public defendants in which the Human Rights Act applied, and one to exist for other cases in which both parties are private, the Human Rights Act will have an indirect influence throughout the law. Thus, the common law will evolve indirectly pursuant to the Human Rights Act.

Finally, the lesson from the United States is that the question of immunities and the relevance of fault will determine who can in practice be sued under Section 8: should a good faith immunity be applied, then to all intents and purposes, almost nobody will be amenable to suit. It is

111 Human Rights Act s 6. See Law Commission (n 2 above) 9–10.

112 *Parochial Church Council of the Parish of Aston Cantlow and Wilmcote with Billesley, Warwickshire v Wallbank* (HL) [2003] UKHL 37, para 6.

113 R Clayton, A Ruck Keene and R Dunlop, 'Key Human Rights Act Cases in the Last 12 Months' [2004] *EHRLR* 614, 617.

114 Eg Hunt (n 15 above); Markesinis (n 15 above); Buxton (n 15 above); Phillipson (n 15 above); and Oliver (n 15 above).

unlikely that a wide good faith immunity would be implied in relation to the actions of officials in England, given that *Z v United Kingdom* suggests that the United Kingdom government would then be at risk of breaching Section 13 of the ECHR.[115] In any event, the European jurisprudence suggests that fault is unnecessary.[116] In addition, as the Act is silent as to immunity, the reasoning of the New Zealand Chief Justice in *Whithair*[117] may well apply, so that United Kingdom judges would resist implying an immunity in the absence of a statutory indication that such a limitation on the cause of action accords with the legislative intent. The fact that the statute provides an express good faith immunity for judicial officers would tend to support this approach, as the legislature clearly considered the question of who should benefit from such an immunity and failed to provide a general good faith immunity.

This is in agreement with the bulk of international decisions which suggest that United States-style immunities are unnecessary. The taxonomy suggests that the courts may be called upon to consider some questions under this heading in the future. In particular, the question of the relevance of fault to the availability of the remedy and amount awarded has not been considered by the courts to date. Further, the question of the importance of the nature of the pleadings, that is, who is named defendant, has not been canvassed and may become relevant in the future. Finally, should a remedy be ordered, the question of who pays the award has been an important issue in other jurisdictions.

5. What does the Court Order?

The survey of the United States, Indian and New Zealand causes of action for breach of human rights sounding in monetary remedies suggests that there are many approaches that could be taken to determining remedy. At a basic level, the first step will be to determine whether or not an award should be made, and the second step will be to determine the amount of any award.

The Human Rights Act requires monetary awards to be 'just and appropriate' and, possibly, 'effective'.[118] Such an award should only be made if, after having taken into account the principles of the ECHR and all the circumstances of the case, including other relief granted and the consequences of the decision, the court is satisfied that a monetary award is necessary to afford just satisfaction.[119] Clayton has suggested that the

115 Z (n 35 above).
116 Fairgrieve (n 4 above) 7–8.
117 *Whithair* [1996] 2 NZLR 45.
118 Amos (n 6 above).
119 Human Rights Act s 8; Amos (n 6 above).

burden will be on the claimant to justify the necessity of the award to achieve just satisfaction.[120]

In any event, the remedy will be discretionary, a point emphasised by the first cases decided considering Section 8: there is no right to a remedy under the Human Rights Act. The Act expressly excludes Article 13 of the Convention, which provides such a right. It may be that the statutory limitations on the award of damages continued the English law's reluctance to award damages in public law cases.[121] Clearly, the statutory directions limit the occasions on which the remedy will be available, but do not amount to a requirement for all other remedies to be exhausted first.[122] There will be no tariff which the court will apply in all cases to come up with the amount of damages that should be awarded.[123]

The existence of the just satisfaction jurisprudence means that the cause of action will include consideration of pragmatic elements, indicating that various matters will be taken into account in determining whether a remedy should be awarded at all and, if an award is to be made, the appropriate amount.

There is a suggestion that elements such as fault—seemingly not relevant in determining liability—will be calculated into quantum.[124] Lord Woolf stated, extra-judicially, that fault should not be a condition precedent to an award of damages, but 'should be a factor making it more appropriate to award damages'.[125] A 'principled approach' to remedy is proposed. It is likely that the applicant's conduct and the nature of the breach will have an equivalent impact.[126] This suggests a remedial approach that is similar to the pragmatic New Zealand response, mixing the principles of the English common law with those of the Strasbourg Court.

The Strasbourg Court's approach to determining quantum is likely to be followed so that damages will usually divide into what in Europe is termed pecuniary damages, non-pecuniary damages and costs, and there will be a general aim of *restitutio in integrum*.[127] The usual 'well-established principles' of compensation aiming to provide restitution for the victim are likely to be followed in relation to pecuniary damages.[128]

120 Clayton (n 7 above) 1433–44.

121 H Fenwick, *Civil Rights: New Labour, Freedom and the HRA* (London, Longman, 2000) 56.

122 Law Commission (n 2 above) 14.

123 Clayton (n 7 above) 1428. The Court does not utilise a strict doctrine of precedent: Law Commission (n 2 above) 20.

124 Fairgrieve (n 4 above) 698; Law Commission (n 2 above).

125 Lord Woolf (n 41 above) 433.

126 Shelton (n 68 above) 205 suggests that decisions in which the judgment alone was considered to afford just satisfaction usually concerned applicants guilty of criminal conduct or procedural, rather than substantive, breaches.

127 Law Commission (n 2 above) 24–25.

128 Clayton (n 7 above) 1434.

In relation to non-pecuniary damages, it is likely that the ECHR principles will be interpreted in light of the English common law's approach. The Law Commission concluded that in the majority of cases under the Human Rights Act, English and Welsh courts may apply the rules by which damages are awarded in tort: 'indeed, they may find it appropriate to treat those rules as the prima facie measure to be applied unless the results appear inconsistent with the principles applied by the Court in Strasbourg'.[129] The Commission believed that tort principles did not differ greatly from the principles of the Strasbourg Court.

Non-pecuniary loss will include 'feelings of distress, anxiety and humiliation, and may include the loss of a relationship'.[130] A finding that the declaration of a breach provides 'just satisfaction' will mean that in some cases no monetary remedy will be awarded, and in other cases, the amount awarded will be low.[131] A causal connection will be required.[132] In relation to costs, it is possible that the usual rule that costs will follow the cause may be altered on occasion in this context.[133] Generally, costs will be awarded where they compensate for expenses incurred to prevent or obtain redress and are reasonable.[134]

Despite the distinction between pecuniary and non-pecuniary damages, awards are often arbitrary and not separated into those heads: 'Far too often, a global sum is simply awarded "on an equitable basis" without further explanation'.[135] This mirrors much of the conclusion of the earlier comparison and may mean that it will always be difficult to predict the amounts likely to be awarded.

It should be noted that the principles of the European Court suggest low awards. The fact that the statutory directions likewise point towards moderate awards will obviously effect the amounts of awards. Further, it is unlikely that punitive or exemplary damages will be awarded in this public law cause of action, although it may be that courts will include a general sense of outrage within the global sum awarded.[136] Finally, like the New Zealand situation, it is likely that quantum under other causes of action will be considered when awarding the monetary remedy through the Human Rights Act.[137] For all these reasons, awards are unlikely to be extravagant.

The indications given by the House of Lords in their first consideration of damages claims under Section 8 strongly emphasise that the Strasbourg

129 Law Commission (n 2 above) 56.
130 *Ibid*, p 47.
131 *Ibid*, pp 32–35.
132 *Ibid*, pp 40–45.
133 G Davies, 'Costs and the Human Rights Act' [2000] *NLJ* 280.
134 Law Commission (n 2 above) 28.
135 Leigh and Lustgarten (n 24 above) 529–30; Law Commission (n 2 above) 19–23.
136 Clayton (n 7 above) 1436.
137 Human Rights Act s 8(3); Law Commission (n 2 above) 14–15.

decisions will be the guiding principles against which quantum will be measured in Section 8 damages cases.[138] While warning of the 'risk of error if Strasbourg decisions given in relation to one article of the Convention are read across as applicable to another',[139] Lord Bingham noted that '[t]he routine treatment of a finding of violation as, in itself, just satisfaction for the violation found reflects the point already made that the focus of the Convention is on the protection of human rights and not the award of compensation.'[140] The Court of Appeal in *Anufrijeva*, therefore, was correct to state that the primary purpose was to bring the infringement of the human right to an end, with compensation being of 'secondary, if any, importance'.[141]

In relation to the Strasbourg Court's jurisprudence concerning the need for a sufficient causal connection to warrant an award of non-pecuniary damages, the House of Lords considered it wise not to 'lay down hard and fast rules in a field which pre-eminently calls for a case by case judgment'.[142] The decision in *Greenfield* noted that the European Court has been 'very sparing' in making awards for physical and mental suffering,[143] and that in making Article 41 awards for breach of Article 6, the sums awarded had been 'noteworthy for their modesty'.[144]

Lord Bingham disagreed with the submission that domestic cases should act as a comparator for Section 8 damages awards for three reasons: in comparison with a tort statute, the objectives of the Human Rights Act mean that damages need not ordinarily be awarded; the purpose of the Act was to give victims the same remedies as they would have at Strasbourg without the delay and expense; and Section 8 itself requires the domestic courts to take into account the Strasbourg Court's principles both in determining whether or not to award damages, and also in determining the amount of any award.[145] Thus, without being inflexibly bound by Strasbourg awards, United Kingdom judges 'should not aim to be significantly more or less generous than the Court might be expected to be, in a case where it was willing to make an award at all'.[146]

In the instant case, the appeal failed as there was no special feature which warranted an award of damages. Lord Bingham ended his speech by confirming the Court of Appeal's strictures in *Anufrijeva*, that the costs of such cases should not be disproportionate to any damages awarded, particularly as damages will often not be awarded even in successful

138 *Greenfield* (n 1 above) para 6.
139 *Ibid*, para 7.
140 *Ibid*, para 9.
141 *Ibid*, referring to *Anufrijeva* (n 34 above) para 53.
142 *Greenfield* (n 1 above) para 15.
143 *Ibid*, para 16.
144 *Ibid*, para 17.
145 *Ibid*, para 19.
146 *Ibid*.

cases.[147] The decision in *Anufrijeva* had set out certain suggestions to ensure the proportionate resolution of Section 8 claims for damages in future cases, including an emphasis on use of the Administrative and Summary Courts, and alternative dispute resolution.[148]

Clearly, the early cases of principle considering the awarding of damages pursuant to Section 8 of the Human Rights Act have determined that the remedy will be highly discretionary, and that decisions as to both whether or not it will be awarded and the amount, if any, that will be awarded will be taken following consideration of various elements specific to the particular case.

6. Summary

Without attempting to predict the details of the English cause of action sounding in a monetary remedy, the framework has schematised it, so as to identify the questions that the English courts will be called upon to answer, and the prevalent influences on those answers. The view afforded is of a cause of action greatly influenced by its position in Europe and its position as a 'late-starter' in terms of such a cause of action. It is likely that the English courts will take advantage of the strengths of Europe and other jurisdictions when developing what will be an undoubtedly unique remedy in English law. Most of the sub-questions identified in the generic taxonomy have been raised already or are partially answered by the statutory context, while other matters are likely to be raised in the future. The generic structure provides a framework against which these, and other developments, can be assessed and understood.

D. CONCLUSIONS

This overview allows for two main observations. First, it is interesting to observe how much of the taxonomy developed by consideration of the three jurisdictions has already been raised in relation to the English cause of action. The international comparison illustrates the number of options that the courts may take on different aspects of the cause of action, some of which the courts have already considered, and other of which may arise in the future.

Second, in application it is obvious that the individual aspects of the cause of action in each of the jurisdictions studied is less relevant than the overall impression given. The schematised framework provides structure

147 *Ibid*, para 30, referring to *Anufrijeva* (n 34 above) para 79.
148 *Anufrijeva* (n 34 above) para 81.

and clarity to the cause of action, simplifying the case law and allowing the commonality to be clearly seen. While the English cause of action is unlikely to resemble any of the three causes of action out of which the structure was developed, it is very probable that it will be called upon to address the general questions making up the taxonomy.

The result of this exercise, therefore, confirms that the generic outline developed from the domestic causes of action for breach of human rights in the United States of America, India and New Zealand has a wider application than those three countries alone. In fact, the inclusion of the overarching influences, allowing jurisdiction-specific differences, suggests that the framework has further applicability beyond England. Consequently, viewing the causes of action as an international phenomenon is both valid and fruitful.

8

Conclusion

THIS BOOK CONSIDERED the domestic cause of action for breach of constitutional rights sounding in the monetary remedy in the United States, India and New Zealand. The first part of the book described the causes of action in the three jurisdictions. There are two causes of action in the United States, existing within a highly defined and complex set of rules concerning suits for the breach of constitutional rights. The Indian cause of action is extremely wide and stands out for its generous public interest litigation rules and distressing fact situations. The cause of action in New Zealand was recently implied and has had few limitations grafted onto it.

The second part of the book presented two results from a comparative analysis. These arose from the perhaps contradictory observation that the three causes of action are at the same time both very similar and very different. Chapter 5 set out four common questions that provide an outline of the structure of the cause of action: what the cause of action protects, who the cause of action protects, against whom the cause of action is directed, and what the court orders. While the questions are often asked differently or approached in different ways in the three jurisdictions, the issues at their heart are equivalent.

Chapter 6 considered the reasons for the different ways of approaching and answering the questions and proposed four overarching influences as the reasons. These influences concern the cause of action's source, age, wider context and internal context. They are overarching in the sense that they cut across the common questions, and the three jurisdictions, affecting them all. These influences provided an explanation of the differences that exist between the United States, India and New Zealand.

Putting the two chapters together provides a generalized framework of the domestic cause of action for breach of constitutional rights sounding in the monetary remedy. In this way, it describes what amounts to a template or taxonomy for the domestic cause of action when viewed as an international phenomenon.

The third part of the book tested the template by turning the analysis around, to 'apply' it to the developing cause of action under the United Kingdom Human Rights Act. To do this, it was necessary to determine the content of the four overarching influences in the English context. This showed that the European aspect of the statute, the wording of the statute, and the international human rights common law were likely to be the most important influences on the monetary remedy under the Human Rights Act. The framework for England was completed by considering the effect of the influences on the four common questions. While some idea of the shape of the Section 8 cause of action was suggested, the intention was not to provide predictions, but to highlight likely issues and problems, and to illustrate how the generalized framework could work in application.

The two main conclusions that can be drawn from the book have been foreshadowed in this summary of the book. Both build on the observation in the introduction that domestic legal developments are interwoven with the law and practices of other jurisdictions.[1]

The first is that a generalized framework can be used to describe the cause of action in the three jurisdictions. Most aspects of the causes of action fall within the four basic level questions that provide a generic structure. This explains the similarities between the jurisdictions. The differences between the jurisdictions could be explained by four overarching influences, that are also common to some extent, but that affect the causes of action in different ways and result in causes of action that appear quite different. Combining the questions with the influences creates an outline of the causes of action.

This framework aims to explain, simplify and provide an order to these causes of action. It not only describes what exists currently, but also illuminates the potential areas of development and debate in each jurisdiction. At a practical level, it can operate as a checklist for individual cases. In other words, the outline created by the book could be used to ensure that all aspects are addressed in argument and argued with the influences in mind.

The overarching influences are interesting in that they seem to affect the entire cause of action, in each of the three jurisdictions, so that they are common to a certain extent. Each of the specific differences in the cause of action is not caused by different influences, but by influences that seem to exist at a higher level and cut across the entire cause of action. While their existence is common, however, their content will be specific to individual jurisdictions.

An unexpected note of interest is the striking similarity between the four overarching influences developed here, and the five factors set out in

1 B Opeskin, 'Constitutional Modelling: The Domestic Effect of International Law in Commonwealth Countries—Part I' [2000] *PL* 607. See further C McCrudden, 'A Common Law of Human Rights? Transnational Judicial Conversations on Constitutional Rights' (2000) 20 *OJLS* 499.

Zweigert and Kotz's seminal text as the way in which stylistic legal families can be identified.[2] In fact, each of Zweigert and Kotz's factors relates to one of the influences developed in the overarching influences chapter of the book.

The first of Zweigert and Kotz's factors is the historical background and development of jurisdictions; this is clearly similar to considering the age of the cause of action. The second of Zweigert and Kotz's factors concerns the mode of legal thought; this equates to the fourth influence, the internal legal context. The third of Zweigert and Kotz's factors is the jurisdiction's especially distinctive institutions; this is part of the analysis in this book under the internal legal context factor. The fourth Zweigert and Kotz factor concerns the kind of legal sources the legal system acknowledges and the way in which they are handled; this is the same as considering the legal sources of the causes of action in this book. The final factor Zweigert and Kotz set out is ideology, which falls within the wider context influence, although it is perhaps a narrower concept. Zweigert and Kotz state that 'the weight to be given to each of these factors varies according to the circumstances'.[3] Thus, not only are the factors themselves similar, but the way in which the assessment is made also resembles that of this book.

While Zweigert and Kotz use these five factors to divide the world's legal systems into families for the purposes of comparative law, this book has deliberately chosen jurisdictions from one legal family only—the Anglo–American family—to ensure limited differences between the causes of action. Even so, the factors suggested by Zweigert and Kotz are evident as the major influences causing differences between the causes of action of these jurisdictions.

The idea of an international human rights common law, as discussed within the issue of the age of the cause of action, perhaps orders the analysis of the book. This means that the domestic causes of action can be viewed as part of a larger whole, one that exists internationally and is bigger than each individual cause of action. The book has illustrated a certain amount of commonality internationally in relation to the domestic monetary remedy for breach of constitutional rights. It has also suggested that the international consensus exerts a pull on domestic causes of action so that the similarities between jurisdictions have become more pronounced over time.

The second conclusion that may be drawn from this book relates to the international consensus, that is that the generalized framework will have value for other domestic causes of action. The interplay of the questions

[2] H Zweigert and H Kotz, T Weir, (tr), *Introduction to Comparative Law*, 3rd edn, (Oxford, Clarendon Press, 1998) 68–72. I am grateful to Professor Jan-Michiel Otto for drawing this similarity to my attention during a useful discussion at the University of Leiden.

[3] *Ibid*, p 72.

and the influences amounts to a checklist with international practical use. While the framework was developed merely as the best way to describe the cause of action in the United States, India and New Zealand, it can be of use in other jurisdictions in which the cause of action either exists or will develop in the future. Thus, it may serve to order and explain the cause of action in other jurisdictions, and it may provide preliminary suggestions of the general development of new causes of action and remedy. This is the way it was used in relation to England in this book. By identifying both the common features of the causes of action internationally, and the site of differences, jurisdictions may be able to borrow insights from one another that are appropriate and avoid wholesale transplants.

One issue must be emphasized. This is a generalized framework gleaned from an analysis of three jurisdictions. It indicates what may be considered relevant in other jurisdictions but cannot conclusively predict the shape of the cause of action. Any cause of action and remedy is largely a creation of a jurisdiction's judiciary. Regardless of its statutory or constitutional basis, judges retain a great power in interpretation and definition of detail. Thus, the shape of a cause of action will be finally determined over time and in response to the individual cases which are brought to court. This is exacerbated in constitutional rights law which is clearly highly discretionary. Judicial attitudes, fact situations, and legal issues are all largely unpredictable; in turn, this means that much of a cause of action and remedy will remain unknown until successive cases are decided. The analysis developed here, however, shows that many questions and issues that will arise as the cause of action develops can be predicted in advance when causes of action are viewed as an international phenomenon.

Index